ASIAN AMERICANS

O P P O S I N G   V I E W P O I N T S ®

Other Books of Related Interest:

ASIAN AMERICANS
OPPOSING VIEWPOINTS®

David L. Bender, *Publisher*
Bruno Leone, *Executive Editor*

William Dudley, *Series Editor*
John C. Chalberg, Ph.D., professor of history,
Normandale Community College, *Consulting Editor*

William Dudley, *Book Editor*

Greenhaven Press, Inc.
San Diego, California

Cover photographs, clockwise from top: 1) World War II internment camp for Japanese Americans (Archive Photos); 2) Chinese market in San Francisco at the turn of the century, (The Bancroft Library); 3) Chinese new year's celebration, (Archive Photos); 4) Filipino contract workers in Hawaii (State of Hawaii)

Library of Congress Cataloging-in-Publication Data

Asian Americans : opposing viewpoints / William Dudley, book editor.
    p.   cm. — (American history series)
    Includes bibliographical references and index.
    ISBN 1-56510-524-9 (lib. bdg. : alk. paper). —
ISBN 1-56510-523-0 (pbk. : alk. paper)
    1. Asian Americans—History.   I. Dudley, William, 1964– .
    II. Series: American history series (San Diego, Calif.)
E184.06A8445   1997   96-30439
973'.0495—dc20   CIP

"America was born of revolt, flourished in dissent, became great through experimentation."

Henry Steele Commager, American Historian

Contents

Chapter 3: The World War II Internment of Japanese Americans

Chapter 4: The "Model Minority": Asian Americans After 1965

Foreword

Aboard the *Arbella* as it lurched across the cold, gray Atlantic, John Winthrop was as calm as the waters surrounding him were wild. With the confidence of a leader, Winthrop gathered his Puritan companions around him. It was time to offer a sermon. England lay behind them, and years of strife and persecution for their religious beliefs were over, he said. But the Puritan abandonment of England, he reminded his followers, did not mean that England was beyond redemption. Winthrop wanted his followers to remember England even as they were leaving it behind. Their goal should be to create a new England, one far removed from the authority of the Anglican church and King Charles I. In Winthrop's words, their settlement in the New World ought to be "a city upon a hill," a just society for corrupt England to emulate.

A Chance to Start Over

One June 8, 1630, John Winthrop and his company of refugees had their first glimpse of what they came to call New England. High on the surrounding hills stood a welcoming band of fir trees whose fragrance drifted to the *Arbella* on a morning breeze. To Winthrop, the "smell off the shore [was] like the smell of a garden." This new world would, in fact, often be compared to the Garden of Eden. Here, John Winthrop would have his opportunity to start life over again. So would his family and his shipmates. So would all those who came after them. These victims of conflict in old England hoped to find peace in New England.

Winthrop, for one, had experienced much conflict in his life. As a Puritan, he was opposed to Catholicism and Anglicanism, both of which, he believed, were burdened by distracting rituals and distant hierarchies. A parliamentarian by conviction, he despised Charles I, who had spurned Parliament and created a private army to do his bidding. Winthrop believed in individual responsibility and fought against the loss of religious and political freedom. A gentleman landowner, he feared the rising economic power of a merchant class that seemed to value only money. Once Winthrop stepped aboard the *Arbella*, he hoped, these conflicts would not be a part of his American future.

Yet his Puritan religion told Winthrop that human beings are fallen creatures and that perfection, whether communal or individual, is unachievable on this earth. Therefore, he faced a paradox: On the one hand, his religion demanded that he attempt to live a perfect life in an imperfect world. On the other hand, it told him that he was destined to fail.

Soon after Winthrop disembarked from the *Arbella*, he came face-to-face with this maddening dilemma. He found himself presiding not over a utopia but over a colony caught up in disputes as troubling as any he had confronted in his English past. John Winthrop, it seems, was not the only Puritan with a dream of a heaven on earth. But others in the community saw the dream differently. They wanted greater political and religious freedom than their leader was prepared to grant. Often, Winthrop was able to handle this conflict diplomatically. For example, he expanded, participation in elections and allowed the voters of Massachusetts Bay greater power.

But religious conflict was another matter because it was grounded in competing visions of the Puritan utopia. In Roger Williams and Anne Hutchinson, two of his fellow colonists, John Winthrop faced rivals unprepared to accept his definition of the perfect community. To Williams, perfection demanded that he separate himself from the Puritan institutions in his community and create an even "purer" church. Winthrop, however, disagreed and exiled Williams to Rhode Island. Hutchinson presumed that she could interpret God's will without a minister. Again, Winthrop did not agree. Hutchinson was tried on charges of heresy, convicted, and banished from Massachusetts.

John Winthrop's Massachusetts colony was the first but far from the last American attempt to build a unified, peaceful community that, in the end, only provoked a discord. This glimpse at its history reveals what Winthrop confronted: the unavoidable presence of conflict in American life.

American Assumptions

From America's origins in the early seventeenth century, Americans have often held several interrelated assumptions about their country. First, people believe that to be American is to be free. Second, because Americans did not have to free themselves from feudal lords or an entrenched aristocracy, America has been seen as a perpetual haven from the troubles and disputes that are found in the Old World.

John Winthrop lived his life as though these assumptions were true. But the opposing viewpoints presented in the American History Series should reveal that for many Americans, these assumptions were and are myths. Indeed, for numerous Americans, liberty has not always been guaranteed, and disputes have been an integral, sometimes welcome part of their life.

The American landscape has been torn apart again and again by a great variety of clashes—theological, ideological, political, economic, geographical, and social. But such a landscape is not necessarily a hopelessly divided country. If the editors hope to prove anything during the course of this series, it is not that the United States has been destroyed by conflict but rather that it has been enlivened, enriched, and even strengthened by Americans who have disagreed with one another.

Thomas Jefferson was one of the least confrontational of Americans, but he boldly and irrevocably enriched American life with his individualistic views. Like John Winthrop before him, he had a notion of an American Eden. Like Winthrop, he offered a vision of a harmonious society. And like Winthrop, he not only became enmeshed in conflict but eventually presided over a people beset by it. But unlike Winthrop, Jefferson believed this Eden was not located in a specific community but in each individual American. His Declaration of Independence from Great Britain could also be read as a declaration of independence for each individual in American society.

Jefferson's Ideal

Jefferson's ideal world was composed of "yeoman farmers," each of whom was roughly equal to the others in society's eyes, each of whom was free from the restrictions of both government and fellow citizens. Throughout his life, Jefferson offered a continuing challenge to Americans: Advance individualism and equality or see the death of the American experiment. Jefferson believed that the strength of this experiment depended upon a society of autonomous individuals and a society without great gaps between rich and poor. His challenge to his fellow Americans to create—and sustain—such a society has itself produced both economic and political conflict.

A society whose guiding document is the Declaration of Independence is a society assured of the freedom to dream—and to disagree. We know that Jefferson hated conflict, both personal and political. His tendency was to avoid confrontations of any sort, to squirrel himself away and write rather than to stand up and speak his mind. It is only through his written words that we can grasp Jefferson's utopian dream of a society of independent farmers, all pursuing their private dreams and all leading lives of middling prosperity.

Jefferson, this man of wealth and intellect, lived an essentially happy private life. But his public life was much more troublesome. From the first rumblings of the American Revolution in the 1760s to the North-South skirmishes of the 1820s that ultimately produced the Civil War, Jefferson was at or near the center of American political history. The issues were almost too many—and too crucial—for one lifetime: Jefferson had to choose between sup-

11

porting or rejecting the path of revolution. During and after the ensuing war, he was at the forefront of the battle for religious liberty. After endorsing the Constitution, he opposed the economic plans of Alexander Hamilton. At the end of the century, he fought the infamous Alien and Sedition Acts, which limited civil liberties. As president, he opposed the Federalist court, conspiracies to divide the union, and calls for a new war against England. Throughout his life, Thomas Jefferson, slaveholder, pondered the conflict between American freedom and American slavery. And from retirement at his Monticello retreat, he frowned at the rising spirit of commercialism he feared was dividing Americans and destroying his dream of American harmony.

No matter the issue, however, Thomas Jefferson invariably supported the rights of the individual. Worried as he was about the excesses of commercialism, he accepted them because his main concern was to live in a society where liberty and individualism could flourish. To Jefferson, Americans had to be free to worship as they desired. They also deserved to be free from an over-reaching government. To Jefferson, Americans should also be free to possess slaves.

Harmony, an Elusive Goal

Before reading the articles in this anthology, the editors ask readers to ponder the lives of John Winthrop and Thomas Jefferson. Each held a utopian vision, one based upon the demands of community and the other on the autonomy of the individual. Each dreamed of a country of perpetual new beginnings. Each found himself thrust into a position of leadership and found that conflict could not be avoided. Harmony, whether communal or individual, was a forever elusive goal.

The opposing visions of Winthrop and Jefferson have been at the heart of many differences among Americans from many backgrounds through the whole of American history. Moreover, their visions have provoked important responses that have helped shape American society, the American character, and many an American battle.

The editors of the American History Series have done extensive research to find representative opinions on the issues included in these volumes. They have found numerous outstanding opposing viewpoints from people of all times, classes, and genders in American history. From those, they have selected commentaries that best fit the nature and flavor of the period and topic under consideration. Every attempt was made to include the most important and relevant viewpoints in each chapter. Obviously, not every notable viewpoint could be included. Therefore, a selective, annotated bibliography has been provided at the end of each book to aid readers in seeking additional information.

The editors are confident that as this series reveals past conflicts, it will help revitalize the reader's views of the American present. In that spirit, the American History Series is dedicated to the proposition that American history is more complicated, more fascinating, and more troubling than John Winthrop or Thomas Jefferson ever dared to imagine.

John C. Chalberg
Consulting Editor

Introduction

"The history of Asian Americans combines the immigrant's quest for the American dream and the racial minority's confrontation with discriminatory laws and attitudes."

In the book *Making Waves: An Anthology of Writings by and About Asian American Women*, historian and writer Connie Young Yu tells the story of her maternal grandmother. Jeong Hing Tong ("Grandmother Lee") was born in China to a distinguished family fallen on hard times. Sometime around the turn of the century she married Lee Yoke Suey, an American-born son of a Chinese merchant, and accompanied him to San Francisco, California. Like her mother-in-law, who had come to America in 1875, the new bride seldom ventured out of her apartment in San Francisco's Chinatown—both because of her bound feet (which, being only 3 ½ inches long, hampered her standing for long periods and walking) and because Chinese women in America, at that time few in number, were often assumed to be prostitutes and abused as such. Yu writes:

> Once in San Francisco, Grandmother lived a life of confinement, as did her mother-in-law before her. When she went out, even in Chinatown, she was ridiculed for her bound feet. People called out mockingly to her, *"Jhat!"* meaning bound.

After several years in America, during which Yu's grandmother bore several children and survived the 1906 San Francisco earthquake, the family moved back to China because her husband believed that that was the only way for their children to receive a good education. (Chinese children in San Francisco were then taught in a segregated school.) After her husband's death, Grandmother Lee decided to return with her seven children to America. The year was 1924, and Congress had revised and tightened its immigration laws. At the Angel Island immigration station in San Francisco, she was ordered to be deported after a health inspection found that she had filariasis, or liver fluke. She was detained on Angel Island for fifteen months. Yu writes:

> While her distraught children had to fend for themselves in San Francisco (my mother, then fifteen, and her older sister had found work in a sewing factory), a lawyer was hired to fight for Grandmother's release from the detention barracks. . . .

Waiting month after month in the bleak barracks, Grandmother heard many heart-rending stories from women awaiting deportation. They spoke of the suicides of several despondent women who hanged themselves in the shower stalls. Grandmother could see the calligraphy carved on the walls by other detained immigrants, eloquent poems expressing homesickness, sorrow, and a sense of injustice.

After fifteen months she was cured of liver fluke and allowed to enter the United States. (Her case was used as a precedent in 1927 by Dr. Frederick Lam to convince federal health officials that liver fluke disease was noncommunicable and should not be used as a reason for exclusion or deportation.)

Yu's grandmother lived the rest of her years in America. Despite her longtime residence she was, as were all Asian-born immigrants, considered an "alien ineligible for citizenship" according to federal naturalization laws. In 1943, Congress passed a law allowing Chinese-born aliens to become naturalized U.S. citizens—provided that applicants had documented proof of their legal entry to the United States and could pass tests in English, American history, and the U.S. Constitution. Yu recalls:

My most vivid memory of Grandmother Lee is when she was in her seventies and studying for her citizenship. She had asked me to test her on the three branches of government and how to pronounce them correctly. I was a sophomore in high school and had entered the "What American Democracy Means to Me" speech contest of the Chinese American Citizens Alliance. When I said the words "judicial, executive, and legislative," I looked directly at my grandmother in the audience. She didn't smile, and afterwards, didn't comment much on my patriotic words. She had never told me about being on Angel Island. . . . It wasn't in my textbooks either.

Yu remembers walking her grandmother through Chinatown, "a small, slim figure always dressed in black," trying to ignore tourists staring at her tiny feet. "She exclaimed once that the size of my growing feet were 'like boats.'" But Yu also notes that her grandmother lived to see her children and grandchildren graduate from college and pursue careers in America and wonders "what she would have said of my own daughter who is now attending a university on an athletic scholarship. Feet like boats travel far?"

Grandmother Lee's story reveals to some extent how the public debates, policies, and controversies over Asian Americans that are the primary focus of this volume could and did affect individual lives. And, while the story of one person cannot encompass the history of all Asian Americans, Grandmother Lee's life history contains experiences common to many, including a struggle with cultural traditions alien to America (bound feet), conflicts of opinion and cultural differences between immigrants and their

Americanized children, and confrontation with immigration officials and policies. Vast numbers of Asians have immigrated to America to pursue opportunities lacking in their homeland because of gender customs, poverty, political oppression, and other reasons; many have encountered severe treatment by the populace as well as by U.S. laws after their arrival. Thus, the history of Asian Americans combines the immigrant's quest for the American dream and the racial minority's confrontation with discriminatory laws and attitudes.

It can be argued that Asian Americans have been shaped more by their American experiences than by their Asian heritage. Historian Sucheng Chan, in her introduction to *Asian Americans: An Interpretive History*, writes:

> Though it is often thought that these various groups are lumped together as "Asian Americans" because they or their ancestors have all come from Asia, there is a more important reason for treating them as a collective entity: for the most part, the host society has treated them all alike, regardless of what differences might have existed in their cultures, religions, and languages.

The treatment Asian Americans received from their "host society" was often far from welcoming. Asian immigrants "were the first to be singled out for discriminatory treatment by our immigration laws, and they were the only ethnic groups ever to be totally excluded," writes historian Roger Daniels in *Asian America*.

Such exclusionary laws are now a thing of the past. Immigration regulations, and other laws and policies that affect Asian immigrants to America and their descendants, have undergone several sweeping changes since the first Chinese Exclusion Act was passed in 1882. These changes have been both the cause and result of different "waves" of Asian immigration, and they are useful reference points in constructing a brief outline and overview of the history of Asian Americans.

The First Asian Immigrants

Prior to the second half of the nineteenth century Asians in the United States were exotic curiosities. These included Filipino sailors who escaped Spanish ships and arrived in Louisiana (then a French colony) in the 1760s, three shipwrecked Japanese sailors who were brought to a community north of present-day Santa Barbara, California, in 1815, and a group of Chinese students who came to study in the United States in 1847. One of their number, Yung Wing, graduated from Yale University and later became the first naturalized U.S. citizen of Chinese ancestry.

During this time no immigration laws existed barring entry of Asians or any other ethnic group. However, in 1790 Congress did pass a federal naturalization law governing how foreign immigrants could become U.S. citizens—providing that they were "free, white persons." This exclusion of nonwhite peoples from U.S. citizenship would have a profound impact on Asian Americans.

The first group of Asians to arrive in America in significant numbers were Chinese immigrants to California in the wake of the discovery of gold in that state in 1848. Between 1850 and 1870, about sixty thousand Chinese, most of them men, settled in California and neighboring territories, usually in segregated "Chinatowns." A few were wealthy merchants engaged in trade; most were impoverished farmers and workers fleeing harsh conditions in China. They labored as miners, often working claims abandoned by whites. In many frontier mining communities where women were scarce, Chinese took up "women's work," such as laundering clothes and cooking. In the 1860s the Central Pacific Railroad employed thousands of Chinese workers to construct the western half of the transcontinental railroad. Many employers at railroads, mining operations, and farms found Chinese laborers to be relatively cheap, dependable, and less likely than whites to form unions and to strike for higher wages. In the 1870s a few Chinese were employed by factories in New England and by plantations in the South.

The Anti-Chinese Movement and Exclusion

Despite some economic successes, Chinese immigrants faced several difficulties as a result of their ethnicity. Because they, with very few exceptions, were not eligible for U.S. citizenship (and the voting rights and other powers that came with it), full inclusion in U.S. society was denied to them. They were victims of both fraud and violence; and because their testimony was not allowed in U.S. courts, they had little legal recourse. In 1871 twenty-one Chinese were killed in a riot in Los Angeles; similar incidents of mob violence would plague the Chinese in ensuing decades.

State and municipal leaders in California, where most Chinese lived, enacted numerous laws and taxes aimed specifically at them. The arguments made against the Chinese were cultural, economic, and racial. The Chinese, it was argued, could never assimilate within American society or comprehend American democracy. Labor leaders argued that Chinese workers threatened their livelihood by working for lower wages, thereby undermining American living standards. Some spoke of the "yellow peril," predicting that an overpopulated China would swamp California with Chinese aliens. Others emphasized the moral threat Chinese opium addicts and prostitutes carried to America. Prostitution among Chinese undoubtedly did exist; historian Sucheta Mazumdar writes that many Chinese women "had been sold, kidnapped, and enticed under false pretenses by brothel owners." She goes on to write, however, that

> the unusually detailed information available on the lives of Chinese prostitutes in San Francisco was not inspired by purely humanitarian concerns. Rather, the publicity about "debauched" Chinese women who only came to work as prostitutes fueled the fears and hostility held by many California residents against the "unassimilable Chinese."

Not all Californians and Americans took part in the anti-Chinese movement. Among those expressing support for the Chinese in California were some missionaries, social reformers, and, to some extent, railroad magnates and other employers. Many Americans harbored contradictory views toward the Chinese—a reality expressed by Charles Nordhoff, an eastern journalist, who wrote of what he heard about the Chinese following a visit to San Francisco in the 1870s:

> He is patient, docile, persevering, quick to learn, . . .the best cook or waiter you ever saw.

> Last week he stole $600 out of my drawer, and is now in State Prison.

> He is sober.

> Last night you saw him smoking opium in the most horrible of dens.

> He saves his money.

> And takes it out of the State to spend in China.

> He is indispensable.

> But he is a curse to the community.

> He will make a useful citizen.

> His whole race is vicious and degraded.

In 1882 Congress passed the Chinese Exclusion Act, the first restrictive immigration law aimed at a specific nationality. Chinese workers were barred from entry for ten years (exceptions were made for a select few, including merchants, students, diplomats, and visitors). The ban, extended and tightened over the next decades, remained in effect until 1943. The Chinese Exclusion Act also declared Chinese residents already in the United States ineligible for naturalization, reaffirming the principle of the 1790 law limiting naturalization to "free, white persons." However, in an ultimately important development for Chinese and other Asian Americans, children born in the United States of alien parents became U.S. citizens under the Fourteenth Amendment to the Constitution, ratified in 1868.

The exclusion by law of Chinese laborers did not change the underlying economic and social conditions that had made them attractive to some employers—and had made America an attractive destination for Chinese and other Asians. Between 1882 (the year Chinese were excluded) and 1924 (by which time most other Asians were barred from immigration), thousands of immigrants from Japan, Korea, India, and the Philippines came to the United States. Many were actively recruited to work on farms, in fish canneries, and at other enterprises in California and other western states. As John Spreckels, an agriculture magnate, told Congress in 1907, "If we do not have the Japs to do the field labor, we would be in a bad fix, because you know American labor will not go into the fields." Some, especially the Japanese, were highly successful in establishing their own farms and businesses.

However, these other immigrants soon sparked a negative backlash similar to the one Chinese had endured previously. Complaints like those made against the Chinese could be heard once again: the new immigrants were unassimilable; their low wages undermined the living standards of American workers; they did not understand American democracy. Labor leaders such as Samuel Gompers of the American Federation of Labor (AFL) refused to include Asian workers in unionization efforts and instead sought their exclusion. Gompers once stated that every Asian immigrant "means the displacement of an American, and the lowering of the American standard of living."

In 1907 the United States negotiated a "Gentleman's Agreement" with Japan, limiting Japanese immigration (although not enough for some critics). People from most Asian countries were barred from immigrating in 1917; the 1924 immigration law, which restricted immigration in general, effectively excluded all Asians, including Japanese.

The Japanese, who by 1910 had surpassed the Chinese as the largest Asian American ethnic group, also replaced the Chinese as the main target of anti-Asian arguments. In addition to older assertions that they were unassimilable and that they forced down living standards, Japanese immigrants and their children faced new charges. One such charge focused on the penchant of many Japanese immigrants for saving money and buying agricultural land (often abandoned or unused). In a series of articles in 1905 the *San Francisco Chronicle* argued that "the Chinese are faithful laborers and do not buy land," but "the Japanese are unfaithful laborers and do buy land." California and other states soon passed statutes forbidding the Japanese (and all other "aliens ineligible for citizenship") from land ownership. Another main charge against the Japanese was a result of the growing international tension between the United States and Japan, prompting some to warn of an enemy alien presence. "Every one of these immigrants . . . ," said the *Chronicle* in 1905, "is a Japanese spy." Japanese Americans and their supporters attempted to refute such arguments by stressing their positive qualities. John P. Irish, an opponent of alien land laws, wrote in 1921 that the Japanese were "honest, law-abiding, and very industrious" people who by their "genius and industry" had transformed previously barren land into productive farms and vineyards.

Fear and resentment of the Japanese did not dissipate after immigration from Japan was stopped in 1924; in fact, they reached a high level of intensity during World War II. Following Japan's attack on Pearl Harbor in 1941, many community and political leaders, some of whom were veterans of previous anti-Japanese movements, expressed much fear and anger at Japanese Americans. Under President Franklin D. Roosevelt's Executive Order 9066, the U.S. military evacuated and relocated more than 110,000 Japanese Americans, two-thirds of them American citizens, and kept them in guarded detention centers. This massive and unprecedented governmental action against an entire ethnic group (for which the United States government formally apologized in 1988) was defended on the grounds that because America was at war with Japan, the Japanese in America posed a military and sabotage threat. "A Jap's a Jap," argued the commanding general of the region, John L. DeWitt. "It makes no difference whether he is an American citizen or not. . . . I don't want any of them."

The Special Case of Hawaii

While California and other mainland states were arguing over the exclusion and detention of Asian Americans, a different story was being played out in Hawaii. These Pacific islands were an independent kingdom from 1810 to 1894 and an independent republic (and U.S. protectorate) from 1894 to 1898. Officially annexed by the United States in 1898 and made a U.S. territory in 1901 (after decades of essentially U.S. economic control), Hawaii became the nation's fiftieth state in 1959. The experiences of Asian immigrants in Hawaii were in many respects quite different from those of Asians on the mainland, both before and after Hawaii's annexation by the United States.

Hawaii's indigenous Polynesian inhabitants are now classified as Pacific Islanders and are considered a subset of Asian Americans in many contemporary studies and surveys. However, their population declined greatly in the nineteenth century due to disease and other factors; by 1920 they comprised only 16 percent of the population. The majority of Hawaii's population was and is made up of Asian Americans of Chinese, Japanese, Filipino, and Korean background. Between 1850 and 1920, three hundred thousand Asian laborers immigrated to Hawaii, where they were employed in large sugar plantations owned predominantly by white Americans. By 1920 Asians comprised 62 percent of Hawaii's population—a situation far different from California (3.5 percent Asian) and the continental United States (.17 percent).

The experiences of Asians in Hawaii differed from those of mainland Asians in other ways as well. Unlike the United States, which discouraged female immigration (the 1875 Page Law, aimed at preventing the importation of prostitutes, effectively limited most female immigration from China), immigration policies in Hawaii encouraged female and family immigration. An anti-Asian movement such as California's anti-Chinese movement of the 1870s failed to attain broad popular support in Hawaii, partly because there was no large class of poor whites who resented competing for jobs with Asians.

The differences between Hawaii and the rest of the United States continued during World War II. Following Pearl Harbor, Hawaii was placed under martial law, and several hundred Japanese community leaders were immediately detained. But in sharp contrast to the situation on the mainland, Hawaii's 150,000 people of Japanese descent, about one third of the area's population, were largely left alone. Military authorities in Hawaii resisted calls from Washington for mass detention and evacuation, citing the impracticality of such an undertaking and the importance of Japanese American labor for the war effort. Newspapers in Hawaii, unlike many in California and other states, did not stir up fears that the Japanese would sabotage the U.S. war effort against Japan.

World War II and Immigration Reform

With the significant exception of the government evacuation and internment of Japanese Americans, World War II had some positive ramifications for Asian Americans. Filipino and Chinese Americans gained new stature as their countries of origin were allied with America against Japan; naturalization statutes were ignored as the U.S. Army conducted mass naturalization ceremonies before inducting Filipino and Chinese soldiers. Japanese Americans, at first barred from U.S. military service, eventually were recruited and drafted into the U.S. Army. Their military service, both as Japanese translators and interpreters in the Pacific and as members of the famous 442nd Regimental Combat Team in Europe, gained them lasting gratitude in the eyes of many Americans. Due in part to wartime labor shortages—and to an executive order by President Roosevelt barring racial discrimination in defense plants—Asian Americans were employed in technical, clerical, and industrial jobs from which they had previously been barred.

Many legal barriers to Asian American citizenship and immigration fell during and after World War II. In 1943 the official exclusion of Chinese was lifted, and Chinese Americans were allowed to become naturalized U.S. citizens. Racial bars to citizenship were lifted for Filipinos and East Indians in 1946 and for Japanese in 1952. Finally, in 1965, Congress abolished national quotas for immigration, placing Asian countries on an equal footing with other nations.

The 1965 immigration reforms resulted in massive and unforeseen demographic changes among Asian Americans. The population of Asian Americans grew from 878,000 in 1960 to nearly 7,000,000 in 1990. Chinese and Filipino Americans have overtaken the Japanese to become the two largest Asian ethnic groups. In addition, large numbers of immigrants and refugees from India, Korea, and Southeast Asia have come to the United States.

At the same time, the public image of Asian Americans has undergone dramatic shifts, sparked by growing recognition that both new Asian immigrants and third- and fourth-generation Asian Americans have achieved remarkable successes in education, in business, and in revitalizing American communities. Sociologist Peter I. Rose, writing in 1985 about Asian Americans, argues that

> no longer viewed as kowtowing inferiors . . . or as inscrutable heathens, Mongolian scabs, or untrustworthy neighbors loyal only to their motherlands, they are now seen by many as members of "model minorities" . . . . The pariahs have become paragons, lauded for their ingenuity and industry and for embodying the truest fulfillment of the "American Dream."

Scholars of Asian American history have differed on whether recent changes represent a fundamental break with America's past record of discrimination and exclusion and whether Asians are now fully accepted in American society. Do Asian Americans past and present represent the classic immigrant success story first embodied by European immigrants, many of whom, after being greeted by the Statue of Liberty, were initially scorned and discriminated against before they were accepted? Some observers argue that they do; others agree with Diana Fong, who wrote in the *New York Times* of May 1, 1982, that despite the successes of Asian Americans, "We're still not fully integrated into the mainstream because of our yellow skin . . . we still cannot escape the distinction of race."

While in detention in Angel Island, separated from her family, Grandmother Lee was both geographically and symbolically far distant from the Statue of Liberty that greeted her European immigrant counterparts. She was, like all Asian immigrants, what historian Ronald Takaki has called a "stranger from a different shore." The story of these "strangers" and the debates over public policy toward them are explored in the viewpoints of this volume.

CHAPTER 1

Chinese Immigrants and the American Response

Chapter Preface

The first significant wave of Asian immigration to the United States consisted of the tens of thousands of Chinese who arrived in California between 1850 and 1882. Chinese immigrants played a notable part in the economic development of the American West. However, they also became the first group of voluntary immigrants to be shut out of the United States by federal law (the 1882 Chinese Exclusion Act). The viewpoints in this chapter present some of the controversies surrounding Chinese immigration. The majority of the viewpoints center around California, the destination of most Chinese immigrants and the site of most anti-Chinese political activity.

The typical Chinese immigrants of this period were impoverished adult males from the southern province of Guangdong (Kwangtung) who were unmarried or had left their wives in China and who often paid for their passage to America by means of a credit-ticket system. Under this system, the immigrants borrowed money from Chinese brokers to be paid off with interest out of their earnings in America. These arrangements led some opponents of Chinese immigrants to attack them as "coolies" or bound laborers.

Chinese immigrants to America were a part of a larger development that saw an estimated two-and-a-half million people leave China between 1840 and 1900 and settle in Australia, Southeast Asia, Canada, Latin America, and other parts of the world. Most were fleeing severe conditions in China caused by civil war, famine, and heavy taxation. The Chinese who came to California (the Chinese name for the state was Gam Saan or golden mountain) generally sought to make their fortune and return to their native home. In this respect they were similar to many of their immigrant counterparts from Europe. In addition to prospecting for gold, many labored in miner's camps as cooks, servants, and laundrymen. Ninety percent of the workers on the Central Pacific Railroad laying track eastward through the Rocky Mountains were Chinese. Chinese were also imported in limited numbers to work in New England factories and in southern plantations. Cut off from their families in China and shunned by much of American society, the overwhelmingly male Chinese population tended to cluster in their own communities (Chinatowns) of which the one in San Francisco, California, became the largest and most famous.

Fearing Chinese cultural differences and resenting labor competition, many Americans in California and other parts of the United States subjected the Chinese to harassment and, in some cases, violence. Following an 1854 California Supreme Court ruling, California courts refused to admit the testimony of Chinese witnesses, leaving them with no legal recourse against attacks and fraud. States and cities passed a variety of discriminatory laws and taxes aimed specifically at the Chinese. Mob riots, such as the one that killed twenty-eight Chinese in Rock Springs, Wyoming, in 1885, killed or drove away numerous Chinese immigrants.

Efforts by the state of California to limit the numbers of Chinese immigrants were frustrated by Supreme Court rulings making immigration policy solely a federal government responsibility. In addition, China and the United States negotiated and signed the Burlingame Treaty in 1868. Valued by American merchants for the trading privileges it secured in China, the treaty also guaranteed to both countries the right of immigration.

These barriers were eventually overcome, however. In 1880 the two countries negotiated a new treaty giving the United States the right to "regulate, limit, or suspend" Chinese immigration. In 1882 Congress passed the Chinese Exclusion Act. The nation's first general immigration restriction bill, it banned the entry of Chinese laborers (while allowing limited immigration of Chinese scholars and merchants). Subsequent pieces of legislation tightened immigration restrictions. An 1888 law abruptly removed the right of Chinese American residents visiting China to return to the United States. The 1892 Geary Act required all Chinese to register with the federal government.

Chinese continued to enter the country, in some cases illegally or under false pretenses (by pretending to be sons of U.S.-born American citizens, for instance). However, because of U.S. immigration restrictions and the heavily imbalanced sex ratio of the Chinese American population, the numbers of Chinese in America steadily declined from 125,000 in 1882 to a little over 60,000 in 1920.

VIEWPOINT 1

"I am deeply impressed with the conviction that, in order to enhance the prosperity and preserve the tranquility of the State, measures must be adopted to check this tide of Asiatic immigration."

Chinese Immigration Must Be Restricted

John Bigler (1805–1871)

The first Asians to arrive in the United States in significant numbers were the Chinese immigrants who landed in California in the mid-1800s. Like people from many other places, the Chinese were drawn by the discovery of gold there in 1848. Historical records indicate that they were welcomed by some leaders of the new and thinly populated state; in 1851 Governor John Mc-Dougal called for "further immigration and settlement of Chinese—one of our most worthy classes of newly adopted citizens."

Anti-Chinese sentiment was quick to develop, however, especially among miners who blamed the Chinese for depressing their wages. A special committee of the California legislature issued a report in April 1852 urging legislative action to deal with "the concentration, within our State limits, of vast numbers of Asiatic races." The committee suggested subjecting the Chinese to a foreign miner's license tax (a tax passed in 1850 for all foreign miners had expired in 1851 due to enforcement difficulties). On April 23, 1852, California's third governor, John Bigler, presented a special message on Asian immigration to the California legislature. The following viewpoint consists of excerpts from the governor's address, which according to historian Roger Daniels "marks the formal beginning of the anti-Chinese movement."

Bigler, a lawyer and Democrat, had moved to California in 1849,

Excerpts of John Bigler's speech to the California legislature, reprinted from "Governor's Special Address," *Daily Alta California*, April 25, 1852.

26

and was a member of the California Assembly before being elected governor. He served two terms as governor, from 1852 to 1856. In his 1852 address, Bigler makes several arguments concerning the undesirability of Chinese immigrants ("Asiatics"), which then numbered about ten thousand in the state. He argues that most of them are "Coolies" bound to long contracts of indentured servitude, that they cannot be trusted to tell the truth at criminal trials, and that they are ineligible for U.S. citizenship because of their race. Among his proposals for restricting Asian immigration was a program of taxation and a federal law making "coolie contracts" unenforceable. Bigler also defends the right of the state of California to regulate and restrict immigration, despite Supreme Court decisions stating that immigration policy was under the sole jurisdiction of the national government. Most of Bigler's proposals in this address were eventually enacted into law.

The subject which I deem it my duty to present for your consideration before our final separation, is the present wholesale importation to this country, of immigrants from the Asiatic quarter of the globe. I am deeply impressed with the conviction that, in order to enhance the prosperity and to preserve the tranquility of the State, measures must be adopted to check this tide of Asiatic immigration, and prevent the exportation by them of the precious metals which they dig up from our soil without charge, and without assuming any of the obligations imposed upon citizens. I allude, particularly, to a class of Asiatics known as "Coolies," who are sent here, as I am assured, and as is generally believed, under contract to work in our mines for a term; and who, at the expiration of the term, return to their native country. I am sensible that a proposition to restrict international intercourse, or to check the immigration of even Asiatics, would appear to conflict with the long cherished benevolent policy of our Government. That Government has opened its paternal arms to the "oppressed of all nations," and it has offered them an asylum and a shelter from the iron rigor of despotism. The exile pilgrim and the weary immigrant, have been recipients of its noble hospitalities. In this generous policy, so far as it effects Europeans, or others capable of becoming citizens under our laws, I desire to see no change; nor do I desire to see any diminution of that spirit of liberality which pervades the naturalization laws of the United States.

A question around which there has been thrown some doubt, is whether Asiatics could, with safety, be admitted to the enjoyments of all the rights of citizens in our Courts of Justice. If they are ignorant of the solemn character of the oath or affirmation, in the form prescribed by the Constitution and Statutes, or if they are indifferent to the solemn obligation which an oath imposes to speak the truth, it would be unwise to receive them as jurors or permit them to testify in courts of law, more especially in cases affecting the rights of others than Asiatics.

Citizenship and Race

Congress, possessing the exclusive power to establish a uniform rule of naturalization, has enacted that "every alien, being a *free white person*, may become a citizen of the United State," by complying with certain conditions. Of the construction of this law, Chancellor Kent remarks, that "the Act of Congress confines the description of Aliens capable of naturalization to *free white persons*." "I presume," continues the learned writer, that "this excludes the inhabitants of Africa and their descendants; and it may become a question, to what extent persons of mixed blood are excluded, and what shades and degrees of mixture of color disqualify an alien from application for the benefits of the Act of naturalization. Perhaps there might be difficulties, also, as to the copper-colored natives of America, or the yellow or tawny races of the Asiatics; and it may be well doubted whether any of them are white persons in the purview of the law. It is the declared law of New York, South Carolina, Tennessee, (and other States,) that Indians are not citizens, but distinct tribes, living under the protection of the Government, and consequently they never can be citizens under the Act of Congress."

It is certain that no Asiatic has yet applied for, or has received the benefits of this Act. Indeed, I am not aware that a single subject of the Chinese Empire ever acquired a residence or a domicil in any of the States of the Union, except, perhaps, in this. In this State their habits have been migratory; and so far as I can learn, very few of them have evinced a disposition to acquire a domicil, or, as citizens, to identify themselves with the country. Gold, with a talismanic power, has overcome these national habits of reserve and non-intercourse which the Chinese and their neighbors have hitherto exhibited; and under the impulse which the discovery of the precious metals in California has given to their cupidity, vast numbers of them are immigrating hither, not, however, to avail themselves of the blessings of a free Government. They do not seek our land as "the asylum for the oppressed of all nations." They have no desire (even if permitted by the constitution and laws) to absolve themselves from allegiance to other powers, and, under the laws of the United States, become American citizens. They come to acquire a certain amount of the precious metals, and then return to their native country.

I invite your attention, for a moment, to results which may ensue, if by inaction we give further encouragement to the mania for emigration which pervades several of the Asiatic States, and which it may be presumed, is being rapidly diffused throughout all continental Asia. The area of Asia is 17,865,000 English square miles, and the total population is computed by the best authorities at three hundred and seventy-five millions two hundred and thirty thousand. The population of the Chinese Empire and dependent States alone is 168,000,000. It will be readily perceived that millions might be detached from such myriads, without any perceptible diminution of the aggregate population; and that vast numbers may be induced, under contracts, to emigrate to a country which they are told contains inexhaustible mines of gold and silver. The facilities afforded them for emigration are rapidly increasing, and few vessels now enter our ports from Asiatic countries which are not crowded with these peculiar people. I have received intelligence, from reliable sources, that the average rate charged an Asiatic from China to California, is forty dollars; that over two thousand of their number have arrived at San Francisco, within the last few weeks, and that at least five thousand are now on their way hither. Letters from Canton to the end of January, estimate the immigration from that port to California, for 1852, at over twenty thousand, nearly all of whom will be hired by Chinese masters, to come here and collect gold under the direction and control of the master himself, who accompanies them, or of an agent.

I have mentioned in the preceding portion of this communication, that numbers of Asiatics have been and are being sent here, under contracts to labor for a term of years in our mines at merely nominal wages, and their families have been retained as hostages for the faithful performances of the contracts. . . .

If it be admitted that the introduction of one hundred thousand, or a less number of "Coolies" into this State, under such contracts with nonresidents, may endanger the public tranquility and injuriously affect the interests of our people, then we are bound to adopt measures to avert such evils. I therefore respectfully submit for your consideration two distinct propositions:

1st. Such an exercise of the taxing power by the State as will check the present system of discriminate and unlimited Asiatic immigration.

2d. A demand by the State of California for the prompt interposition of Congress, by the passage of an Act prohibiting "Coolies" shipped to California under contracts, from laboring in the mines of this State. With the consent of the State, Congress would have the clear right to interpose such safeguards as in their wisdom might be deemed necessary. The power to tax as well as to entirely exclude this class of Asiatic immigrants, it is believed, can be constitutionally exercised by the State. As the subject is one of great magnitude, I have deemed it my duty to examine the opinions of eminent writers on international law, as well as the written opinions of the Judges of the Supreme Court of the United States.

An Inferior Race

In his 1862 inaugural message, California's first Republican governor, Leland Stanford, characterized Chinese immigration as a threat to the future of the state. Ironically, Stanford later employed thousands of Chinese when he was president of the Central Pacific Railroad.

While the settlement of our State is of the first importance, the character of those who shall become settlers is worthy of scarcely less consideration. To my mind it is clear that the settlement among us of an inferior race is to be discouraged by every legitimate means. Asia, with her numberless millions, sends to our shores the dregs of her population. Large numbers of this class are already here; and, unless we do something early to check their immigration, the question which of the two tides of immigration meeting upon the shores of the Pacific shall be turned back will be forced upon our consideration, when far more difficult than now of disposal. There can be no doubt but that the presence of numbers among us of a degraded and distinct people must exercise a deleterious influence upon the superior race, and, to a certain extent, repel desirable immigration. It will afford me great pleasure to confer with the Legislature in any constitutional action, having for its object the impression of the immigration of the Asiatic races.

It might be urged, as an objection to the imposition of a tax, that such a statute would be a regulation of commerce, and that the power to regulate commerce is exclusively reposed in Congress. I am aware that a majority of the Judges composing the Supreme Court of the United States, have decided that statutes passed by the Legislatures of New York and Massachusetts, imposing a tax on passengers of a ship from a foreign port, were regulations of foreign commerce; and that the power to regulate commerce being exclusively reposed in Congress, the statutes were void. But the whole Court were understood to concede the right of the State to tax immigrants after they were on shore. The power of States to exclude immigrants is also shown by the best writers on international law, as well as by the decisions of the Supreme Court of the United States. . . .

I will remark that the principle involved in the recommendation which I have made, does not appear to me to be entirely analogous to that contained in the statutes of New York and Massachusetts, and declared to be unconstitutional by the Supreme Court of the United States. In those cases it was proposed to impose a tax upon "free white persons," who could acquire the rights of American citizens. But, in the present instance, it is proposed to tax persons who, it is believed, cannot assume the obligations imposed upon, nor acquire the civil or political privileges of citizens of the United States. In those cases, the public health merely was endangered; but it is believed that in this instance the most vital interests of the State and people—and, perhaps, the public peace are at stake. Whether the objection raised by the Supreme Court to the statute of New York, that it was a regulation of commerce, and that, therefore, it was void, would apply to a statute of this State, imposing a similar tax upon Asiatics, I must leave it to you and to other tribunals, to determine.

There is no official information in this department, touching the nature of the contracts said to have been made with Asiatics, by their own countrymen, or by foreign residents in the Chinese Empire, to work in our mines. It is not officially known to this department whether those persons are here in a state of voluntary or involuntary servitude. But if it be ascertained that their immigration and servitude is voluntary, I am still of the opinion that the Legislature may enact laws to prevent or discourage shipments of vast bodies of "Coolies" into this State. I am convinced not only that such a measure is necessary, but I am also convinced that there is nothing in the Federal Constitution which forbids the enactment of such laws. . . .

California's Situation

It must be conceded that the extraordinary wants of this State will demand novel if not extraordinary legislation. The history and condition of California is peculiar—it is without parallel. Her resources, like her exigencies, are without precedent. In framing laws, therefore, to meet such exigencies, it is clear that we cannot be guided entirely by precedents which have been established in the common course of events in other States. But, though our condition may sometimes require departures from precedents in the enactment as well as in the execution of laws, we should not fail to follow the Constitution, both as our chart and as the palladium of our liberties.

Having thus performed one of the most important duties which will perhaps devolve upon me during my term of office, I commit this subject to your care, and entreat for it your careful consideration.

"We are not the degraded race you would make us."

A Defense of Chinese Immigrants

Norman Asing (dates unknown)

On May 5, 1852, the *Daily Alta California*, a San Francisco newspaper, published an open letter to California governor John Bigler responding to his recent message concerning Chinese immigrants. The writer of the letter was Norman Asing, a Chinese merchant in San Francisco. Little is known about Asing (sometimes spelled Assing) aside from the fact that he was considered by outsiders to be a powerful leader in and spokesman for the Chinese community in San Francisco. In his letter, excerpted here, Asing defends the character and history of the Chinese people, asserts that he and others are living disproof of Bigler's assertion that the Chinese cannot become naturalized U.S. citizens, and argues that as state governor Bigler has no authority to regulate immigration.

To His Excellency Gov. Bigler

Sir: I am a Chinaman, a republican, and a lover of free institutions; am much attached to the principles of the government of the United States, and therefore take the liberty of addressing you as the chief of the government of this State. . . . The effect of your late message has been thus far to prejudice the public mind against my people, to enable those who wait the opportunity to hunt them down, and rob them of the rewards of their toil. . . .

I am not much acquainted with your logic, that by excluding population from this State you enhance its wealth. I have always

From Norman Asing, "To His Excellency Gov. Bigler," *Daily Alta California*, May 5, 1852.

considered that population was wealth; particularly a population of producers, of men who by the labor of their hands or intellect, enrich the warehouses or the granaries of the country with the products of nature and art. You are deeply convinced you say "that to enhance the prosperity and preserve the tranquility of this State, Asiatic immigration must be checked." This, your Excellency, is but one step towards a retrograde movement of the government. . . . It was one of the principal causes of quarrel between you (when colonies) and England; when the latter pressed laws against emigration, you looked for immigration; it came, and immigration made *you what you are*—your nation what it is. It transferred you at once from childhood to manhood and made you great and respectable throughout the nations of the earth. I am sure your Excellency cannot, if you would, prevent your being called the descendant of an immigrant, for I am sure you do not boast of being a descendant of the red man. But your further logic is more reprehensible. You argue that this is a republic of a particular race— that the Constitution of the United States admits of no asylum to any other than the pale face. This proposition is false in the extreme, and you know it. The declaration of your independence, and all the acts of your government, your people, and your history are all against you.

We Are Not a Degraded Race

It is true, you have degraded the Negro because of your holding him in involuntary servitude, and because for the sake of union in some of your states such was tolerated, and amongst this class you would endeavor to place us; and no doubt it would be pleasing to some would-be freemen to mark the brand of servitude upon us. But we would beg to remind you that when your nation was a wilderness, and the nation from which you sprung *barbarous*, we exercised most of the arts and virtues of civilized life; that we are possessed of a language and a literature, and that men skilled in science and the arts are numerous among us; that the productions of our manufactories, our sail, and workshops, form no small share of the commerce of the world; and that for centuries, colleges, schools, charitable institutions, asylums, and hospitals, have been as common as in your own land. . . . And we beg to remark, that so far as the history of our race in California goes, it stamps with the test of truth the fact that we are not the degraded race you would make us. We came amongst you as mechanics or traders, and following every honorable business of life. You do not find us pursuing occupations of degrading character, except you consider labor degrading, which I am sure you do not; and if our countrymen save the proceeds of their industry from the tavern and the gambling house to spend it on farms or town lots or on their families, surely you will admit that even these are virtues. You say "you desire to see no change in the generous policy of this government as far as regards Europeans." It is out of your power to say, however, in what way or to whom the doctrines of the Constitution shall apply. You have no more right to propose a measure for checking immigration, than you have the right of sending a message to the Legislature on the subject. As far as regards the color and complexion of our race, we are perfectly aware that our population have been a little more tan than yours.

Chinese Workers Are Not Slaves

In a letter to Governor John Bigler dated April 29, 1852, and published in the San Francisco Herald *and other California newspapers, Chinese immigrants deny Bigler's charge that they are bound laborers.*

"Cooly" is not a Chinese word: it has been imported into China from foreign parts, as it has been into this country. What its original signification was, we do not know; but with us it means a common laborer, and nothing more. We have never known it used among us as a designation of a class, such as you have in view—persons bound to labor under contracts which they can be forcibly compelled to comply with. The Irishmen who are engaged in digging down your hills, the men who unload ships, who clean your streets, or even drive your drays, would, if they were in China, be considered "Coolies;" tradesman, mechanics of every kind, and professional men, would not. If you mean by "Coolies" laborers, many of our countrymen in the mines are "Coolies," and many again are not. There are among them tradesmen, mechanics, gentry, (being persons of respectability and who enjoy a certain rank and privilege,) and schoolmasters, who are reckoned with the gentry, and with us considered a respectable class of people. None are "Coolies," if by that word you mean bound men or *contract slaves*.

Your Excellency will discover, however, that we are as much allied to the African race and the red man as you are yourself, and that as far as the aristocracy of *skin* is concerned, ours might compare with many of the European races; nor do we consider that your Excellency, as a Democrat, will make us believe that the framers of your declaration of rights ever suggested the propriety of establishing an aristocracy of *skin*. I am a naturalized citizen, your Excellency, of Charleston, South Carolina, and a Christian, too; and so hope you will stand corrected in your assertion "that none of the Asiatic class" as you are pleased to term them, have applied for benefits under our naturalization act. I could point out to you numbers of citizens, all over the whole continent, who have taken advantage of your hospitality and citizenship, and I defy you to say that our race have ever abused that hospitality or forfeited their claim on this or any of the governments of South America, by an infringement on the laws of the countries into which they pass. You find us peculiarly peaceable and orderly. It does not cost your state much for our criminal prosecution. We apply less to your courts for redress, and so far as I know, there are none who are a charge upon the state, as paupers.

Gold and Migration

You say that "gold, with its talismanic power, has overcome those natural habits of non-intercourse we have exhibited." I ask you, has not gold had the same effect upon your people, and the people of other countries, who have migrated hither? Why, it was gold that filled your country (formerly a desert) with people, filled your harbors with ships and opened our much-coveted trade to the enterprise of your merchants.

You cannot, in the face of facts that stare you in the face, assert that the cupidity of which you speak is ours alone; so that your Excellency will perceive that in this age a change of cupidity would not tell. Thousands of your own citizens come here to dig gold, with the idea of returning as speedily as they can.

We think you are in error, however, in this respect, as many of us, and many more, will acquire a domicile amongst you.

But, for the present, I shall take leave of your Excellency, and shall resume this question upon another occasion which I hope you will take into consideration in a spirit of candor. Your predecessor pursued a different line of conduct towards us, as will appear by reference to his message.

I have the honor to be your Excellency's very obedient servant.

Norman Asing

*"California needs population, but it would be far better
for her future prosperity—aye, for her safety—to be
content with her present population, than to increase it
manifold by inviting Chinese immigration."*

Chinese Immigrants
Are Harming California

California Legislature

By 1870 the population of Chinese immigrants in the United
States had reached 60,000, with nearly 50,000 residing in California. Over the next decade (a time of economic hardship in the
American West), that population continued to grow, as did anti-
Chinese sentiment and violence. Much of the anti-Chinese movement's support came from white workers anxious over labor
competition with Chinese immigrants. The issue of Chinese labor
received much attention in the eastern United States in June 1870
when about seventy-five Chinese were imported to replace striking workers at a shoe factory in North Adams, Massachusetts.
Chinese workers during this time were also imported to the
South in limited numbers by planters in the wake of the abolition
of black slavery. California, however, remained both the site of
most of America's Chinese population and the center of the anti-
Chinese movement.

In 1876 a committee of the California state legislature conducted
investigative hearings on Chinese immigration in San Francisco
and Sacramento. Most of the witnesses selected to testify favored
excluding Chinese immigrants. The committee published its findings in an 1877 pamphlet titled *An Address to People of the United
States upon the Evils of Chinese Immigration*. The pamphlet was dis-
tributed across the nation. A condensed form of the pamphlet,

From the California Legislature's Anti-Chinese Memorial to Congress, 1877. Reprinted from
Chinese Immigration (Washington, DC: R.O. Polkinhorn, 1882).

submitted to Congress as a "Memorial," is reprinted here.

In their report, the members of the California legislature express their concerns over the threat that Chinese immigrants ("Mongolians") pose to California's white working class. The ideal American society, they argue, is one in which labor is valued and the population is racially homogeneous. Continued Chinese immigration, they conclude, will result in the "degrading of labor," unavoidable racial conflict, and the formation of a society in which the wealthy few oversee masses of Chinese slaves.

The Legislature of the State of California, at its thirteenth session, respectfully represents to the Senate and House of Representatives in Congress assembled, as follows:

A perfect equality of political rights, and a universal cooperation of the entire people, or at least its moral capability of cooperating in the making and administering the laws, being the cornerstone of the permanence of every republic, your memorialists deem it of the most vital importance that we should not invite a national element into our midst whose social character and moral relations are so repulsive to those fundamental principles upon which our society, and indeed every civilized society, is founded, that we can neither socially amalgamate with it, nor entrust it with the prerogatives and duties of participation in the administration of our Government. It is neither a shortsighted policy of national exclusiveness, nor a lack of charity for inferior nationalities, that impels California to lift her voice against the unrestricted influx of a race in every respect more undesirable than that population, for the absolute exclusion of which, the National Administration and Congress have already manifested their willingness to cooperate with those States which desire to rid themselves of this element of national discord.

In appealing to Congress for protection against the contingency of an overwhelming immigration of Mongolians, the Legislature of California is solely actuated by the love and care for the safety and maintenance of our institutions, and the consciousness that a condition of slavery in our midst must unavoidably be the result of an unrestrained immigration of Mongolians. The Representatives of the people of California deem it a solemn duty to manifest to the National Congress the conviction that, if this immigration be not discouraged, the time is not far when degraded labor will have become as identified with the pecuniary interests of a portion of the people of this State, and as inimical to the

37

fundamental principles of a democratic government, as Negro labor in the now rebellious States.

Even the position of the small number of free Negroes in the free States teaches us that no republican government ought to suffer the presence of a race which must, socially and politically, be always separate and distinct, and the antipathy to which is stronger in regulating its position and disabilities in society than the laws of the land. In the conviction of your memorialists, it is not alone a legalized state of slavery, which undermines the foundation of a republic, but that social relation which is the necessary consequence of the settlement in *one* community of two entirely uncongenial races, and which tends to produce, though the inferior race may be nominally free, the respective positions of a governing and a servile class, is just as dangerous to the permanence of republican institutions and ought to be as much guarded against as slavery itself.

The Threat to California

Your memorialists assert that California is in a position far different from that of her sister States in regard to the settlement within the United States of races which, as long as self-respect and conservatism govern the Anglo-Saxon race in America, can never be admitted to social amalgamation or political equality. The free States in the East could only then fully appreciate the evils and complications which threaten the social system of California, if they were as much exposed to the danger of becoming colonies of free Negroes as California to the immigration of millions of Mongolians. Though the free Negro speaks our language, though he grows up among us, worships the same God as ourselves, and is accustomed to our institutions, yet the free States find the presence of a comparatively small population of this race exceedingly annoying, and fraught with dangers not only to the peace of their own community, but to the harmony between their laws and the constitutional policy of the National Legislature. What may be the difficulties and dangers which California will have to encounter, if she is not to be protected from the unlimited influx of a race which already comprises the eighth part of her entire population, which is utterly a stranger to our language, to the fundamental principles of enlightened religion, to our consciousness of moral obligations, and, with a few individual exceptions, even to a sense of the most common proprieties of life. Does it not deserve the serious consideration of the National Legislature and of the treaty-making power, that not the slightest barrier exists for the protection of California against immigration from a contiguous semicivilized empire, which counts its slaves by hundreds of millions?

The Congress of seventeen hundred and ninety and seventeen

The purported consequences of Chinese labor competition are depicted in an illustration and accompanying article excerpted from the November 7, 1885, issue of the San Francisco magazine the Wasp.

But it is not alone in the field of labor that the evils of the Asiatic interloper are felt. He is the ruin of the household. Our artist has pictured on the last page a panorama of distress which is by no means a work of imagination. The wreck of the white working-man's family is graphically depicted. The leering, idiotic and immodest attitude of the daughter of the house shows the damning influence of the opium-pipe; the father, driven from employment, despairingly seeks relief in a suicide's death, leaving his widow destitute, famished and despondent; the son, driven to stealing bread for himself and mother, finds himself a felon. In the clutches of the law; while near by in a huge manufactory may be seen the cause of all the evil in the fact that Chinese are driving the white men from employment, hurling them from the windows and kicking them out of the doors. Surely such a spectacle must stir the blood in the veins of either Saxon or Celt.

hundred and ninety-five, when no American statesman had the slightest anticipation that the domain of the Union would stretch to the Pacific Ocean, and when the people of the United States came but little into personal contact with the nations of Asia, believed sufficiently to provide against the contingency of other than congenial and desirable immigration, by excluding from the rights of citizenship all but free white aliens. It is due to the wisdom of our forefathers and to the care and foresight with which they planted institutions intended to be permanent and beyond contingencies which human sagacity might provide against, that they would have put other restrictions upon the immigration of inferior races, besides the disability of acquiring the rights of citizenship, could they have but anticipated so near a geographical relation between the United States and China, that the former would be liable to a continual and unlimited influx of population from the latter. It is, therefore, in the belief of your memorialists, no extravagant hope which California entertains, that at the present time the same Congress and the same Administration, which believe it to be their duty to offer the Federal aid to States desirous to entirely exclude Negroes from their soil, will not refuse to her the same cooperation against a race much more uncongenial to us than the other, and much more dangerous on account of the facility with which countless millions may at any time be thrust upon us by the pleasure of a barbarian potentate.

Whilst the influence of slavery is losing territory in our Eastern sister States, the unrestrained settlement of Mongolians in California is slowly but surely building up such social relations as will soon place the two races practically in the position of masters and unfree servants. A race so degraded, that it is stated by the committee of this Legislature appointed to confer with the Chinese companies at San Francisco, that according to the information from these leaders of the Chinese, there are but one hundred respectable families (i.e., married women with children) among a population of fifty thousand Chinese, a large proportion of which number consists of females—a race so devoid of a sense of truth and veracity that the testimony of ever so many individuals to the same facts has no weight upon the minds of our juries—such a race can certainly not reside long in our midst without awakening all those selfish interests which desire the introduction of cheap labor, and the immediate cultivation of articles heretofore produced by slave labor in the South, even at the cost of an irradicable system of involuntary servitude.

Endangering the White Working Class

Degradation of labor and the impoverishment of the laboring classes are poisons which destroy the lifeblood of a republic. There are enough resources in the almost unbounded domains of the Union to support the dignity of labor for centuries, unless it is brought into competition with slave labor. Chinese labor ranks no higher in the public respect than slave labor. Its compensation is so low in proportion to the necessities of life in California that the white laborer cannot compete with the Chinaman, who needs neither a civilized abode, nor decent clothing, nor education for his children. The larger portion of the Chinese has been engaged in mining. During the early years after the discovery of gold in this State, when our population was sparse, and when there was no lack of rich surface mines, the American and European miner experienced no hardship from the presence of the Chinese; but, as in the course of time, the rich surface diggings became more and more exhausted, and the chances of generous reward for individual labor in mining claims became rare, the antipathies of our own race against the Mongolians were aroused, and grew daily stronger in proportion as the mines occupied by Mongolians became of increasing importance to American citizens or Europeans, who sought the means of a modest and toilsome subsistence for a permanent settlement upon our soil.

As a natural consequence, California has witnessed those collisions of races which are deplorable, but which will always manifest themselves between a superior and an inferior race, which are forced into permanent contact, and whose mutual antipathies are strengthened by a conflict of pecuniary interests. In many mining sections, organizations were formed for the purpose of forcibly preventing Chinese from working in places where they had not yet made their appearance, and to eject them from districts where the mineral would reward the labor of white persons. These arbitrary mining regulations were enforced by the miners, and as the Executive authorities of the State were not desirous to produce civil strife by forcibly resisting the popular will, laws have existed and still exist in this State, outside of the legal power, in restriction of the right of Chinese to work the mines.

By such treatment, and by such oppressive and tyrannical bearing, as the rude and passionate classes of a superior race will always assume towards a race residing among them, whose settlement is highly undesirable, a large portion of the Chinese in the mines was induced to resort to our towns and cities, whereby the share of the latter in the great social evil—for as such we consider the settling of the Chinese among us—has been disproportionally increased. Although the Chinese in the cities have so far not met with that spirit of persecution which discouraged their settlement in the mines, yet it is manifest that a bitter hostility against them is a marked and growing feeling among the laboring classes of our cities. This feeling is mainly due to the intrusion of the Chinese into several branches of industry, to the serious detriment of the white workingmen heretofore engaged in them. The latter, being unable to maintain a decent and civilized subsistence upon wages which afford the Chinaman a comfortable living, were compelled, in every case where Chinese competition made its appearance, to retire from their profession, and abandon its exercise to their Chinese competitors. Several of our industrial professions, which but a few years ago afforded a profitable employment to a large number of persons of our own race, and which were yearly growing in importance and in their capacity of employing white workingmen and their families, are now monopolized by Chinese, to the exclusion of our own citizens. Our working classes look, therefore, anxiously into the future, for they feel that the Chinese, with their skill for mechanical imitation, will slowly but surely push themselves into one profession after another, and reduce the value of labor to the level which it occupies in monarchies, and which makes it equivalent to pauperism and degradation. This apprehension is well founded, if the success heretofore enjoyed by Chinese competition with our working classes may be considered as a fair criterion of the position of Chinese labor to white labor in the future.

Your memorialists are aware that the Legislature of a republic ought always to encourage rather than discourage competition of labor, so long as this labor emanates from congenial or homogeneous races; but if her working classes are forced to compete with a race entirely foreign to all our moral, social, and political interests, and independent of the necessities which a civilized life imposes, then it becomes certainly the duty of the Government to shield the labor of her citizens, and to anticipate, by wise legislation, the violent collision which must be the unavoidable result of an unrestricted encroachment of an inferior race upon the self-respect, the dignity, and, above all, upon the indispensable resources of the working classes of the governing race. California needs population, but it would be far better for her future prosperity—aye, for her safety—to be content with her present population, than to increase it manifold by inviting Chinese immigration.

The Mongolian is not only by degrees diminishing the means of subsistence of our white workingmen, but he is a serious impediment in the way of the immigration of the poor and humble classes of our own race from the Eastern States and Europe. As labor is undignified and despised in the slave States, because it is performed by a race which is inferior in nature and in social standing, the unrestrained immigration of Mongolians to this State, and their intrusion into every mechanical profession, will have the same humiliating and demoralizing influence upon the working classes of our citizens. No American or European workman, even if he could work for the wages of the Mongolian, will work with him at the same workbench, in the same workshop, or, in those branches which the Chinaman does succeed in monopolizing, even in the same profession. The Chinese will infinitely more degrade labor than the Negro in the slave States has done. The statement of the Chinese companies themselves, that there are but one hundred respectable families in the State, among fifty thousand Chinese, is a correct guide to their moral condition—if such a term can be at all applied to a people who have not the least consciousness of truth and veracity, and whose entire female population (with the exception of one hundred, according to the statement of the Chinese) are engaged in the business of prostitution.

The Social Habits of the Chinese

The social habits and customs of the Chinese, if we except the merchants, are so loathsome that even the atmosphere becomes pregnant with the effluvia of their abodes, and that entire streets in which they have settled—some of which in the speedy course of California progress have become most eligible business sites—are held in disrepute, and prevent the natural growth of commercial thoroughfares and of wholesome traffic.

Such, with the exception of some respectable Chinese merchants in our larger cities, is the character of the Chinese who are in our midst and who continue to come. The Chinese population among us forms a State within a State; they are under the secret control of the five organizations which are known as companies, whose orders and decisions they implicitly obey. All indications tend to show that there exists between themselves a relation of involuntary servitude, but the slavish subjection of the Mongolian to his social system and the fear of the revenge of his superiors are so great that nothing can induce him to disclose the nature of the power which holds him to strict obedience, even against the police and judicial authorities of this State. The presence of hordes of Mongolians would at present undoubtedly be advantageous to the capitalist and the manufacturer. These classes, although very necessary to the development of a young State, are generally not as careful of the preservation of the principles of freedom and of the exclusion of every element dangerous to the maintenance and the purity of republican institutions, as they are anxious of reaping immediate and unusual profits. Better, far better, that our manufacturing interests should sleep a few years longer, until the natural decrease of the value of labor will make the employment of white laborers profitable, than to develop them by a race which we shall not be able to exclude when the time will have arrived when white workmen will gladly cooperate with the capitalists who desire to experiment in this State with the cultivation of Southern products.

But your memorialists assert that even the *present* value of the labor of our own workingmen is not in the way of the profitable development of new resources in this State. Laborers of our own race have been successfully and profitably employed in experiments of manufacture. Only, then, when a capitalist, desiring to underbid his competitors, introduced Chinese labor—only then it became impossible for others engaged in the same business to continue employing the labor of our own citizens.

It is only lately that it has become known to the people of Europe that California has all the necessary elements to become one of the richest vineyards in the world. The efforts which have been made to attract the vine-growing people of Europe to the reward which their labor and skill would reap in the southern portion of our State are just beginning to be successful. The question arises—Shall the State invite to its shores thousands of families from the wine-growing borders of the Rhine, which will be a valuable addition to the intelligent, liberty-loving, congenial population of the State, and which will, in developing the resources of our soil, build up homesteads for themselves, or shall we have hordes of Mongolians create large plantations for a few owners of immense tracts of land; and thus, in enriching a few, degrade the value and dignity of labor, and keep away from our shores the desirable working classes of Europe?

For Their Own Protection

It is as well for the protection of the Chinese who reside among us, as for our own protection, that we earnestly urge the Congress to put some barrier in the way of Chinese immigration. We entreat the National Congress to consider that antipathies of races cannot be equalized or counteracted by police laws. The law has not the power of preventing the innumerable acts of brutality and violence which the lower classes of our own population exercise toward the Chinese whenever a favorable opportunity offers itself; for Chinese cannot testify against white persons, and, for fear of the revenge of their persecutors, do not dare to seek the protection of the Courts. These evils, so dangerous as well in their existing force as in their prospective consequences, call certainly for the serious consideration of the power which regulates our intercourse with foreign nations.

The Congress will in its wisdom determine whether the existing treaties interfere with such relief as California expects. If such obstacles exist, the Legislature of California begs to submit that such a revision of the treaties as would protect California from the unlimited influx of Mongolian hordes is most essential to her safety and welfare. All real advantages to be derived from a mutual intercourse of commerce with China may be enjoyed without encouraging any longer the immigration of the lowest and most degraded population of China. If the United States will henceforth admit but those Chinese who are engaged in mercantile pursuits, and either entirely exclude other Mongolians, the commercial intercourse with China, as far as it is of genuine and permanent value to California, would, in our opinion, be by no means depreciated. The Mongolians in California subsist largely on the imported products of their native country. Of our products they consume none but the most indispensable. But whatever pecuniary profits the presence of a large population of Mongolians might offer, California is willing to forego them; for she values the safety of her social and political institutions higher than the immediate cultivation upon her soil of sugar, rice, tea, and cotton.

Former Legislatures of California have also felt the greatness of the evil against which your memorialists urgently solicit the aid and cooperation of the National authorities. They repeatedly instructed their Senators and their Representatives to lay this important matter before the Congress, and invite its attention to the dangers which threaten the welfare, perhaps the existence, of the Caucasian race in the States bordering upon the Pacific. Yet, heretofore, the wishes of California have in this respect been wholly neglected by her representatives in Congress.

Trusting in the sincerity and zeal with which our present Senators and Representatives will submit to Congress the evils but imperfectly indicated in this memorial, the State of California entertains the strong hope that the care and solicitude of Congress for the welfare of every part of the Nation will be directed to the earnest consideration of the great social danger upon the Pacific coast.

VIEWPOINT 4

"The history of the 'Anti-Chinese Crusade' in California . . . [should] cause a blush of shame on the cheek of every intelligent Christian citizen."

The Anti-Chinese Movement Is Harming California

Otis Gibson (1826–1889)

Otis Gibson was a Methodist missionary who lived in China from 1854 to 1865. He was subsequently assigned to San Francisco, where he headed the Methodist Chinatown mission and ran a shelter for former prostitutes. Gibson became a leading spokesman for and defender of Chinese immigrants, pleading their cause in speeches, in pamphlets, and in testimony before a congressional investigative hearing in the fall of 1876. He was burned in effigy in some anti-Chinese demonstrations.

The following viewpoint comes from a chapter of *The Chinese in America*, a book written by Gibson and published in 1877. The chapter focuses on the events of the anti-Chinese movement in San Francisco in 1876. Quoting at length from newspaper accounts and other sources, Gibson argues that the anti-Chinese movement is the result of political demagoguery, and is misinformed and prejudiced in its accusations against Chinese immigrants. He contends that this movement has resulted in tragic violence against Chinese immigrants and has damaged America's standing abroad.

From Otis Gibson, *The Chinese in America* (Cincinnati: Hitchcock & Walden, 1877).

It is a humiliating fact that the greatest enthusiasm is often manifested upon issues where ignorance, bigotry, prejudice and selfishness play the principal parts. The history of the "Anti-Chinese Crusade" in California, during this Centennial year of American independence; the grounds upon which it has been waged; the character and spirit of its leaders and active agents; the methods of the campaign, the willful misrepresentations made concerning helpless and defenseless strangers who have come to us by special invitation; the criminal perversion of testimony given under oath; the ill-concealed effort to blacken the character of Protestant Missions and missionaries, in order to make a case against the Chinamen; the proud arrogance and assumption of superior virtue and morality by a class of men, many of whom, in daily life and practice, fall far below the average Chinaman—all these things conspire to cause a blush of shame on the cheek of every intelligent Christian citizen, who understands the case, whenever the subject is mentioned.

Indeed, the whole discussion of this question, so far as these political demagogues are concerned, has been so puerile, so utterly destitute of logic and sound argument,—in its spirit and intent so subversive of the fundamental principles of liberty upon which the whole fabric of our government is built,—so blind to patent facts, so utterly regardless of truth, honor, and justice, that it requires no ordinary patience to arrange the shameful facts in hand, and write out an impartial sketch of its history.

Two Developments

In the Spring of the present year (1876), two facts conspired to give certain political aspirants a coveted occasion to inaugurate a bitter and wide-spread Anti-Chinese agitation. First, the decision of the Supreme Court of the United States, that the State legislations of California, prohibiting the importation of lewd Chinese women was unconstitutional. Second, the fact that an unusually large number of Chinese immigrants were arriving each month, with *rumors* that multitudes more were only waiting an opportunity to come. These two facts furnished an immediate occasion, and fresh material for an appeal to the selfishness, bigotry, and race prejudices of the people, in order to excite their hostility against the Chinese, and thereby secure their adherence to the political school of the agitators and lift them into office. The result has been that, for political purposes alone, the leaders of both political parties, and the secular press generally, have declared war upon the Chinamen. The press has deprecated the constant, violent assaults and abuses heaped upon the Chinamen, not because of the injustice and brutality of such conduct, but simply on the low, selfish ground that these acts of violence would injure the Anti-Chinese cause in the Eastern States. And before the Commissioners appointed by the municipal government of San Francisco could reach Washington, with the address and resolutions of the famous Anti-Chinese Mass-meeting of April 5th, a California Senator, Mr. A[aron] A. Sargent, had anticipated all they had to say in a speech before the Senate, May 2, 1876.

A large portion of the press of California devoted itself to fanning the flames of excitement. The people were daily treated to editorials and correspondence setting forth in exaggerated and highly colored phrases the vices and crimes of the Chinese people, the ruin caused by Chinese cheap labor, and the tremendous impending evils of further Chinese immigration. All the existing evils which affect the morals of our own people were charged home upon the Chinese. All the sufferings of the poor and wretched were the results of Chinese immigration. The very vices and crimes of our hoodlum element were traced to the presence and competition of Chinese cheap labor. The people were admonished to remember that China had a population of four hundred millions, an alien race, incapable of assimilating with and of attaining to our higher forms of civilization, and that a constant stream from such a source would soon overrun and devastate the whole land. With admirable sophistry and flattery it was maintained that a "European after being in this country a few years, becomes as good a citizen, and as patriotic as a native born; a Chinaman never." (But the *fact* is, *some* Europeans make bad citizens, some Chinamen make good ones.) The working classes were easily made the dupes and tools of the demagogues. They were made to believe that if the Chinese were removed out of the way, thousands of white laborers, more than now, would immediately find employment at greatly increased wages. The Chinese laboring men were all called coolie slaves, and for a white man to be a common laborer beside a servile class, was disgraceful in the extreme, and utterly repugnant to the noble instincts of the intelligent yeomanry of this free land.

Anti-Chinese Clubs

The organization of Anti-Chinese clubs throughout the city and country was strongly recommended. The frantic cry was raised, "Organize, organize, *organize*." And organize they did. Politicians organized. The various classes of craftsmen organized. Loafers, tramps, and bummers organized. Hoodlum boys of ten and fifteen years of age were encouraged to join some of these organizations, and have been found very useful in teaching the Chinese that they are not wanted in this country. We give a specimen of the proceedings of these Anti-Chinese clubs as reported in the daily papers. It is quite suggestive:

"The Seventh Ward Anti-Coolie Club met last evening. After the business was through with, a gentleman, who has felt the evils of Chinese invasion, asked permission of the Club to make a few remarks, and said:

> Mr. Gintlemin and Prisidint, I have some remarks to make on this great thing. I've been wurruckin amongst these hathens as foremin and head boss over some iv'em, and you bet your life I knocked 'em down whiniver they tuk any airs on thimsilves wid me. I am a white man, as is a white man, and Mr. Prisidint, I claims as how when a man is a white man, he should aither be a white man or lave the country. I showed thim 'are hathens as I was a white man, and forninst such employed Chinamens. Why, sur, I seed them men who employed these Chinamen, actually give 'em a chaw of terbacker, and indulgin' 'em in every way and manner as was possable to indulge 'em, and I was discharged because I knocked 'em down when they tuk too many liberties wid me. Yis, sur."

Acts of violence against the Chinese have been shamefully numerous, but for some reason, the newspaper reporters have not always thought them worthy of mention. One day some eight or ten of the Chinese girls of the Asylum of the Methodist Mission, accompanied by three American ladies, were rudely assaulted by a large crowd of men and boys in broad daylight within a few blocks of the City Hall. Mud, sand, and stones were thrown at them, and they were followed by a jeering, insulting crowd till they were compelled to seek refuge in the house of an Irish woman, who not only sheltered them but went out and tried to disperse the mob. The managers of the school have not since dared to take the girls out for recreation or observation without the special protection of the police.

The municipal authorities of San Francisco were early aroused to this question. The mayor has seemed to be the principal leader in the whole Anti-Chinese movement. He presented an address to the Board of Supervisors of the city, setting forth in no mild terms the evils, present and impending, of this Chinese immigration, and recommended some action on their part which should open up a general agitation of the subject whose influence should be felt in Congress. The Board acted promptly on the suggestion, and immediately took action which culminated in the "Grand Anti-Chinese Mass-meeting," of April 5th, and the appointment of three commissioners to go to Washington to present to the general Government the case against the Chinamen. . . .

The excitement ran so high that at last even the conservative, stolid Chinamen began to be alarmed, and on April 1st, issued the following *Manifesto:*

The United States has been open to Chinese emigration for more than twenty years. Many Chinamen have come; few have returned. Why is this? Because among our Chinese people, a few in California have acquired a fortune and returned home with joy. A desire to obtain a competency having arisen in the heart, our people have not shrunk from toil and trouble. They have expected to come here for one or two years and make a little fortune and return. Who among them ever thought of all these difficulties,—expensive rents, expensive living? A day without work means a day without food. For this reason, though wages are low, yet they are compelled to labor and live in daily poverty, quite unable to return to their native land. Now this honorable country is discussing the importance of prohibiting the further emigration of the Chinese. That is very good indeed. First, because it will relieve the American people of trouble and anxiety of mind; secondly, the Chinese will no longer be wanderers in a foreign land. Both parties will thus be benefited. But this result should be brought about in a reasonable manner. It is said that the six companies buy and import Chinaman into this country. How can such things be said? Our six companies have, year after year, sent letters discouraging our people from coming to this country, but the people have not believed us, and have continued to come. The necessary expense of these poor new comers is a constant drain upon the resources of those already settled here, so that the Chinese residents of this country, are also opposed to this rapid Chinese emigration.

But the capitalists of this honorable country are constantly calling for Chinese cheap labor. The white laboring men of this country are very angry because the Chinese obtain employment which they claim belongs to white men alone, and so they hate the Chinamen, sometimes throw stones at them, sometimes strike them on the street, and constantly curse them. The Chinese people can not return such treatment in the same kind, lest other nations hearing of such things should ridicule the laws of this honorable country as of no use.

To prohibit the Chinese from coming to this country is not a difficult matter. Formerly His Imperial Majesty, our August Emperor, made a treaty of amity and friendship with the Government of this honorable country, opening commercial relations and permitting free intercommunication between the people of the two countries. This treaty is in accordance with the law of all nations.

And now if the American people do not desire the Chinese to come here, why not go to the Emperor and ask a repeal of the treaty, or why not limit the number of immigrants on each steamer to a very few? Then more would return and fewer would come, and not ten years would elapse before not a trace of the Chinamen would be left in this greet and honorable country. Would not that be well indeed? But let there be counsel and consideration. It can not be said that Chinese labor impoverishes this country, and are not the customs paid by the Chinese a benefit to this country? Now let the Government of the United States propose to the Government of China a repeal or change of the treaty, prohibiting the people of either country from crossing the ocean, then shall we Chinese forever remain at home and enjoy the happiness of fathers, mothers, wives, and children and no longer remain strangers in a strange land. Then the white laborer of this country shall no longer be troubled by the competition of the Chinese, and our Chinese people no longer be subjected to the abuses and indignities now daily heaped upon them in the open streets of this so-called Christian land. If this can be accomplished, we Chinese will continually offer to the virtue of this honorable country our deepest gratitude and thanks.

They also, the same day, addressed the following letter to the Chief of Police:

SAN FRANCISCO, April 1, 1876.
"To H.H. ELLIS, *Chief of Police of City and County of San Francisco:*

SIR:—We wish to call your attention to the fact, that at the present time frequent and unprovoked assaults are made upon our Chinese people while walking peacefully the streets of this city. The assaulting party is seldom arrested by your officers, but if a Chinaman resist the assault, he is frequently arrested and punished by fine or by imprisonment. Inflammatory and incendiary addresses against the Chinese, delivered on the public streets to the idle and irresponsible element of this great city, have already produced unprovoked and unpunished assaults upon some of our people, and we fear, that if such things are permitted to go on unchecked, a bloody riot against the Chinese may be the result. Regretting, that the Chinese are so obnoxious to the citizens of this country, and quite willing to aid in seeking a repeal or modification of the existing treaty between China and the United States, yet being here under sacred treaty stipulations, we simply ask to be protected in our treaty rights.

Respectfully submitted,

THE SIX COMPANIES.

To show that the Chinamen had not exaggerated the abuses heaped upon them, we give an item from a daily paper of the same date as the above note to the Chief of Police:

A RIOTOUS ASSEMBLY.

An inflammatory Anti-Chinese meeting was held last evening on Kerney Street, and addressed by an incendiary orator. Under his heated harangue, the crowd was wrought up to the highest pitch of excitement, and increased in numbers until the street

51

was blocked by a surging mass. The speaker read a long series of resolutions condemning the importation of coolies, demanding a remedy from the lawmaking power, and ended by proclaiming that if no measures were taken to suppress the plague, the people were justified in taking summary vengeance on the Mongolians. The resolutions were received with yells by the listeners, and several unlucky Chinamen who passed by at the moment, were knocked down and kicked, to emphasize the verdict. The speaker then resumed his address in a more incendiary strain than before, calling on the populace, in the name of humanity, and their families, and as American citizens, to "drive every greasy-faced coolie from the land." "We must take this insidious monster by the throat," shouted the speaker, "and throttle it—choke it until its heart ceases to beat, and then hurl it into the sea!" At the conclusion of his speech he called upon every man to sign the resolutions, which about two hundred of those present did. During the crowding up to accomplish this, a car passed along on which a Chinaman was riding. Yells of "Pull him off!" "Lynch him!" "Kill the greasy slave!" etc., rent the air; but the Mongolian escaped with only a few cuffs and a vigorous kick or two.

Things got to such a pass that the sensational papers which had been fanning the flames of popular excitement began to find that "Fears of an Anti-Chinese riot were expressed in various quarters," and to "call upon the Mayor and the Chief of Police to give their attention to the matter in time." They further trusted "that at the Anti-Chinese mass-meeting to-night there will be no sensational clap-trap eloquence," designed to fire the popular heart. "The popular heart is already sufficiently *fired*." Thousands of the best citizens feared a bloody riot. The Chinese themselves became exceedingly nervous, and prepared, as best they could, to defend themselves in case of an attack. The pawnbroker shops reaped a rich harvest from the sale of revolvers and bowie-knives to Chinamen. One dealer alone sold sixty pistols to Chinamen in one day at good prices. . . .

In [April] a committee of California Senators, appointed to investigate the whole question of Chinese immigration, and report at the next meeting of the Legislature, held its sessions in San Francisco and Sacramento. The committee professed to seek all facts bearing on the Chinese question. But the class of questions constantly proposed by this committee to the witnesses and the direction seemingly given to the investigation had the tendency to bring into notice all the testimony unfavorable to the Chinese, and to throw into the shade important and reliable testimony in their favor.

It seems to have been a part of the design or scheme of this committee to destroy, if possible, the confidence, and to modify the views, of the Christian public in the Eastern States, with regard to the influence of Christian missions upon the Chinese people. Wicked, godless men, of infamous reputation in the communities where they live, and heathen of bitter hostility to the Christian religion, were called upon to testify as to the character of Protestant missionaries among the Chinese in California, and as to the number and character of the Chinese converts to Christianity. The testimony of such men has been reported and published in all the land, and has added fuel to the flames of prejudice and bigotry. . . .

The anti-Chinese movement is depicted in a negative light in this Thomas Nast cartoon for Harper's Weekly, *February 18, 1871.*

Since the great meeting [on April 5], and as one of its legitimate results, and during the session of the Senate Investigating Committee, assaults and riots upon the Chinese people have been more numerous than before. A newspaper correspondent from Truckee, says:

> Last night an armed, masked party, numbering about fifteen, proceeded about a mile back of town to a Chinese camp situated on Front Creek, burned their cabins, and deliberately shot down three of them, killing two outright. The other was mortally wounded.

The same correspondent adds the following suggestive paragraph:

> Now that our mill-owners and others heretofore employing Chinese laborers have discharged them, and employed white laborers, the latter will not avail themselves of the inducements held out to them, and the consequence is that Chinese labor is again resorted to.

A curious state of things, indeed. White men are engaged upon a job, but refuse to work. Chinamen, of necessity, are employed, and the white men, masked and under cover of night, go and shoot down the Chinamen and burn their cabins. They will neither work themselves nor let any body else. But Mr. Pixley and Mr. Roach are sent by the municipal government of San Francisco to memorialize Congress on the virtues of these white men and the vices of these Chinamen!! At Antioch a mob of white men drove the Chinamen out of town one day, and burned their houses the next, and the newspaper correspondent when narrating the affair, piously said, "This Chinese nuisance has become a disgrace which the *law-abiding* population will not much longer *permit* to eat away the foundations of Christianity!!!"

The next day the South San Francisco Anti-Chinese Club passed a resolution admitting "boys of the ward to the meetings on the ground that they could be useful in working out the desired end," and passed a vote of *thanks "to the people of Antioch for the noble stand they had taken and the rousing example they had set."*

A morning paper said:

> It is scarcely safe for a Chinaman to walk the streets in certain parts of this city. When seen, whether by day or night, they are mercilessly pelted with stones by the young scape-graces who now, there being no schools, have nothing else to do, while older hoodlums look on approvingly, and, if the Chinamen venture to resist the assaults, take a hand in and assist the youngsters. Chinese wash-houses are sacked almost nightly. A Chinaman apparently has no rights which a white hoodlum, big or little, is bound to respect.

. . . During the intense heat of the Anti-Chinese Crusade, in April and May, 1876, the municipal government of San Francisco demonstrated its ability to close Chinese gambling-houses, but they were only closed temporarily, for in August, after three or four months only had elapsed, these dens were all open again, and rumors floated around among my Chinese friends, to the effect that the Chinese gambling fraternity had paid large moneys for the privilege of resuming their business.

Such is the character and history of the present Anti-Chinese excitement. An able editorial in the New York *World*, of June 5th, well and truthfully said:

The Anti-Chinese agitation on the Pacific Coast has, in all likelihood, been given more prominence than it deserves. Those who participated in it are generally of the brawling class, made up of small politicians, anxious to curry favor with laborers and artisans, who are apprehensive, especially in a time of commercial depression, and always easily aroused; and sensation mongers eager to accept the offered opportunity to write up Chinatown again, and invent a few details to suit the occasion. Behind them is the hoodlum element on the alert for any thing which promises a riot and occasion for pillage.

In the midst of the turmoil raised by these agitators, it is not easy that the voice of common sense is heard, and principle is very apt to be swayed or silenced by prejudice. Nevertheless, we venture the prediction that if the respectable citizens of California could be polled, they would by an overwhelming majority declare that the present Mongolian crusade is as undesirable as it is unjust.

Besides, the Anti-Chinese argument defeats itself, for in the same breath it is urged that the Celestials pour in there by myriads. It is also charged that they don't come to stay and be Americanized, but as soon as they have made a little money take it and themselves home to the Flowery Kingdom. The positions are inconsistent, and till we have elected to stand on one we must reject them both. If the Chinese pay taxes, rents, and fares, and earn and purchase that which they wear and consume, the community must be the gainer. If they work for less wages than other people, there is a saving of capital which will find other investment. Inasmuch as the most rabid denunciations of the Chinese come from people who do not work, except when menaced by starvation, the Chinese have rather the better of the argument. So with the moral feature of the question. The prison statistics of the State of California and San Francisco show the average of crime among the Chinamen to be lower than among the rest of the population. If Chinese prostitutes are inoculating the guileless youths of San Francisco with terrible disease does not the fault rest with the guileless youth? It is by no means flattering to our national pride that in this Centennial year such a discussion as this should be waged and that all the courtesy and cogency should be displayed on the side of the uncivilized heathens.

This crusade against the Chinese in America is already beginning to bear fruit in China. A correspondent from China writes:

The Chinese excitement in San Francisco is now pretty generally known throughout the open ports, and has created a bad feeling against the Americans. Educated natives characterize it as a gross infringement on the treaty, and sure to find speedy retaliation on Americans here.

VIEWPOINT 5

"The fact . . . that acts of Congress . . . have not permitted Chinese persons born out of this country to become citizens by naturalization, cannot exclude Chinese persons born in this country from the operation of the broad and clear words of the Constitution."

U.S.-Born Children of Chinese Immigrants Are American Citizens

Horace Gray (1828–1902)

The Fourteenth Amendment to the Constitution, adopted in 1868 following the Civil War, states that "All persons born or naturalized in the United States, and subject to the jurisdiction thereof, are citizens of the United States and of the State wherein they reside." Written to secure the citizenship rights of African Americans newly freed from slavery, the Fourteenth Amendment has also played a pivotal role in the history of Asian Americans. Until the middle of the twentieth century virtually all Asian immigrants were barred by federal law from becoming naturalized U.S. citizens. As "aliens ineligible for citizenship" they could not vote, often could not own land, and were not always given the same constitutional protections as American citizens by the federal courts. However, because of the Fourteenth Amendment, the alien status of Asian immigrants and the disadvantages that went with it were not passed down to their children born on U.S. soil.

The Supreme Court issued no rulings on whether children born in the United States of Asian parents were American citizens under the Fourteenth Amendment until the 1898 decision of *Wong Kim Ark v. United States*. Wong Kim Ark was born in San Fran-

From Horace Gray, the majority opinion in *Wong Kim Ark v. United States*, 169 U.S. 652 (1898).

cisco, California, in 1873, to Chinese immigrant parents. In 1890 he visited China and returned to the United States. However, following a subsequent visit to China, he was denied permission to reenter the United States in August 1895 on the grounds that he was not a citizen (at the time, Chinese immigrant workers were excluded from America). The case reached the Supreme Court after a lower court ruled that he was a U.S. citizen.

In March 1898 the Supreme Court upheld the lower court ruling in favor of Wong Kim Ark. The following viewpoint is excerpted from that decision, written and delivered by Horace Gray, an associate justice on the Supreme Court from 1882 to 1902. He argues that citizenship under the Constitution should be interpreted according to English common law precedent, which held that, under a doctrine known as *jus soli*, a person born within the king's domain was held to be the king's subject. He concludes that this legal history, coupled with the language of the Fourteenth Amendment, clearly establishes the American citizenship of Wong Kim Ark and all other U.S.-born children of immigrants.

The facts of this case, as agreed by the parties, are as follows: Wong Kim Ark was born in 1873 in the city of San Francisco, in the State of California and United States of America, and was and is a laborer. His father and mother were persons of Chinese descent, and subjects of the Emperor of China; they were at the time of his birth domiciled residents of the United States, having previously established and still enjoying a permanent domicil and residence therein at San Francisco; they continued to reside and remain in the United States until 1890, when they departed for China; and during all the time of their residence in the United States they were engaged in business, and were never employed in any diplomatic or official capacity under the Emperor of China. Wong Kim Ark, ever since his birth, has had but one residence, to wit, in California, within the United States, and has there resided, claiming to be a citizen of the United States, and has never lost or changed that residence, or gained or acquired another residence; and neither he, nor his parents acting for him, ever renounced his allegiance to the United States, or did or committed any act or thing to exclude him therefrom. In 1890 (when he must have been about seventeen years of age) he departed for China on a temporary visit and with the intention of returning to the United States, and did return thereto by sea in the same year, and was permitted by the collector of customs to enter the United

States, upon the sole ground that he was a native-born citizen of the United States. After such return, he remained in the United States, claiming to be a citizen thereof, until 1894, when he (being about twenty-one years of age, but whether a little above or a little under that age does not appear) again departed for China on a temporary visit and with the intention of returning to the United States; and he did return thereto by sea in August, 1895, and applied to the collector of customs for permission to land; and was denied such permission, upon the sole ground that he was not a citizen of the United States.

It is conceded that, if he is a citizen of the United States, the acts of Congress, known as the Chinese Exclusion Acts, prohibiting persons of the Chinese race, and especially Chinese laborers, from coming into the United States, do not and cannot apply to him.

The question presented by the record is whether a child born in the United States, of parents of Chinese descent, who, at the time of his birth, are subjects of the Emperor of China, but have a permanent domicil and residence in the United States, and are there carrying on business, and are not employed in any diplomatic or official capacity under the Emperor of China, becomes at the time of his birth a citizen of the United States, by virtue of the first clause of the Fourteenth Amendment of the Constitution, "All persons born or naturalized in the United States, and subject to the jurisdiction thereof, are citizens of the United States and of the State wherein they reside."

The Common Law

I. In construing any act of legislation, whether a statute enacted by the legislature, or a constitution established by the people as the supreme law of the land, regard is to be had, not only to all parts of the act itself, and of any former act of the same law-making power, of which the act in question is an amendment; but also to the condition, and to the history, of the law as previously existing, and in the light of which the new act must be read and interpreted.

The Constitution of the United States, as originally adopted, uses the words "citizen of the United States," and "natural-born citizen of the United States." By the original Constitution, every representative in Congress is required to have been "seven years a citizen of the United States," and every Senator to have been "nine years a citizen of the United States;" and "no person except a natural-born citizen, or a citizen of the United States at the time of the adoption of this Constitution, shall be eligible to the office of President." The Fourteenth Article of Amendment, besides declaring that "all persons born or naturalized in the United States, and subject to the jurisdiction thereof, are citizens of the United States and of the State wherein they reside," also declares that "no State shall make or enforce any law which shall abridge the privileges or immunities of citizens of the United States; nor shall any State deprive any person of life, liberty or property, without due process of law; nor deny to any person within its jurisdiction the equal protection of the laws." And the Fifteenth Article of Amendment declares that "the right of citizens of the United States to vote shall not be denied or abridged by the United States, or by any State, on account of race, color or previous condition of servitude."

The Constitution nowhere defines the meaning of these words, either by way of inclusion or of exclusion, except in so far as this is done by the affirmative declaration that "all persons born or naturalized in the United States, and subject to the jurisdiction thereof, are citizens of the United States." In this, as in other respects, it must be interpreted in the light of the common law, the principles and history of which were familiarly known to the framers of the Constitution. . . .

In *Smith v. Alabama*, Mr. Justice [Stanley] Matthews, delivering the judgment of the court, said: "There is no common law of the United States, in the sense of a national customary law, distinct from the common law of England as adopted by the several States each for itself, applied as its local law, and subject to such alteration as may be provided by its own statutes." "There is, however, one clear exception to the statement that there is no national common law. The interpretation of the Constitution of the United States is necessarily influenced by the fact that its provisions are framed in the language of the English common law, and are to be read in the light of its history.". . .

English Law and Nationality

II. The fundamental principle of the common law with regard to English nationality was birth within the allegiance, also called "ligealty," "obedience," "faith" or "power," of the King. The principle embraced all persons born within the King's allegiance and subject to his protection. Such allegiance and protection were mutual . . . and were not restricted to natural-born subjects and naturalized subjects, or to those who had taken an oath of allegiance; but were predicable of aliens in amity, so long as they were within the kingdom. Children, born in England, of such aliens, were therefore natural-born subjects. But the children, born within the realm, of foreign ambassadors, or the children of alien enemies, born during and within their hostile occupation of part of the King's dominions, were not natural-born subjects, because not born within the allegiance, the obedience, or the power, or, as would be said at this day, within the jurisdiction of the King. . . .

It thus clearly appears that by the law of England for the last three centuries, beginning before the settlement of this country, and continuing to the present day, aliens, while residing in the dominions possessed by the Crown of England, were within the allegiance, the obedience, the faith or loyalty, the protection, the power, the jurisdiction, of the English Sovereign, and therefore every child born in England of alien parents was a natural-born subject, unless the child of an ambassador or other diplomatic agent of a foreign State, or of an alien enemy in hostile occupation of the place where the child was born.

III. The same rule was in force in all the English Colonies upon this continent down to the time of the Declaration of Independence, and in the United States afterwards, and continued to prevail under the Constitution as originally established.

In the early case of *The Charming Betsy* (1804), it appears to have been assumed by this court that all persons born in the United States were citizens of the United States; Chief Justice [John] Marshall saying: "Whether a person born within the United States, or becoming a citizen according to the established laws of the country, can divest himself absolutely of that character otherwise than in such manner as may be prescribed by law, is a question which it is not necessary at present to decide.". . .

In *Inglis v. Sailors' Snug Harbor* (1830), in which the plaintiff was born in the city of New York, about the time of the Declaration of Independence, the justices of this court (while differing in opinion upon other points) all agreed that the law of England as to citizenship by birth was the law of the English Colonies in America. . . .

The Civil Rights Act and the Fourteenth Amendment

V. In the fore front, both of the Fourteenth Amendment of the Constitution, and of the Civil Rights Act of 1866, the fundamental principle of citizenship by birth within the dominion was reaffirmed in the most explicit and comprehensive terms.

The Civil Rights Act, passed at the first session of the Thirty-ninth Congress, began by enacting that "all persons born in the United States, and not subject to any foreign power, excluding Indians not taxed, are hereby declared to be citizens of the United States; and such citizens, of every race and color, without regard to any previous condition of slavery or involuntary servitude, except as a punishment for crime whereof the party shall have been duly convicted, shall have the same right, in every State and Territory in the United States, to make and enforce contracts, to sue, be parties and give evidence, to inherit, purchase, lease, sell, hold and convey real and personal property, and to full and equal benefit of all laws and proceedings for the security of person and property, as is enjoyed by white citizens, and shall be subject to like punishment, pains and penalties, and to none other, any law, statute, ordinance, regulation or custom, to the contrary notwithstanding.". . .

The same Congress, shortly afterwards, evidently thinking it unwise, and perhaps unsafe, to leave so important a declaration of rights to depend upon an ordinary act of legislation, which might be repealed by any subsequent Congress, framed the Fourteenth Amendment of the Constitution, and on June 16, 1866, by joint resolution proposed it to the legislatures of the several States; and on July 28, 1868, the Secretary of State issued a proclamation showing it to have been ratified by the legislatures of the requisite number of States. . . .

A Scrap of Paper

Possession of U.S. citizenship by virtue of birth on American soil did not necessarily protect Chinese American citizens from discriminatory treatment. In a letter published in the Honolulu Star Bulletin *on August 26, 1931, a Hawaiian-born student at the Chicago Theological Seminary describes his experiences while attending a YMCA conference in Canada.*

I was detained at Windsor, Canada, for eight hours, just on account of my being of Chinese descent. The fault was of the {Canadian} official. He was dumb, and he didn't follow instructions to allow delegates to the Conference to go through. Anyway I was impressed with the fact that I am a Chinese. My American citizenship didn't mean a thing. It was just a scrap of paper. If a Negro says he is an American, and has no paper to show, he will be allowed to go through, no matter how ignorant he is, but if I am a Chinese with all my papers to prove that I am an American citizen, I am still taken off the train.

The situation that burned me up the most was the treatment I received from the American officials at Niagara Falls. I was impressed more there that I am a Chinaman. I, an American citizen, was not allowed to visit the Falls because I was of Chinese descent! That takes the cake for insult and discrimination. I was too mad to do anything. I could have torn up my citizenship papers right then and there. If my government is not going to protect my rights and treat me as any other citizen, I would rather be a Chinaman and be treated like hell than be hypocritical about it.

The first section of the Fourteenth Amendment of the Constitution begins with the words, "All persons born or naturalized in the United States, and subject to the jurisdiction thereof, are citizens of the United States and of the State wherein they reside." As appears upon the face of the amendment, as well as from the history of the times, this was not intended to impose any new restrictions upon citizenship, or to prevent any persons from becoming citizens by the fact of birth within the United States, who would thereby have become citizens according to the law existing before its adoption. It is declaratory in form, and enabling and extending in effect. Its main purpose doubtless was, as has been often recognized by this court, to establish the citizenship of free negroes, which had been denied in the opinion delivered by Chief Justice Taney in *Dred Scott v. Sandford* (1857) . . . ; and to put it beyond doubt that all blacks, as well as whites, born or naturalized within the jurisdiction of the United States, are citizens of the United States. . . . But the opening words, "All persons born," are general, not to say universal, restricted only by place and jurisdiction, and not by color or race—as was clearly recognized in all the opinions delivered in *The Slaughterhouse Cases* [1873]. . . .

The real object of the Fourteenth Amendment of the Constitution, in qualifying the words, "All persons born in the United States," by the addition, "and subject to the jurisdiction thereof," would appear to have been to exclude, by the fewest and fittest words, (besides children of members of the Indian tribes, standing in a peculiar relation to the National Government, unknown to the common law,) the two classes of cases—children born of alien enemies in hostile occupation, and children of diplomatic representatives of a foreign State—both of which, as has already been shown, by the law of England, and by our own law, from the time of the first settlement of the English colonies in America, had been recognized exceptions to the fundamental rule of citizenship by birth within the country. . . .

The Fourteenth Amendment affirms the ancient and fundamental rule of citizenship by birth within the territory, in the allegiance and under the protection of the country, including all children here born of resident aliens, with the exceptions or qualifications (as old as the rule itself) of children of foreign sovereigns or their ministers, or born on foreign public ships, or of enemies within and during a hostile occupation of part of our territory, and with the single additional exception of children of members of the Indian tribes owing direct allegiance to their several tribes. The Amendment, in clear words and in manifest intent, includes the children born, within the territory of the United States, of all other persons, of whatever race or color, domiciled within the United States. Every citizen or subject of another country, while domiciled here, is within the allegiance and the protection, and consequently subject to the jurisdiction, of the United States. . . .

To hold that the Fourteenth Amendment of the Constitution excludes from citizenship the children, born in the United States, of citizens or subjects of other countries, would be to deny citizenship to thousands of persons of English, Scotch, Irish, German or other European parentage, who have always been considered and treated as citizens of the United States.

VI. Whatever considerations, in the absence of a controlling provision of the Constitution, might influence the legislative or the executive branch of the Government to decline to admit persons of the Chinese race to the status of citizens of the United States, there are none that can constrain or permit the judiciary to refuse to give full effect to the peremptory and explicit language of the Fourteenth Amendment, which declares and ordains that "All persons born or naturalized in the United States, and subject to the jurisdiction thereof, are citizens of the United States."

Chinese Persons

Chinese persons, born out of the United States, remaining subjects of the Emperor of China, and not having become citizens of the United States, are entitled to the protection of and owe allegiance to the United States, so long as they are permitted by the United States to reside here; and are "subjects to the jurisdiction thereof," in the same sense as all other aliens residing in the United States. . . .

In *Yick Wo v. Hopkins* the decision was that an ordinance of the city of San Francisco, regulating a certain business, and which, as executed by the board of supervisors, made an arbitrary discrimination between natives of China, still subjects of the Emperor of China, but domiciled in the United States, and all other persons, was contrary to the Fourteenth Amendment of the Constitution. Mr. Justice Matthews, in delivering the opinion of the court, said: "The rights of the petitioners, as affected by the proceedings of which they complain, are not less, because they are aliens and subjects of the Emperor of China." "The Fourteenth Amendment to the Constitution is not confined to the protection of citizens. It says, 'Nor shall any State deprive any person of life, liberty or property, without due process of law; nor deny to any person within its jurisdiction the equal protection of the laws.' These provisions are universal in their application, to all persons within the territorial jurisdiction, without regard to any differences of race, of color, or of nationality; and the equal protection of the laws is a pledge of the protection of equal laws. . . . The questions we have to consider and decide in these cases, therefore, are to be treated as involving the rights of every citizen of the United States, equally with those of the strangers and aliens who now invoke the jurisdiction of this court.". . .

Persons born in China, subjects of the Emperor of China, but domiciled in the United States, having been adjudged, in *Yick Wo v. Hopkins*, to be within the jurisdiction of the State, within the meaning of the concluding sentence, must be held to be subject to the jurisdiction of the United States, within the meaning of the first sentence of this section of the Constitution; and their children, "born in the United States," cannot be less "subject to the jurisdiction thereof.". . .

Congressional Debates

During the debates in the Senate in January and February, 1866, upon the Civil Rights Bill, Mr. [Lyman] Trumbull, the chairman of the committee which reported the bill, moved to amend the first sentence thereof so as to read, "All persons born in the United States, and not subject to any foreign power, are hereby declared to be citizens of the United States, without distinction of color." Mr. Cowan, of Pennsylvania, asked, "Whether it will not have the effect of naturalizing the children of Chinese and Gypsies, born in this country?" Mr. Trumbull answered, "Undoubtedly;" and asked, "Is not the child born in this country of German parents a citizen?" Mr. Cowan replied, "The children of German parents are citizens; but Germans are not Chinese." Mr. Trumbull rejoined: "The law makes no such distinction; and the child of an Asiatic is just as much a citizen as the child of a European. "Mr. Reverdy Johnson suggested that the words, "without distinction of color," should be omitted as unnecessary; and said: "The amendment, as it stands, is that all persons born in the United States, and not subject to a foreign power, shall by virtue of birth, be citizens. To that I am willing to consent; and that comprehends all persons, without any reference to race or color, who may be so born." And Mr. Trumbull agreed that striking out those words would make no difference in the meaning, but thought it better that they should be retained, to remove all possible doubt. . . .

The Fourteenth Amendment of the Constitution, as originally framed by the House of Representatives, lacked the opening sentence. When it came before the Senate in May, 1866, Mr. Howard, of Michigan, moved to amend by prefixing the sentence in its present form, (less the words "or naturalized,") and reading; "All persons born in the United States, and subject to the jurisdiction thereof, are citizens of the United States and of the State wherein they reside." Mr. Cowan objected, upon the ground that the Mongolian race ought to be excluded; and said: "Is the child of the Chinese immigrant in California a citizen?" "I do not know how my honorable friend from California looks upon Chinese, but I do know how some of his fellow-citizens regard them. I have no doubt that now they are useful, and I have no doubt that within proper restraints, allowing that State and the other Pacific States to manage them as they may see fit, they may be useful; but I would not tie their hands by the Constitution of the United States so as to prevent them hereafter from dealing with them as in their wisdom they see fit." Mr. Conness, of California, replied: "The proposition before us relates simply, in that respect, to the children begotten of Chinese parents in California, and it is proposed to declare that they shall be citizens. We have declared that by law; now it is proposed to incorporate the same provision in the fundamental instrument of the Nation. I am in favor of doing so. I voted for the proposition to declare that the children of all parentage whatever, born in California, should be regarded and treated as citizens of the United States, entitled to equal civil rights with other citizens of the United States." "We are entirely ready to accept the provision proposed in this Constitutional Amendment, that the children born here of Mongolian parents shall be declared by the Constitution of the United States to be entitled to civil rights and to equal protection before the law with others.". . . It does not appear to have been suggested, in either House of Congress, that children born in the United States of Chinese parents would not come within the terms and effect of the leading sentence of the Fourteenth Amendment.

Doubtless, the intention of the Congress which framed and of the States which adopted this Amendment of the Constitution must be sought in the words of the Amendment; and the debates in Congress are not admissible as evidence to control the meaning of those words. But the statements above quoted are valuable as contemporaneous opinions of jurists and statesmen upon the legal meaning of the words themselves; and are, at the least, interesting as showing that the application of the Amendment to the Chinese race was considered and not overlooked. . . .

Naturalization Laws

It is true that Chinese persons born in China cannot be naturalized, like other aliens, by proceedings under the naturalization laws. But this is for want of any statute or treaty authorizing or permitting such naturalization, as will appear by tracing the history of the statutes, treaties and decisions upon that subject—always bearing in mind that statutes enacted by Congress, as well as treaties made by the President and Senate, must yield to the paramount and supreme law of the Constitution. . . .

The Fourteenth Amendment of the Constitution, in the declaration that "all persons born or naturalized in the United States, and subject to the jurisdiction thereof, are citizens of the United States and of the State wherein they reside," contemplates two sources of citizenship, and two only: birth and naturalization. Citizenship by naturalization can only be acquired by naturalization under the authority and in the forms of law. But citizenship by birth is established by the mere fact of birth under the circumstances defined in the Constitution. Every person born in the

United States, and subject to the jurisdiction thereof, becomes at once a citizen of the United States, and needs no naturalization. A person born out of the jurisdiction of the United States can only become a citizen by being naturalized, either by treaty, as in the case of the annexation of foreign territory; or by authority of Congress, exercised either by declaring certain classes of persons to be citizens, as in the enactments conferring citizenship upon foreign-born children of citizens, or by enabling foreigners individually to become citizens by proceedings in the judicial tribunals, as in the ordinary provisions of the naturalization acts.

The power of naturalization, vested in Congress by the Constitution, is a power to confer citizenship, not a power to take it away. "A naturalized citizen," said Chief Justice Marshall, "becomes a member of the society, possessing all the rights of a native citizen, and standing, in the view of the Constitution, on the footing of a native. The Constitution does not authorize Congress to enlarge or abridge those rights. The simple power of the National Legislature is to prescribe a uniform rule of naturalization, and the exercise of this power exhausts it, so far as respects the individual. . . . The Fourteenth Amendment, while it leaves the power where it was before, in Congress, to regulate naturalization, has conferred no authority upon Congress to restrict the effect of birth, declared by the Constitution to constitute a sufficient and complete right to citizenship.

No one doubts that the Amendment, as soon as it was promulgated, applied to persons of African descent born in the United States, wherever the birthplace of their parents might have been; and yet, for two years afterwards, there was no statute authorizing persons of that race to be naturalized. If the omission or the refusal of Congress to permit certain classes of persons to be made citizens by naturalization could be allowed the effect of correspondingly restricting the classes of persons who should become citizens by birth, it would be in the power of Congress, at any time, by striking negroes out of the naturalization laws, and limiting those laws, as they were formerly limited, to white persons only, to defeat the main purpose of the Constitutional Amendment.

The fact, therefore, that acts of Congress or treaties have not permitted Chinese persons born out of this country to become citizens by naturalization, cannot exclude Chinese persons born in this country from the operation of the broad and clear words of the Constitution, "All persons born in the United States, and subject to the jurisdiction thereof, are citizens of the United States."

VII. Upon the facts agreed in this case, the American citizenship which Wong Kim Ark acquired by birth within the United States has not been lost or taken away by anything happening since his birth. No doubt he might himself, after coming of age, renounce this citizenship, and become a citizen of the country of his parents, or of any other country; for by our law, as solemnly declared by Congress, "the right of expatriation is a natural and inherent right of all people," and "any declaration, instruction, opinion, order or direction of any officer of the United States, which denies, restricts, impairs or questions the right of expatriation, is declared inconsistent with the fundamental principles of the Republic.". . . Whether any act of himself, or of his parents, during his minority, could have the same effect, is at least doubtful. But it would be out of place to pursue that inquiry; inasmuch as it is expressly agreed that his residence has always been in the United States, and not elsewhere; that each of his temporary visits to China, the one for some months when he was about seventeen years old, and the other for something like a year about the time of his coming of age, was made with the intention of returning, and was followed by his actual return, to the United States; and "that said Wong Kim Ark has not, either by himself or his parents acting for him, ever renounced his allegiance to the United States, and that he has never done or committed any act or thing to exclude him therefrom."

The evident intention, and the necessary effect, of the submission of this case to the decision of the court upon the facts agreed by the parties, were to present for determination the single question, stated at the beginning of this opinion, namely, whether a child born in the United States, of parents of Chinese descent, who, at the time of his birth, are subjects of the Emperor of China, but have a permanent domicil and residence in the United States, and are there carrying on business, and are not employed in any diplomatic or official capacity under the Emperor of China, becomes at the time of his birth a citizen of the United States. For the reasons above stated, this court is of opinion that the question must be answered in the affirmative.

VIEWPOINT 6

"The Fourteenth Amendment does not . . . arbitrarily make citizens of children born in the United States of parents who, according to the will of . . . this Government, are and must remain aliens."

U.S.-Born Children of Chinese Immigrants Are Not Necessarily American Citizens

Melville W. Fuller (1833–1910)

For much of Asian American history the first generation of Asian immigrants was barred by federal law from U.S. citizenship. However, the U.S.-born children of these immigrants automatically became citizens. This somewhat paradoxical situation resulted from the Fourteenth Amendment to the Constitution. Passed in 1868 to define the status of freed black slaves, it stated that "All persons born or naturalized in the United States, and subject to the jurisdiction thereof, are citizens of the United States." The Fourteenth Amendment was interpreted to include Chinese children in the 1894 case of *Wong Kim Ark v. United States*, in which the Supreme Court ruled that Wong Kim Ark, a Chinese American born in California who was refused entry into the United States after visiting China, was a lawful U.S. citizen and could not be excluded. The case was one of the few legal victories in the more than fifty cases Chinese litigants brought before the Supreme Court between 1882 and 1921.

The two dissenters in this ruling were Melville W. Fuller, chief

From Melville W. Fuller, the dissenting opinion in *Wong Kim Ark v. United States*, 169 U.S. 705 (1898).

justice from 1888 to 1910, and John Harlan, associate justice from 1874 to 1911. The following viewpoint is excerpted from their minority opinion, written by Fuller and joined by Harlan. Fuller argues that the other Supreme Court justices had misinterpreted the Fourteenth Amendment and the 1866 Civil Rights Act when they concluded that Wong Kim Ark was a U.S. citizen. Wong Kim Ark, being born of alien Chinese parents who were subjects of the Chinese emperor, was never fully "subject to the jurisdiction" of the United States, he argues, and thus the Fourteenth Amendment does not apply. To grant citizenship in such circumstances, he concludes, deprives the U.S. government of necessary powers to regulate immigration.

I cannot concur in the opinion and judgment of the court in this case.

The proposition is that a child born in this country of parents who were not citizens of the United States, and under the laws of their own country and of the United States could not become such—as was the fact from the beginning of the Government in respect of the class of aliens to which the parents in this instance belonged—is, from the moment of his birth a citizen of the United States, by virtue of the first clause of the Fourteenth Amendment, any act of Congress to the contrary notwithstanding.

The argument is, that although the Constitution prior to that amendment nowhere attempted to define the words "citizens of the United States" and "natural-born citizen" as used therein, yet that it must be interpreted in the light of the English common law rule which made the place of birth the criterion of nationality; that that rule "was in force in all the English colonies upon this continent down to the time of the Declaration of Independence, and in the United States afterwards, and continued to prevail under the Constitution as originally established;" and "that before the enactment of the Civil Rights Act of 1866 and the adoption of the Constitutional Amendment, all white persons, at least, born within the sovereignty of the United States, whether children of citizens or of foreigners, excepting only children of ambassadors or public ministers of a foreign Government, were native-born citizens of the United States."

Thus the Fourteenth Amendment is held to be merely declaratory except that it brings all persons, irrespective of color, within the scope of the alleged rule, and puts that rule beyond the control of the legislative power. . . .

Obviously, where the Constitution deals with common law rights and uses common law phraseology, its language should be read in the light of the common law; but when the question arises as to what constitutes citizenship of the nation, involving as it does international relations, and political as contradistinguished from civil status, international principles must be considered, and, unless the municipal law of England appears to have been affirmatively accepted, it cannot be allowed to control in the matter of construction.

Nationality is essentially a political idea, and belongs to the sphere of public law. . . .

Manifestly, when the sovereignty of the Crown was thrown off and an independent government established, every rule of the common law and every statute of England obtaining in the Colonies, in derogation of the principles on which the new government was founded, was abrogated. . . .

The Constitution

Considering the circumstances surrounding the framing of the Constitution, I submit that it is unreasonable to conclude that "natural-born citizen" applied to everybody born within the geographical tract known as the United States, irrespective of circumstances; and that the children of foreigners, happening to be born to them while passing through the country, whether of royal parentage or not, or whether of the Mongolian, Malay or other race, were eligible to the Presidency, while children of our citizens, born abroad, were not. . . .

Undoubtedly all persons born in a country are presumptively citizens thereof, but the presumption is not irrefutable.

In his Lectures on Constitutional Law, p. 279, Mr. Justice [Samuel F.] Miller remarked: "If a stranger or traveller passing through, or temporarily residing in this country, who has not himself been naturalized, and who claims to owe no allegiance to our Government, has a child born here which goes out of the country with its father, such child is not a citizen of the United States, because it was not subject to its jurisdiction." . . .

The 1866 Civil Rights Act

The Civil Rights Act became a law April 9, 1866 . . . and provided: "That all persons born in the United States and not subject to any foreign power, excluding Indians not taxed, are hereby declared to be citizens of the United States." And this was reënacted June 22, 1874, in the Revised Statutes, section 1992.

The words "not subject to any foreign power" do not in themselves refer to mere territorial jurisdiction, for the persons referred to are persons born in the United States. All such persons are undoubtedly subject to the territorial jurisdiction of the United States, and yet the act concedes that nevertheless they may be subject to the political jurisdiction of a foreign government. In other words, by the terms of the act all persons born in the United States, and not owing allegiance to any foreign power, are citizens.

Paper Sons

After Congress passed the 1882 Chinese Exclusion Act and subsequent laws banning most Chinese immigration, some Chinese continued to enter the United States illegally. Since U.S. citizens were permitted to bring their children into the country, one method of gaining entry was to claim to be sons of Chinese American citizens born in the United States who had visited China (presumably to begin a family). The inflow of these "paper sons" increased following the 1906 San Francisco earthquake, which destroyed most hospital and immigration records in the city and thus enabled Chinese immigrants to claim American birth. Hay Ming Lee, interviewed in the book Longtime Californ', *recounts how he was able to enter America.*

In the beginning my father came in as a laborer. But the 1906 earthquake came along and destroyed all those immigration things. So that was a big chance for a lot of Chinese. They forged themselves certificates saying that they were born in this country, and then when the time came, they could go back to China and bring back four or five sons, just like that! They might make a little money off it, not much, but the main thing was to bring a son or a nephew or a cousin in.

Now my father thought he was even smarter than that. When he came in the second time he didn't use that native-born certificate he had. He got a certificate saying he was a student. But that didn't make sense at all. He thought he was so smart being a student, but then, if you come in as a student, how could you bring a son into this country? If he had used his birth certificate, I could have come in as a native son. Instead, we had to go back to the same old thing, "paper son." They had to send me over not as my own father's son, but as the son of another cousin from our village.

The allegiance of children so born is not the local allegiance arising from their parents merely being domiciled in the country, and it is single and not double allegiance. Indeed double allegiance in the sense of double nationality has no place in our law, and the existence of a man without a country is not recognized.

But it is argued that the words "and not subject to any foreign power" should be construed as excepting from the operation of the statute only the children of public ministers and of aliens born during hostile occupation.

Was there any necessity of excepting them? And if there were others described by the words, why should the language be construed to exclude them?

Whether the immunity of foreign ministers from local allegiance rests on the fiction of extra-territoriality or on the waiver of territorial jurisdiction by receiving them as representatives of other sovereignties, the result is the same.

They do not owe allegiance otherwise than to their own governments, and their children cannot be regarded as born within any other.

And this is true as to the children of aliens within territory in hostile occupation, who necessarily are not under the protection of, nor bound to render obedience to, the sovereign whose domains are invaded; but it is not pretended that the children of citizens of a government so situated would not become its citizens at their birth, as the permanent allegiance of their parents would not be severed by the mere fact of the enemy's possession.

If the act of 1866 had not contained the words, "and not subject to any foreign power," the children neither of public ministers nor of aliens in territory in hostile occupation would have been included within its terms on any proper construction, for their birth would not have subjected them to ties of allegiance, whether local and temporary, or general and permanent.

There was no necessity as to them for the insertion of the words although they were embraced by them.

But there were others in respect of whom the exception was needed, namely, the children of aliens, whose parents owed local and temporary allegiance merely, remaining subject to a foreign power by virtue of the tie of permanent allegiance, which they had not severed by formal abjuration or equivalent conduct, and some of whom were not permitted to do so if they would.

And it was to prevent the acquisition of citizenship by the children of such aliens merely by birth within the geographical limits of the United States that the words were inserted.

The Fourteenth Amendment

Two months after the statute was enacted, on June 16, 1866, the Fourteenth Amendment was proposed, and declared ratified July 28, 1868. The first clause of the first section reads: "All persons born or naturalized in the United States and subject to the jurisdiction thereof, are citizens of the United States and of the State wherein they reside." The act was passed and the amendment proposed by the same Congress, and it is not open to reasonable doubt that the words "subject to the jurisdiction thereof" in the amendment were used as synonymous with the words "and not subject to any foreign power" of the act.

The jurists and statesmen referred to in the majority opinion, notably Senators [Lyman] Trumbull and Reverdy Johnson, concurred in that view, Senator Trumbull saying: "What do we mean by 'subject to the jurisdiction of the United States'? Not owing allegiance to anybody else; that is what it means." And Senator Johnson: "Now, all that this amendment provides is that all persons born within the United States and not subject to some foreign power—for that no doubt is the meaning of the committee who have brought the matter before us—shall be considered as citizens of the United States.". . .

The Fourteenth Amendment came before the court in *The Slaughterhouse Cases* . . . at December term, 1872. . . .

Mr. Justice Miller, delivering the opinion of the court, in analyzing the first clause, observed that "the phrase 'subject to the jurisdiction thereof' was intended to exclude from its operation children of ministers, consuls and citizens or subjects of foreign States, born within the United States."

That eminent judge did not have in mind the distinction between persons charged with diplomatic functions and those who were not, but was well aware that consuls are usually the citizens or subjects of the foreign States from which they come, and that, indeed, the appointment of natives of the places where the consular service is required, though permissible, has been pronounced objectionable in principle.

His view was that the children of "citizens or subjects of foreign States," owing permanent allegiance elsewhere and only local obedience here, are not otherwise subject to the jurisdiction of the United States than are their parents. . . .

I do not insist that, although what was said was deemed essential to the argument and a necessary part of it, the point was definitively disposed of in the *Slaughterhouse Cases*, particularly as Chief Justice [Morrison R.] Waite in *Minor v. Happersett* . . . remarked that there were doubts, which for the purposes of the case then in hand it was not necessary to solve. But that solution is furnished in *Elk v. Wilkins* . . . where the subject received great consideration and it was said:

"By the Thirteenth Amendment of the Constitution slavery was prohibited. The main object of the opening sentence of the Fourteenth Amendment was to settle the question, upon which there had been a difference of opinion throughout the country and in this court, as to the citizenship of free negroes, . . . and to put it beyond doubt that all persons, white or black, and whether formerly slaves or not, born or naturalized in the United States, and *owing no allegiance to any alien power*, should be citizens of the United States, and of the State in which they reside. . . .

73

"This section contemplates two sources of citizenship, and two sources only: birth and naturalization. The persons declared to be citizens are 'all persons born or naturalized in the United States, and subject to the jurisdiction thereof.' The evident meaning of these last words is, not merely subject in some respect or degree to the jurisdiction of the United States, but *completely subject to their political jurisdiction*, and *owing them direct and immediate allegiance*. And the words relate to the time of birth in the one case, as they do to the time of naturalization in the other. *Persons not thus subject to the jurisdiction of the United States at the time of birth* cannot become so afterwards, except by being naturalized, either individually, as by proceedings under the naturalization acts, or collectively, as by the force of a treaty by which foreign territory is acquired."

To be "completely subject" to the political jurisdiction of the United States is to be in no respect or degree subject to the political jurisdiction of any other government.

Now I take it that the children of aliens, whose parents have not only not renounced their allegiance to their native country, but are forbidden by its system of government, as well as by its positive laws, from doing so, and are not permitted to acquire another citizenship by the laws of the country into which they come, must necessarily remain themselves subject to the same sovereignty as their parents, and cannot, in the nature of things, be, any more than their parents, completely subject to the jurisdiction of such other country.

Chinese Subjects

Generally speaking, I understand the subjects of the Emperor of China—that ancient Empire, with its history of thousands of years and its unbroken continuity in belief, traditions and government, in spite of revolutions and changes of dynasty—to be bound to him by every conception of duty and by every principle of their religion, of which filial piety is the first and greatest commandment; and formerly, perhaps still, their penal laws denounced the severest penalties on those who renounced their country and allegiance, and their abettors; and, in effect, held the relatives at home of Chinese in foreign lands as hostages for their loyalty. And whatever concession may have been made by treaty in the direction of admitting the right of expatriation in some sense, they seem in the United States to have remained pilgrims and sojourners as all their fathers were. . . . At all events, they have never been allowed by our laws to acquire our nationality, and, except in sporadic instances, do not appear ever to have desired to do so.

The Fourteenth Amendment was not designed to accord citizenship to persons so situated and to cut off the legislative power from dealing with the subject.

The right of a nation to expel or deport foreigners who have not been naturalized or taken any steps toward becoming citizens of a country, is as absolute and unqualified as the right to prohibit and prevent their entrance into the country. . . .

But can the persons expelled be subjected to "cruel and unusual punishments" in the process of expulsion, as would be the case if children born to them in this country were separated from them on their departure, because citizens of the United States? Was it intended by this amendment to tear up parental relations by the roots?

The Fifteenth Amendment provides that "the right of citizens of the United States to vote shall not be denied or abridged by the United States or by any State on account of race, color or previous condition of servitude." Was it intended thereby that children of aliens should, by virtue of being born in the United States, be entitled on attaining majority to vote irrespective of the treaties and laws of the United States in regard to such aliens?

In providing that persons born or naturalized in the United States, and subject to the jurisdiction thereof, are citizens, the Fourteenth Amendment undoubtedly had particular reference to securing citizenship to the members of the colored race, whose servile status had been obliterated by the Thirteenth Amendment, and who had been born in the United States, but were not and never had been subject to any foreign power. They were not aliens, (and even if they could be so regarded, this operated as a collective naturalization,) and their political status could not be affected by any change of the laws for the naturalization of individuals.

Nobody can deny that the question of citizenship in a nation is of the most vital importance. It is a precious heritage, as well as an inestimable acquisition; and I cannot think that any safeguard surrounding it was intended to be thrown down by the amendment. . . .

The President's Treaty Powers

Did the Fourteenth Amendment impose the original English common law rule as a rigid rule on this country?

Did the amendment operate to abridge the treaty-making power, or the power to establish an uniform rule of naturalization?

I insist that it cannot be maintained that this Government is unable through the action of the President, concurred in by the Senate, to make a treaty with a foreign government providing that the subjects of that government, although allowed to enter the United States, shall not be made citizens thereof, and that their children shall not become such citizens by reason of being born therein.

A treaty couched in those precise terms would not be incompatible with the Fourteenth Amendment, unless it be held that that amendment has abridged the treaty-making power.

Nor would a naturalization law excepting persons of a certain race and their children be invalid, unless the amendment has abridged the power of naturalization. This cannot apply to our colored fellow-citizens, who never were aliens—were never beyond the jurisdiction of the United States.

"Born in the United States, and subject to the jurisdiction thereof," and "naturalized in the United States, and subject to the jurisdiction thereof," mean born or naturalized under such circumstances as to be completely subject to that jurisdiction, that is, as completely as citizens of the United States, who are of course not subject to any foreign power, and can of right claim the exercise of the power of the United States on their behalf wherever they may be. When, then, children are born in the United States to the subjects of a foreign power, with which it is agreed by treaty that they shall not be naturalized thereby, and as to whom our own law forbids them to be naturalized, such children are not born so subject to the jurisdiction as to become citizens, and entitled on that ground to the interposition of our Government, if they happen to be found in the country of their parents' origin and allegiance, or any other.

Turning to the treaty between the United States and China, concluded July 28, 1868, the ratifications of which were exchanged November 23, 1869, and the proclamation made February 5, 1870, we find that, by its sixth article, it was provided: "Citizens of the United States visiting or residing in China shall enjoy the same privileges, immunities or exemptions in respect of travel or residence as may there be enjoyed by the citizens or subjects of the most favored nation. And, reciprocally, Chinese subjects residing in the United States shall enjoy the same privileges, immunities and exemptions in respect to travel or residence as may there be enjoyed by the citizens or subjects of the most favored nation. But nothing herein contained shall be held to confer naturalization on the citizens of the United States in China, nor upon the subjects of China in the United States.". . .

By the convention of March 17, 1894, it was agreed "that Chinese laborers or Chinese of any other class, either permanently or temporarily residing within the United States, shall have for the protection of their persons and property all rights that are given by the laws of the United States to citizens of the most favored nation, excepting the right to become naturalized citizens."

These treaties show that neither Government desired such change nor assented thereto. Indeed, if the naturalization laws of the United States had provided for the naturalization of Chinese persons, China manifestly would not have been obliged to recognize that her subjects had changed their allegiance thereby. But our laws do not so provide, and, on the contrary, are in entire harmony with the treaties.

I think it follows that the children of Chinese born in this country do not, *ipso facto*, become citizens of the United States unless the Fourteenth Amendment overrides both treaty and statute. Does it bear that construction; or rather is it not the proper construction that all persons born in the United States of parents permanently residing here and susceptible of becoming citizens, and not prevented therefrom by treaty or statute, are citizens, and not otherwise?

But the Chinese under their form of government, the treaties and statutes, cannot become citizens nor acquire a permanent home here, no matter what the length of their stay may be. . . .

In *Fong Yue Ting v. United States*, . . . it was said in respect of the treaty of 1868: "After some years' experience under that treaty, the Government of the United States was brought to the opinion that the presence within our territory of large numbers of Chinese laborers, of a distinct race and religion, remaining strangers in the land, residing apart by themselves tenaciously adhering to the customs and usages of their own country, unfamiliar with our institutions, and apparently incapable of assimilating with our people, might endanger good order, and be injurious to the public interests; and therefore requested and obtained from China a modification of the treaty."

It is not to be admitted that the children of persons so situated become citizens by the accident of birth. On the contrary, I am of opinion that the President and Senate by treaty, and the Congress by naturalization, have the power, notwithstanding the Fourteenth Amendment, to prescribe that all persons of a particular race, or their children, cannot become citizens, and that it results that the consent to allow such persons to come into and reside within our geographical limits does not carry with it the imposition of citizenship upon children born to them while in this country under such consent, in spite of treaty and statute.

In other words, the Fourteenth Amendment does not exclude from citizenship by birth children born in the United States of parents permanently located therein, and who might themselves become citizens; nor, on the other hand, does it arbitrarily make citizens of children born in the United States of parents who, according to the will of their native government and of this Government, are and must remain aliens.

Tested by this rule, Wong Kim Ark never became and is not a citizen of the United States, and the order of the District Court should be reversed.

CHAPTER 2

Asian Americans in the Early Twentieth Century

Chapter Preface

The experience of Chinese immigrants in the nineteenth century—who immigrated to America for economic reasons, found work shunned by other Americans, and became the target of nativist movements and immigration exclusion laws—was repeated to some extent by other Asian immigrant groups in the early twentieth century. The viewpoints in this chapter focus especially on immigrants from Japan and the Philippines. These groups differed from the Chinese in some cultural characteristics and in the status of their country of origin (China was an impotent empire, Japan a rising and modernizing military power, the Philippines an American colony). But both the Japanese and Filipinos were excluded from naturalized U.S. citizenship, were the victims of residential discrimination and racial intermarriage laws, and were eventually banned from further U.S. immigration.

The Japanese arrived in significant numbers in Hawaii (then an independent kingdom) beginning in the 1880s, where they were imported as contract laborers for sugar plantations. In the 1890s Japanese immigrants from Hawaii and Japan began to settle in the United States, concentrating in the states of California, Washington, and Oregon. Like the Chinese before them, most Japanese immigrants were young peasant men who worked at physically demanding and low-paying jobs in agriculture and industry (many replaced the Chinese, whose population was aging and declining because of restrictions on Chinese immigration). Many Japanese opened small businesses; others developed land that had been considered unusable by previous settlers into successful farms.

In the late nineteenth century, an anti-Japanese movement rose in California and neighboring states, with many of the same racial and economic arguments—and some of the same leaders—as the anti-Chinese movement before it. In 1906, the San Francisco city government tried to place all Japanese students in the public school system with Chinese students in a segregated school. Because Japan, unlike China, was a rapidly modernizing military power, San Francisco's move created an international incident after the Japanese consulate protested the city's treatment of Japanese immigrants. President Theodore Roosevelt personally intervened, convinced the San Francisco leadership to reverse its actions, and promised to limit Japanese immigration. The United States and Japan then negotiated the so-called Gentleman's

Agreement, a series of diplomatic notes made in 1907–1908 in which Japan agreed to stop issuing passports to Japanese "laborers." (Japan wanted to prevent a law similar to the 1882 Chinese Exclusion Act, which it regarded as insulting.)

The Gentleman's Agreement did not limit immigration as much as some people hoped. By permitting family unification, it fostered a shift from predominantly male to predominantly female immigration. The female immigrants included wives reuniting with their husbands as well as "picture brides" married by proxy and family arrangement who would then travel to America to join husbands they had never met. Because of this demographic development, the Japanese population in the United States became self-sustaining and continued to grow, a ramification that deeply alarmed many exclusionists who worried about Japanese "takeover." California and other states passed laws designed to prevent Japanese ownership of land. Finally, in 1924 the Gentleman's Agreement was superseded by a new immigration law banning all Japanese immigration (other Asians had been excluded under a 1917 law).

One group of Asian immigrants not affected by these immigration restriction laws were the Filipinos. Classified as "nationals" because the Philippines were then under American colonial rule, Filipinos were imported to work on Hawaiian sugar plantations, on California farms, and in Alaskan fish canneries. Most Filipino immigrants were young men who, more than their Chinese and Japanese predecessors, actively sought female company (whether in commercial dance halls or marriages) and were more involved in labor unions and strikes—qualities that outraged many whites. California and other states rewrote their miscegenation laws to include "members of the Malay race." In 1934 Filipino immigration was finally banned in a measure that also promised independence to the Philippines in ten years.

VIEWPOINT 1

"The Japanese can not, may not and will not provide desirable material for our citizenship."

Japanese Residents Can Never Be Assimilated

V.S. McClatchy (1857–1938)

V.S. McClatchy, publisher of the *Sacramento Bee* and *Fresno Bee*, was one of the foremost leaders of California's anti-Japanese movement during the 1920s. The founder of and driving force behind the California Joint Immigration Committee, a private anti-immigrant organization, McClatchy wrote and published numerous articles, pamphlets, and other writings attacking the Japanese residents of California as a threat to the United States. (McClatchy's concerns about immigration were not limited to the Japanese; in the 1930s he wrote articles against Filipino immigration.) In the following viewpoint, excerpted from a 1921 article, McClatchy argues that the Japanese living in California can never fully assimilate and become true Americans. Among the reasons he gives for the inability of the Japanese to assimilate are cultural differences between Americans and Japanese; Japanese worship of their "Mikado" (emperor); and the restrictive citizenship laws of the Japanese government, which claims all Japanese as its citizens.

There are three principal elements in the menace threatened by Japanese immigration to this country. They are:

1. The non-assimilability of the Japanese race; the practical impossibility of making out of such material valuable and loyal American citizens.

From V.S. McClatchy, "Japanese in the Melting Pot: Can They Assimilate and Make Good Citizens?" *Annals of the American Academy of Political and Social Science*, January 1921.

2. Their unusually large birth-rate per thousand population, already shown in California to be three times that of the whites, notwithstanding that the estimated proportion of adult females to males among the Japanese is only 1 to 4, while among the whites it is, say, 1 to 1.

3. The great advantages which they possess in economic competition, partly due to racial characteristics, and partly to standards of living, organization, direction and aid from their government. These advantages make it hopeless for American whites to compete with them.

It should be evident that we can not encourage or permit in our midst the development of an alien element possessing these characteristics without inviting certain disaster to our institutions and to the nation itself. The evidence on each of these points is apparently incontrovertible.

Three Reasons

As to non-assimilability, the first element mentioned in the Japanese menace, there are three main reasons why it is useless to attempt the making of good American citizens out of Japanese material, save of course in exceptional individual instances. The Japanese can not, may not and will not provide desirable material for our citizenship.

1. The Japanese *can not* assimilate and make good citizens because of their racial characteristics, heredity and religion.

2. The Japanese *may not* assimilate and make good citizens because their Government claims all Japanese, no matter where born, as its citizens.

3. The Japanese *will not* assimilate and make good citizens. In the mass, with opportunity offered, and even when born here, they have shown no disposition to do so, but, on the contrary, pronounced antagonism.

There can be no effective assimilation of Japanese without intermarriage. It is perhaps not desirable for the good of either race that there should be intermarriage between whites and Japanese. The laws of some states forbid such marriages, but even where such marriages are permitted and encouraged, the Japanese themselves will not take advantage thereof. That is best demonstrated in Hawaii, where there is a great commingling of races; but the Japanese, comprising nearly half of the entire population of the Territory, and steadily increasing in number, maintain in wonderful degree their racial purity. With a population of 112,000 or more the Japanese in Hawaii in five years have contracted marriages with other races, according to the report made this year by the Survey Commission—at the request of the Commissioner of Education, at Washington, Bulletin No. 16, 1920—as follows: Thirty-two Japanese men and four women were married to Hawaiians, a few Japanese men to Portuguese women, one Japanese man to an American woman and a few Japanese women to Chinese and Koreans.

Emperor Worship

The Japanese hold that their Mikado is the one living God to whom they owe their very existence, and therefore all obedience. It is not possible to make of an individual in whom that belief is deeply and firmly grounded an American citizen who can be relied upon in a crisis. This worship of the Mikado (Mikadoism, or Shintoism) is a part of the education of each child in Japan, and school children are by government decree forced to worship at the Shinto shrines.

Buddhism, which is tolerated in Japan, has Shintoism grafted onto it. Baron Goto, a prominent Japanese statesman, at a gathering of Foreign Board Mission Secretaries, at New York, in June, 1919, said he was almost persuaded to embrace Christianity; that with slight modifications he could do so.

It is upon such suggestions as this American missionaries hang their hopes that, by placating the Japanese in various ways, and more particularly as to their demands for free immigration and citizenship privileges in the United States, the evangelization of the Japanese, both in Japan and in this country, will be made very much easier through Japanese Government suggestion or influence.

The modification necessary or desirable in Christianity before Baron Goto would embrace it is probably a modification similar to that which has been made in Buddhism; that is to say, the incorporation therein of Mikadoism, or Shintoism, which recognizes the god character of the Mikado, and insures thereby the loyalty of the individual Japanese to the Japanese Empire, through the Mikado. . . .

From a writer long resident in Japan, and fully conversant with its language, its religion and its people, is quoted the following statement on this matter: "Mikadoism, or Emperor worship, is the sheet anchor of patriotic fervor in Japan—the soul of the body politic. The vast majority of the people have no other religion. It is not a relic of bygone days, but the very heart of present-day Japan."

The plea of Sidney Gulick and a number of his Christian friends that we make citizens of the Japanese and then trust to making good citizens of them by Christianizing them, advocates an experiment dangerous in the extreme, doubtful even as to a superficial change in religion, and certain to end in disaster.

The inherent incapacity of the Japanese for assimilation, their religious belief and ideals, bred in them for generations and taught to them the world over, which foreign birth and foreign residence do not modify, create a permanent and insurmountable barrier between them and that real American citizenship which would be of value, and not a grave menace, to this nation. They can not be transmuted into good American citizens.

Japanese Laws on Citizenship

The second point made by me against the possibility of making American citizens out of Japanese is based upon my statement that Japan does not permit it. We come now to the curious and inconsistent policy of our Government as to dual citizenship, the full viciousness of which is most apparent in the case of the Japanese. We recognize as an American citizen and extend all rights and privileges as such to any one born under the American flag, including, of course, the Japanese. Japan, on the other hand, rigidly insists that every Japanese, no matter where his parents were born, and no matter what nation may have conferred citizenship on him, with or without his request, is a Japanese citizen, and must perform all the obligations as such.

Every Japanese born here, even if his forbears for generations were born here, but had not been permitted to expatriate, is subject to orders from Japan; is kept track of through the Japanese Consulate and other organizations, and is subject to call for military duty. Authorities on international law agree that, since the United States confers its citizenship on the Japanese born here, unasked and with full knowledge of Japan's claims, we must, in the event of war, recognize those Japanese as the citizens of Japan.

We are thus conferring upon the Japanese born here all the rights and privileges of citizenship, without any of the obligations; and we are certainly breeding in our midst a class of American citizens whose hand, we know in advance, must be against us in possible case of war.

Japan not only claims as her citizens all Japanese born on American soil, but she also takes great care that they grow up really as Japanese citizens, with all the ideals and loyalty of the race, untouched by the notions prevalent in this country, which would weaken that loyalty.

The Japanese children born under the American flag are compelled to attend Japanese schools, usually after the public school hours, where they are taught the language, the ideals and the religion of Japan, with its basis of Mikado worship. Here they are taught by Japanese teachers, usually Buddhist priests, who frequently speak no English, and who almost invariably know nothing of American citizenship. The text-books used are the Mombusho series, issued under the authority of the Department of Education at Tokio. These schools are located wherever there are

Japanese communities, and teachers in the American public schools testify that the Japanese children frequently are studying their Japanese lessons in their public school hours.

In Hawaii, this system of Japanese schools and its effect in preventing any chance of inculcating the principles of American citizenship in the Japanese upon whom we confer such citizenship, caused such widespread comment that the Hawaiian Legislature in 1919 attempted to pass a law providing that teachers in foreign language schools must know sufficient English and enough American history and civics to ground the pupils in the principles of American citizenship. That bill was defeated on the demand and through the influence of the Japanese who said its effect would be to destroy their schools.

California senator James D. Phelan emphasized the Japanese "invasion" of California in his (unsuccessful) 1920 campaign for reelection.

Now, the survey commission appointed by the Commissioner of Education of the United States, reports in Bulletin No. 16 of 1920, that these Hawaiian-Japanese schools, if not anti-American, are at least not pro-American, and recommends that all foreign language schools in the Hawaiian Islands should be abolished, except for foreign children who can never become American citizens.

It has been shown already why the Japanese *can not* make good citizens, because of their religion and heredity and non-assimilability; it has been shown also why they *may not* make good citizens, because the laws of Japan, efficiently and rigorously administered in the United States, as well as in Japan, do not permit them; it is equally true that they *will not* make good citizens, and that the evidence of the acts of those who have resided under the American Flag for many years is conclusive on this point.

In Hawaii, where their numbers make them independent, and where they are now in a position to practically control the Territory, the Japanese form a separate, alien community, observing the laws, customs and the ideals of Japan; using the Japanese language, both in their business and in their schools, and bringing up their children to be not American but Japanese citizens, with all that loyalty to the Mikado which is a part of the Japanese religion.

The statement made as to Japanese policy in Hawaii is equally true of the Japanese in California, though, because of differences in conditions, the evidence has not forced itself as yet so strongly on public attention. The Japanese schools are found in every Japanese community in California where there are enough children to support them.

The Japanese, however, are not content to depend upon education of their American-born children in this country in order to make them loyal subjects of the Mikado. In the report of the Japanese Association of America, concerning its California census, as quoted by the State Board of Control, appears the statement that there are in Japan at this time about 5,000 California-born Japanese. That statement carries little significance to most people. It means, however, that there are at this time 5,000 of the Japanese born in California, that is to say, 20 per cent of California's Japanese minors, upon whom the United States conferred citizenship, who are now back in Japan being thoroughly instructed in the religion and ideals of Japan; so that when they return here they may serve, not as American citizens, but as loyal subjects of the Mikado, to do his will and serve his interests.

The Japanese writer, C. Kondo, Chief Secretary of the Central Japanese Association of Southern California, in a very able article published in *Nichi Bei* of January 8 and 9 of this year, frankly acknowledges that the Japanese of California show no disposition to Americanize themselves, and that to this fact largely is due the antagonism which they have created. He warns them that this antagonism will increase rather than disappear, and suggests that they should move to the southern states, where their characteristics are as yet unknown. He adds, however, that if they pursue the same methods there that they have in California, they will encounter the same bitter experience that they are now undergoing here.

One reason why the Japanese show no disposition to Americanize themselves lies in their belief, passed down through generations, grounded into them in their schools, and a part of their religion (For is not their nation the only one on earth whose ruler is the living God?), that they are superior to any race on earth. Why, then, should they be willing to expatriate themselves and become citizens of an inferior nation?

The cockiness which many have noticed in the Japanese under certain conditions and on certain occasions, their pride and sensitiveness, their intolerance of criticism or opposition, are all due to this inbred and firmly established belief in their superiority. In the issue of June 10, 1920, of *The Northman*, a Swedish publication printed at Portland, Oregon, Miss Frances Hewett, who spent six years in Japan teaching English to Japanese school children in the public schools there, says: "Neither do the tourists learn that these children are taught that they, being children of the Son of Heaven, are superior to all foreigners, and that their natural destiny is to bring all other peoples to subjection."

A Threat to America

Under such conditions, it is not only probable but practically certain that the majority of Japanese who are now endeavoring to secure for themselves the privileges of American citizenship, are doing it not from any desire to help the American nation, or to become an integral part of it, but that they may better serve Japan and the Mikado. A striking evidence of this is found in an article which appeared in the Sacramento *Daily News*, a Japanese newspaper, February 4, 1920. This calls the attention of the Japanese to the dual citizenship situation, and suggests that for the present they cease registering births with the Japanese authorities, and register only with the American authorities. They are advised that they need not fear thereby to lose Japanese citizenship, because at any time they can make good their claim to it by proof of birth, etc. The article closes with the statement that the American citizen can be used for furthering the purposes of Japan in this country. Following is part of the article:

> It is urged then when as American citizens (by birth) the opportunity comes for them to reinforce the Japanese residents in America who have no citizenship rights, they must on behalf of His Majesty, the Emperor of Japan, become the loyal protectors of the race.

The following is a portion of a statement made on his return to San Francisco from Japan by Dr. Benjamin Ide Wheeler, President Emeritus of the University of California and republished in the *Japan Advertiser* of Tokio on May 22, 1920. Dr. Wheeler had gone to Japan as a member of an unofficial mission headed by Mr. Wallace M. Alexander of the San Francisco Chamber of Commerce to discuss with leading Japanese the feasibility of a friendly understanding between the two countries.

The two civilizations can not mingle, and the leaders in Japan agree that it is not well to attempt to amalgamate them. They can not and will not understand our civilization, and no matter in what part of the world he is, a Japanese always feels himself a subject of the Emperor, with the Imperial Government backing him, much as a feudal retainer had the support of his overlord in exchange for an undivided loyalty.

VIEWPOINT 2

"They are more American than Japanese in their ideas and ideals, their language and manners, their mode of thinking and attitude toward life in general."

Japanese Residents Are Assimilating

Kiichi Kanzaki (dates unknown)

Kiichi Kanzaki was general secretary of the Japanese Association of America from 1915 to 1921, when he returned to Japan. The association, which was formed in 1909 at the suggestion of the Japanese consulate general in San Francisco, functioned as a semiofficial organ of the Japanese government. Japanese immigrants were officially required to be members of the Japanese Association of America, although not all enrolled or paid membership fees. The national organization and its local branches performed some bureaucratic functions for Japanese immigrants, including issuing them the certificates they needed to travel outside the country with the right to reenter and to bring family members to America. Some opponents of Japanese immigration accused the association of being part of a Japanese government plot to maintain control of the Japanese American population.

In addition to its bureaucratic functions and its provision of legal assistance to Japanese Americans, the Japanese Association of America published numerous pamphlets and books. Some were aimed at Japanese immigrants. For example, Japanese women disembarking in San Francisco were given "The Guide for Newcoming Women," which explained American customs and manners. Other publications attempted to influence American public opinion in favor of the Japanese. The following viewpoint is taken from a 1921 pamphlet based on a statement Kanzaki submitted to a congressional committee on immigration. Kanzaki, re-

From Kiichi Kanzaki, *California and the Japanese* (Japanese Association of America, 1921).

sponding in part to the arguments of anti-Japanese activists such as V.S. McClatchy and California senator James D. Phelan, addresses the issue of whether Japanese immigrants and their families are successfully assimilating into American society. He argues that such assimilation is taking place, especially among American-born Japanese, and that the Japanese would be even more successful at fitting in if racial prejudice and legal barriers to U.S. citizenship were removed.

The allegation that the Japanese are non-assimilable is the central argument of the anti-Japanese agitators. But they have never yet explained what they mean by assimilation, nor have they given any reason for their assertions. Mr. V.S. McClatchy, for example, testified before the Committee of Immigration and Naturalization last June [1920] saying: "Now the objections to the Japanese are that they are non-assimilable. They don't intermarry and we don't want them to intermarry. The Japanese is always a Japanese." (Hearing Report p. 253.) Not only does the witness give no reasons for this important assertion, but he mixes the question of assimilation with that of intermarriage, which is utter injustice, for assimilation can take place without intermarriage as I shall endeavor to demonstrate later. Senator James D. Phelan has resorted to the same method of attack. He said during the same hearing: "If there is any way of putting them on an equality in all respects, we would do it. It is an economic proposition because the races are non-assimilable, and we can never have that equality." Further on he said: "It is our duty to exclude the Japanese for economic reasons. Their competition is deadly and their non-assimilability established. Heretofore the Japanese have objected to discrimination, but God made them so and it is the nature of things. If we were to swallow them and could assimilate them as an American community, it would be well and good, but we can not do it. They, therefore, should not complain except against the decree of nature." (Hearing Report, p. 204.)

I should like to note in the first place that Senator Phelan has not given any fact or reason for his assertions, and has not scientifically proved his case.

Defining Assimilation

Assimilation may be defined, for practical purposes, as an art or process by which one is brought into a resemblance, harmony, conformity, or identity with regard to others. More specifically, the Japanese may be brought to such conditions with regard to Americans to the fullest extent of the meaning of the term. It means their adjustment to the new conditions and adaptation to social, political, industrial and cultural institutions of America. If this is true and if this is what assimilation implies, then the whole question of assimilation boils down to *how far and to what degree* the Japanese have been, and can be, assimilated. Nothing absolute can be said on the question, as for example, that the Japanese are non-assimilable. Indeed, assimilation is a relative matter, not an absolute one.

There are two phases to the question of assimilation thus defined, namely, physical and cultural. The physical assimilation of any race is difficult to measure and has not yet been scientifically proved. But the fallacy of such an assertion as "the Creator made the two races different and different they will remain" has been convincingly demonstrated even by the Immigration Commission. It has generally been thought that, under the educational, social, and political conditions now existing in America, European immigrants gradually change their habits of living and their ways of thinking, and thus become Americans. Even changes in bodily form, such as height and weight, the cephalic index, color of the hair, etc., have been admitted as summarized by Franz Boas of Columbia University. (The Report of the Immigration Commission, Vol. 39.) These changes are by no means foreign to Japanese immigrants. We have observed similar changes also among the descendants of Japanese in America. Their hair is becoming lighter and even brownish-black. The yellow or tan appearance of their skin is losing its darker pigment; while their stature is gaining in height and their weight is increasing in proportion. While there has not been a sufficiently careful study made so far to determine the exact extent of these remarkable changes, such a tendency is undeniably shown by actual cases and facts. The racial difference, though it tends to discourage rapid amalgamation, by no means prevents even physical assimilation, and the Japanese immigrants are in an exactly similar position to the American people as any European immigrant race, in the possibility of their physical assimilation. . . .

Cultural Assimilation

The cultural assimilation of the Japanese in America is more illuminating and suggestive. First, take American-born Japanese children and young people, even, who are alleged to be non-assimilable. They are more American than Japanese in their ideas and ideals, their language and manners, their mode of thinking and attitude toward life in general. They speak almost entirely in English in daily conversation. Often the mothers find it difficult to communicate with them, unless they, too, have ample command of English.

When these native sons and daughters are taken back to Japan they never desire to remain there, not even for a short while, and insist upon returning to their "home" in America. Having thus adopted American ideas and ideals, they embrace to the fullest extent Americanism. That this is true is proved, for example, by the eagerness with which they have joined, and are joining, wherever there is an opportunity, the Boy Scouts of America, and the remarkable record which they have made.

During the last Great War our American-born Japanese were eager to serve under the Stars and Stripes and have admirably demonstrated their patriotism and loyalty to America. I was an eye-witness at one of the memorable scenes of departure of one of the native sons enlisted. Several of his friends urged him to stand courageously on the battlefield and to fight valiantly for America. In response, the young soldier, with a smile of American optimism, said: "It is a high honor for me that I can go as the first American-born Japanese to fight for those lofty ideals of which the Stars and Stripes are the symbol. I will do my very best and when duty calls me I will sacrifice my life for the cause of humanity and democracy. I pledge that I will bring no dishonor either to the land of my birth or to the country of my forefathers."

Soon after, another soldier came to bid me farewell and with a cheerful countenance said: "I am exceedingly glad that I am going. Like my friend already gone, I will pledge myself, soul and body, to fight for America's cause. I will do my duty even sacrificing my life under the Stars and Stripes."

These encouraging results are also true among the adult Japanese residents in California. It is appealing to note that their ideals, both social and economic, political and cultural, have been greatly changed, even to the point of "conversion." A sense of brotherhood and social equality and a rising spirit of democracy and internationalism are fast winning the hearts of our fellow countrymen in this State. Thus, contrary to the assertion often made, there is an undeniable tendency to make America their permanent home.

This tendency is gaining ground so firmly that even those who return to the mother country with a determination to remain, are usually found coming back, fully decided to make America their permanent home. It is no exaggeration to state that over eighty per cent of the Japanese here today will find their graves in the land of their adoption. Another bright prospect is further evidenced by the surprisingly high aspiration and firm determination on the part of Japanese parents to educate their children in America, as Americans, useful for America's future.

Again, their mode of living, their attitude of thinking, and their philosophy of life are being Americanized so profoundly that to-day they find no difficulty in performing their new civic duties and in conforming to American laws. Except in rare cases, the observance of Sunday has become a part of their lives, while the spirit of true American home life is becoming more and more understood and appreciated. That the Japanese will sacrifice themselves for American ideals has been conclusively shown by their attitude during the last Great War. We look back, indeed, with a pardonable pride, upon those memorable days when the Japanese in this country stood up in concert with America's hymn of Democracy and contributed handsome sums for war bonds, the Red Cross, and War Savings Stamps.

The following is the approximate estimate of the amounts contributed to the United States War Loans by the Japanese in California:

First Loan	$250,000.00
Second Loan	.280,000.00
Third Loan	.838,000.00
Fourth Loan	.750,000.00
Fifth Loan	.650,000.00
	$2,768,000.00

The figures fluctuated much among the Japanese in the other parts of the United States: For example, the Japanese in New York City contributed $1,589,550 for the Fifth Loan. The total amount may not be large, but contribution per capita is large. . . .

For the actual military service over-seas, the Japanese, despite the fact that they are not allowed to become citizens of the United States, volunteered in large numbers under the American colors. A Japanese graduate of the University of Southern California considered it his duty to fight for the country which gave him shelter and education from boyhood. He volunteered, though he had no citizenship rights. To his great disappointment, however, his application was turned down.

Assimilability of the Japanese

That assimilability is one of Japanese racial characteristics can be proven by the history of the rapid growth of Modern Japan. Upon what else, if assimilability is denied, can we base our explanation of that remarkable growth and complete change, almost revolutionary, which took place within the last fifty years in Japan? The Japanese, indeed, have always shown that they can and are willing to assimilate. Their high respect for Western civilization and their sincere desire to adopt it have been amply demonstrated by the fruits which they are reaping today.

93

The Japanese are assimilable. They have proven that they are assimilable, yet it must be admitted that this process of assimilation among the Japanese in America has been very slow. Who is to blame for this? Even if we admit that there are certain faults on our part, nevertheless, we are tempted to quote Mr. Gregory Mason from *The Outlook* of June 16, 1920, who answered the question in the following convincing language:

"In my opinion, the Americans are mainly to blame for the fact that the Japanese element which comes to this country remains an unkneaded lump in the national dough."

We Have Cast Our Lot in California

George Shima, a Japanese American farmer known as the "Potato King" for his agricultural successes in California, wrote the following in a 1920 editorial.

I am a farmer, who has devoted his life to the development of the delta district of the Sacramento Valley, and know little of politics, diplomacy, or international questions. But it seems to me the part of wisdom and common sense to look upon the treatment of the local Japanese as a purely local matter, which should be considered quite independently of Japanese policy in the Far East.

We live here. We have cast our lot with California. We are drifting farther and farther away from the traditions and ideas of our native country. Our sons and daughters do not know them at all. They do not care to know them. They regard America as their home.

We have little that binds us to Japan. Our interest is here, and our fortune is irrevocably wedded to the state in which we have been privileged to toil and make a modest contribution to the development of its resources. What is more important, we have unconsciously adapted ourselves to the ideals and manners and customs of our adopted country, and we no longer entertain the slightest desire to return to our native country.

Here I would like to call most impartial attention of thinking Americans to an almost neglected phase of the question of assimilation, namely, the barriers of all sorts in the way of Japanese assimilation.

Besides racial prejudice against them, the Japanese are not allowed the privilege of becoming full citizens of the United States, thus being prevented from developing along many lines. Among these, the most noteworthy is the California Alien Land Law and the consequent laws which prohibit Japanese from possessing land unless they are citizens. Under these circumstances, can it justly and fairly be claimed that the Japanese are non-assimilable?

In conclusion it is well to ask the question, Are the Japanese really undesirable people? Do they possess no characteristics worthy of positive effort at assimilation in this country, especially when they have proved that they are assimilable? In spite of the series of alarming allegations made against the Japanese in California, particularly in connection with the charge of undesirability, it is an encouraging fact to find that even the leaders of the anti-Japanese agitators admit that the Japanese possess numerous worthy qualities.

Mr. V.S. McClatchy, for example, testified before the House Committee on Immigration and Naturalization, December 1919, describing this point as follows: "The Japanese is sober and industrious, and I don't entirely agree with my friend Mr. Freeman. He is generally law abiding. He has respect for his superiors and parents, and so far as police records go the cities don't have trouble with Japanese. They are very industrious. They work long hours for little pay when necessary, and they have absolute cooperation. Now the objections are that they don't assimilate—" But, having such good and worthy qualities and having above all demonstrated that they are assimilable, what other qualities are lacking to make good American citizens?

Senator James D. Phelan stated a similar absurdity in the following language: "We admire their (Japanese) industry and cleverness, but for that very reason, *being a masterful people*, they are more dangerous." And because "the Chinese are not a masterful race and are far more tractable and are quite willing to work for wages," Senator Phelan prefers a subservient slavish race to a free and independent race!

The editor of a powerful daily on the Pacific Coast, the San Francisco *Chronicle*, recently gathered courage enough to state the same thing from another angle: "The objection to Japanese immigration is not from any unfriendly feeling or any assumption of superiority. The fact seems to be *that the Japanese adhere to an ability and willingness to do hard work which the American race has lost, so they are too dangerous to be admitted*." What a paradox! It is not necessary to add any further word as to the good qualities of Japanese immigrants, even if there are numerous other yet more plausible points. In the face of all these very statements made by the anti-Japanese agitators, the charge of undesirability of Japanese immigrants crumbles, for the Japanese possess good qualities which even "the American race has lost" and they have shown that they are assimilable. Why not make them worthy members of the United States and transform them into a valuable asset instead of mistreating and persecuting them?

VIEWPOINT 3

"This proposed legislation is an infringement upon the fair play and square deal traditional with the American nation."

Land Ownership Restriction Laws Are Unjust

George Shima (1863–1926)

George Shima (born Kinji Ushijima) moved from Japan to the United States while in his twenties. After initially working as a potato picker and labor contractor, he began leasing and purchasing undeveloped swampland in the San Joaquin delta, which he drained and converted into farmland. His reclamation efforts and his pioneering raising of potatoes for the California market met with great success, and by 1913 the "Potato King" controlled 28,800 acres of land and employed 500 workers. He bought a house and lived in Berkeley, California (despite an organized neighborhood protest against his residence), and sent his children to American universities, including Harvard and Stanford.

Shima's career was perhaps the most spectacular single example of a general pattern in California and other western states—the successful movement of Japanese immigrants into farming. In Idaho, Colorado, and Utah, Japanese farmers helped establish sugar beets as a major cash crop. In Washington and California, Japanese farmers and vendors dominated the market for fresh fruits and vegetables in Seattle, Los Angeles, and other cities. Such successes, however, resulted in a political backlash against the Japanese. In 1913 California passed a law making land ownership illegal for Japanese. Other states followed California's example.

From George Shima, "Appeal to Justice," in *California and the Japanese* by Kiichi Kanzaki (Japanese Association of America, 1921).

Land ownership became an issue again in 1920 when Californians voted on a referendum initiative closing loopholes in the 1913 law. The following viewpoint is taken from a public statement by Shima, speaking as president of the Japanese Association of America, in October 1920, prior to the November elections. Shima argues that the proposed land initiative is fundamentally unfair. He asserts that the Japanese in the United States and the Japanese government have taken steps to respond to American concerns about immigration, including halting the inflow of "picture brides" (women who were married in family-arranged ceremonies in Japan with the grooms absent, and who then sailed to America to join the husbands they had never met). He concludes by arguing that the Japanese in America are industrious and law-abiding neighbors who should not be punished by alien land laws.

There are now being circulated petitions for an important initiative measure. This measure is directed against all peoples from Asia, but especially the Japanese. Its object is:

1. Absolute prohibition of land ownership by Japanese.

2. Absolute prohibition of leasing of farm land by Japanese.

3. Prohibition of the American-born Japanese minor, an American citizen, from acquiring real property under the guardianship of his or her own parent. To put it another way, the Japanese parent is prohibited from being the guardian to his or her own minor son or daughter acquiring real property.

4. Prohibition of the Japanese from becoming a member of, or acquiring any share in, any company or corporation owning farm land.

5. The confiscation of real property upon certain prima facie presumptions.

These are the main points of the proposed measure, which for severity and harshness, has no equal. Around these main points are wound detailed provisions, all evidently conceived in the idea that the Japanese should not be permitted to till the soil, that they should play no part in the development of California's agricultural resources—except as wage laborers.

Obviously these extreme proposals involve the question of constitutionality. Strong argument can be advanced against them upon the ground that they are unconstitutional.

To us, however, the prime consideration is not a legal one, but one of justice and equity.

In our judgment, and we trust, in the judgment of all true Americans, this proposed legislation is an infringement upon the fair play and square deal traditional with the American nation.

The people of Japan, for two generations, have been taught friendship and good-will for the people of America. They have fostered respect for the ideals and institutions of the United States. Your great emancipators, your champions of liberty and equality have been idols of our students and young men. Your missionaries have preached to us not only the Christian gospel of brotherhood but the American ideals of equality and equity.

We know that the Constitution of the United States guarantees to all "persons" under the American flag the equal protection of laws. We have believed, as we still believe, that this is a promise of protection for the homes and fortunes of all who come here under the law and under the treaty to help develop your great resources by their labor and enterprise.

In the face of all this, it is hard for us to believe that the present agitation against us has the sanction of Americanism—that it springs from the heart of the true American.

We know that there is no trouble between Americans and Japanese who come in direct and intimate contact with each other. Americans who employ or are employed by Japanese have no complaint against us. American business men and bankers who have dealt with Japanese have little to say against us. American workmen are willing and eager to work for Japanese. They work harmoniously and friendlily side by side with Japanese laborers. Why allow outsiders, who know little about us, who have their own axes to grind, to stir up ill-feeling and animosity where there is no cause for them?

We recognize that racial difference engenders a race feeling. But no one will deny that this is a feeling which should not be fostered or deliberately stirred up. All sensible men will agree that it is criminal to exploit that feeling for ulterior purposes.

The hope of our age lies in the effort to minimize race feeling. Its spirit, its ideal, its tendency is not to emphasize, but to alleviate racial difference. If we make business of fanning and feeding race feeling, there can be no hope of international peace, and all efforts for a league of nations must be set at naught. Surely race feeling should not be injected where there is no occasion for it.

Permit us to repeat that between Americans, who deal with Japanese, and Japanese, who deal with Americans, there exists little or no cause of trouble. Is it the part of wisdom to permit outsiders to create discord where harmony prevails?

Immigration Is a Separate Issue

We wish it clearly understood that we advocate nothing akin to free immigration. On the contrary, we recognize the wisdom of restricting Japanese immigration. We, therefore, believe that the "gentlemen's agreement" is a wise arrangement. If there be any doubt as to its interpretation or its enforcement, there should be frank and straightforward exchange of views between the two governments.

With this in view we took the initiative in stopping the arrival of "picture brides." Need we say that our minds are always open to friendly, reasonable suggestions and advices calculated to improve our relations with our neighbors?

An Appeal to Vote Against the California Land Law

The American Committee of Justice—an organization based in Oakland, California, whose members included political figures, landowners, members of the clergy, and others—opposed the 1920 initiative restricting Japanese land ownership. In 1920 it published a pamphlet urging California voters to reject the measure.

Initiative No. 1 aims to dispossess a helpless minority of aliens who have come here at our invitation and who are tilling California's soil in compliance with our laws. This Initiative, totally ineffective in restricting future Oriental immigration, merely persecutes the aliens against whom it is directed, and sows the seeds of distrust in their minds. No fair-minded, far-seeing Californian could endorse such a proposition.

Only 2 per cent of California's total population is Japanese. . . . We should not be placed in the ridiculous position of 98 per cent of our population being in fear of 2 per cent. We would be confessing ourselves weaklings and fools if we were to think that our institutions and civilization are being endangered by the presence of such a small number of Japanese, unobtrusive, law-abiding, minding their own business, and bothering nobody.

The area of land cultivated by Japanese in California amounts to only 1.6 per cent of our farm land. Even of this 1.6 per cent only a very small portion is actually owned or controlled by them. No man with a healthy mind can believe that this is a grave menace to the State. . . .

This Initiative is an affront to the American tradition of honor and fair play. Our innate sense of justice revolts against it. It should be defeated because it insults the American people, rather than because it works hardship for the Japanese.

Defeat this Initiative, and we shall be in a stronger position in urging the Federal Government to protect California against further influx of Oriental immigration. Adopt it, and we shall merely embarrass our Government and make the solution of the real trouble all the more difficult.

Our only contention is that those Japanese who, comparatively small in number, are already here, should be treated justly and equitably. A policy of discrimination and persecution will merely complicate the question and render its solution all the more difficult.

We have not neglected to foster Americanism among the Japanese in California. We have always co-operated with the American authorities or organizations in the Americanization movement. We have issued circulars and pamphlets, and sent out lecturers, explaining to the Japanese throughout the State what American ideals stand for.

The Japanese in California never fail to respond, and respond heartily, whenever they are called upon to shoulder their share in patriotic or charitable enterprises. Their economic activities have been deeply curbed by various devices, legislative, and otherwise, making it extremely difficult for them to improve their financial status, and yet they have never shirked their duty in regard to any undertaking calculated to advance public welfare.

The proposed initiative measure, outlined at the outset, will, if adopted, condemn the Japanese in California to a status little better than that of slaves or serfs. It will deprive them of all opportunity for material progress and economic advancement. It will render it impossible for them to provide for the future of their American-born children who are going to remain here as American citizens. Is it wise, is it in conformity with the American tradition of fair play, is it calculated to promote America's own welfare, that such a law should be adopted, virtually compelling the Japanese in California to fling upon the world, upon the American community, their sons and daughters, unprovided, and ill-trained to perform duties as members of a body politic of which these American-born children are destined to be a factor?

As we listen to the passing storm of passion, of denunciation, of abuse and slander, we ask ourselves if we were mistaken in our belief in your honor, in our faith that you would not strip us of the protection of the common law of equity and deny us the equal protection of your laws.

It is a painful question. We are few in numbers, defenseless except by the truth. You are a myriad in numbers and strong. You are taught at your altars to love your neighbors and that it is a scarlet sin to bear false witness against them. Surely you would not heed those who make business of spreading falsehoods about us, and urge you to persecute your peaceable, industrious, and law-abiding neighbors such as the Japanese?

Our good opinion of you and your country may seem of little value to you. But it has been of great value to us. It has guided us on our hard march onward for the past sixty years. It was a march to which your land summoned us, with promise of peace and friendship at its end. If you listen to enemies of the world's good order, and deny us that promise which we have followed as a great light, how can you summon others to trust you?

Many of the foregoing statements undoubtedly require elucidation and amplification. Some should be supported by statistical data. Perhaps, too, there should be an explanation of Japanese laws concerning the expatriation of Japanese abroad and the rights of aliens in Japan, for these Japanese laws are much more liberal than are commonly known to you.

But we feel it advisable to make this appeal as brief as possible. With that consideration in mind we have deliberately omitted such data as might otherwise well have been included herein. But the Japanese Association, whose headquarters are at 444 Bush Street, San Francisco, will undoubtedly be glad to supply any one interested in this question with such information as it possesses or may be able to obtain.

VIEWPOINT 4

"Sacramento County has the state capital. It ought to be a permanent center of white civilization, but more than half of the irrigated land . . . is farmed and controlled by the Japanese."

Land Ownership Restriction Laws Are Necessary

Elwood Mead (1858–1936)

In 1913 the state of California passed a law forbidding future land acquisitions by "aliens ineligible for citizenship"—a phrase aimed at Asian (and especially Japanese) farmers who could not become citizens because of federal naturalization statutes limiting eligibility to "free white persons." (It was widely assumed that under these laws Japanese immigrants were ineligible for citizenship, although such reasoning was not officially confirmed by the Supreme Court until 1922.) Japanese farmers were able to take advantage of loopholes in the 1913 law, including placing farms in the names of their children who were U.S. citizens by virtue of their American birth. However, in 1920 anti-Japanese activists placed a more stringent alien land law on the ballot for popular referendum. Californians voted 3-1 in favor of the measure.

The following viewpoint is taken from a 1921 article by Elwood Mead, a University of California agriculture professor and proponent of the 1920 land initiative. Mead argues that such land restrictions are necessary to avoid the total takeover of California land by foreign owners. He argues that Japanese have success-

From Elwood Mead, "The Japanese Land Problem of California," *Annals of the American Academy of Political and Social Science*, January 1921.

fully evaded the 1913 law, and have also abused the Gentleman's Agreement between the United States and Japan that had sought to limit Japanese immigration.

Alien land laws remained on the books in California until 1956, when Californians passed another initiative repealing them.

The most keenly contested issue of the recent election in California was over the action which should be taken on the initiative amendment prohibiting the selling or leasing of land to Japanese. Compared to this, interest as to who was to be president, or whether America would belong to the League of Nations was vague and remote. To many white farmers the vote on this amendment would determine whether they would continue to live on their farms or have to sell to an Oriental. The vote was therefore large. Public opinion was thoroughly aroused, and the majority of over three to one for the amendment showed clearly the trend of public opinion.

This legislation is a farmers' movement. It was opposed by some landowners and by many who believe in the complete exclusion of the Japanese but who did not believe that this was the way to secure national action. Organized labor was divided on the issue as were business men in cities. The San Francisco Chamber of Commerce opposed the amendment and there were placards in some towns advising laborers and business men to vote "no" since its adoption would, as they naively put it, drive the Japs into town to compete with the townspeople.

There was practically no division of opinion among country people who have to compete with the Japs. They worked and voted for the amendment. The white farm laborer does not like to work with them and still less to work for them. The white tenant farmer knows they have made his lot harder by forcing him to pay higher rent. The farmer living on his own land fears their invasion of his section and their organized campaigns for exclusive control of land and the marketing of products.

For this action, and the feeling that lies back of it, the Japanese are responsible. The California farmer is easy-going and optimistic, not inclined to plan for the future. If during the last ten years the Japanese had gone into the farming districts as individuals and mingled with white farmers as individuals, there would today be no more prejudice against them as a race than there is against Swedes or Italians, which is none at all. The statement that they have not done so, but have sought to establish themselves as racial communities, is not made in the way of criticism but to help explain why Japanese land ownership is objected to.

In Placer County, for example, 15,000 out of 19,000 irrigated acres are leased or owned by Japanese. The fine homes of the former white tenants are empty. They shelter rats and owls. So far as white people are concerned the towns are socially dead. The irrigated part of Placer County is practically a little Japan. The people from Nippon dominate its life. Controlling the land, they can perpetuate the ideas, habits, religion and loyalties of the mother country and do this indefinitely.

If the Italians owned 80 per cent of the tomato crop of the Sacramento District and 79 per cent of the Turlock District, and exercised a similar control over many other important fruit and vegetable products, they would be regarded with the same apprehension as are the Japanese. The good standing of the one and the unpopularity of the other is due quite largely to the fact that the first mingles with Americans and makes himself a part of the American life of California. The other seeks to create and is creating a racial life of his own.

A Farmers' Meeting

Last February, I attended a meeting of farmers called to discuss a resolution pledging landowners in that locality to refuse to lease land to Japanese. There was a considerable sprinkling of business men from the nearest town and most of the landowners were present. Japanese settlement in this area, which is a part of a melon-growing district, dated back only three years. In that time Japanese settlement had grown so rapidly that the previous year over 60 per cent of the melon crop had been grown by this race. Over 60 per cent of the melon shipments were handled by a commission firm with whom the Japanese did business. A similar growth for another two seasons would mean that the melon business would be to the white grower only a memory. The white farmers met to consider whether they would abdicate and move out or take steps to end this invasion.

When the meeting opened the discussion was entirely in favor of the Japanese. The first speaker announced he was there to "declare himself." He said he was renting land to the Japanese as a business proposition and he intended to continue to do so; that before the Japs came he was glad to get $15 an acre cash rent, now he was getting $40 an acre, and he owed the increase to the Japs. He further stated that before brown men came into the neighborhood, land was selling for $100 an acre. They had offered him $250 an acre, and he proposed to deal where he could make the most money. The land was his own. Now was his time to make hay and so far as he was concerned the Japanese were the haymakers. It was not his business to sacrifice money to keep California white.

Other landowners made similar declarations and it looked as though Japanese leasers would dominate the discussion. A change came when an elderly farmer rose and said:

> I came to this district twenty years ago. I live on the farm that I bought then and where my six children were born. They go to the country school. Three years ago all their playmates were white children. Now all the children in that school except mine and those of one other farmer are Japanese. My white neighbors who have sold or leased the land to Japanese have gone to towns. They don't come in contact with these aliens. They simply take their money. I live among them, but am not one of them. I am living there without neighbors. Last week a Japanese family moved into a house across the road in front of my home. That means more Japanese children in the school. It means that my isolation from people of my own race is more complete and I, too, am here to "declare myself."

> My farm is for sale. It is for sale to the first Japanese who will buy it. No white man will buy for none will go into a Japanese neighborhood. When I sell, my white neighbor will leave and it then becomes a Japanese community. When that happens the trade of that community will go into new channels. I have always traded at the white man's store, put my money in the white man's bank, but the Japanese will do neither. They trade with their own race.

The farmer was followed by a member of a commission firm that handled the melons of Japanese growers. He stated at the outset that if he was to consider his own financial interests he would remain silent, but he had decided it was his duty to give his views on the Japanese land problem. As his firm handled Japanese melons he obtained for them the money to finance growing and he knew, from being their banker, how in the short space of three years they had extended their control of melon production. He stated that with these people cooperation is an instinct, that the cooperation in that section was a continuation of their clan relation in Japan. These cooperative units usually had about twenty members. When one was in trouble the others helped him out, and it was a definite practice for those who had money to finance others and thus lift them out of the wage-earning into the employing class. He gave a score of instances where this financial help had been extended during the past season. He said that the Japanese had now secured a large enough share of the business to handle the selling of their melons in the future, that it was comparatively easy for them to make financial arrangements with commission houses in the east, and having done this they would be able to carry on as Japanese concerns.

His statement brought a complete change of sentiment in the meeting. Even the most defiant landowner realized that when the farms of that section were all under Japanese control through ownership or lease, they would be able to fix rents and land prices because white people will not go into sections dominated by Japanese. They saw that high rents were a temporary expedient to be paid long enough only to fix the status of the neighborhood as Oriental. Once this was done, there would be no further need for high rents or high prices. *The resolution was signed by every landowner.*

Previous to the movement for legislation, meetings like this were held all over California. It became evident that the voluntary action of isolated communities was not sufficient, that there were too many places where landowners were being tempted by money profits to ignore ultimate results and were creating a situation fraught with immensurable difficulty in the future.

Japanese Control of Farmland

The report of the Oriental problem by the State Board of Control shows that out of 3,893,500 acres irrigated, the Orientals control 623,753 acres, or about one-sixth and the Japanese alone control 458,056 acres, or about 16 per cent. This control has practically all been secured in the last ten years. The increase in acreage has been 412.9 per cent and the market value of the crops produced by Japanese has increased over tenfold, much of the work being done by hired white labor. With certain products like small fruits, they now have such a monopoly that they are able to dictate prices and control local markets.

San Joaquin County is one of the largest agricultural counties in the state. More than half of the irrigated land is controlled by the Japanese. Sacramento County has the state capital. It ought to be a permanent center of white civilization, but more than half of the irrigated land in that county is farmed and controlled by the Japanese, either as owners or lessees. The growth of their gardens and orchards in Sonoma, Santa Clara, and Solano counties is being watched by white farmers with ever increasing apprehension.

What makes this growth more ominous is the fact that it has occurred while the "Gentlemen's Agreement" was supposed to exclude laborers. It confers no right to own agricultural land, yet in ten years there has been over 100 per cent increase in numbers and more than half of these newcomers have flocked to the country. Farm purchases could only be made through evasion of the law passed in 1913. The Japanese have evaded it by every device which the best lawyers could invent. Japanese farmers have come to California knowing they were not wanted. They have bought land knowing it was contrary to the spirit of the law and the wishes of the people of California. In this they have shown the same spirit as in Korea and China. Yet, when these evasions became so notorious and the economic struggle so severe that white farmers sought to so amend the law as to end these aggressions, the Japanese used their thirty-nine associations and all of their influence to create sympathy for a sensitive, diffident people who were only seeking to contribute to this nation's wealth.

The Struggle for Race Supremacy

Washington was one of several states in addition to California to pass state laws restricting Japanese land ownership. The following passage is excerpted from an editorial in the Seattle Daily Wireless *(reprinted in the Seattle* Star *on February 25, 1921) in support of such legislation.*

The *Wireless* has never made it a point to proclaim its patriotism, but one thing its readers will never see it do is to advocate the surrender of the Pacific Coast to the Japanese.

The *Post-Intelligencer* is doing that very thing when it attempts to prevent the legislature from passing the Anti-Alien Land Bill, for it knows, as every thinking person must know, that the Japanese and American people will never live side by side in harmony. Once the Japanese succeed in establishing themselves here in sufficient numbers, a struggle for race supremacy between them and the American population will be on until one or the other race is driven out.

Like the ostrich which seeks to escape danger by burying its head in the sand, the *Post-Intelligencer* shuts its eyes to what no observing person can fail to see: the startling rapidity with which the Japanese have fastened their hold on the soil of this state and on its economical life.

Nothing could be more misleading. The Japanese are crowding in here because rural California is a paradise compared to the hard conditions of agriculture in their own country. No one can blame them for trying to possess the land and the agriculture of this state, nor ought we to think it strange that the Japanese government should back them up in this endeavor by every device of its adroit, if somewhat devious, diplomacy.

In order to compete with the Japanese, the American farmer, who has to make his way by labor, must sacrifice rest, recreation and the giving of time to civic interests or the development of the higher life of a community. He must change his ideas of what is desirable in life and surrender inherited habits. Only by devoting all of the energy of himself, his wife and children to the hard task of making a living, can he pay the rents and do the other things necessary to withstand the rural competition of the Japanese. The thing which America ought to recognize is that requiring him to do this is not an advance but a backward step in our progress and it will not be made. The American subjected to this competition will go into the cities or to other countries and the Japanese will continue to displace him as he has been displacing him during the last ten years.

These statements are made with no personal dislike for the Japanese, nor have I met with any evidence of a personal hatred toward them. On the contrary, the people of California have a high regard for their achievements, their industry and their surprising cleverness, but this does not blind the people in direct contact with them to what is going on or to the social and political dangers which are being created by this rapid absorption of farming land.

Conflicting Cultures

The land problem of California presents a new issue to America. The state seeks to check the immigration of people who come here for their racial and individual advantage, who seek to create little Japans with schools, newspapers, religion and language of the country they left. They bring a civilization many centuries old which they regard as superior to ours. They retain a loyalty to their own country, to its institutions and life, which prevents their becoming Americans or being assimilated into American life. Ownership of land enables them to secure these desired ends and what they have accomplished in the last ten years shows that unless something is done to check this progress, they will become the agricultural owners of California in a brief time as history runs. It is not a question of which is the superior race or which has the better culture. The objection to the Japanese is that with their coming Anglo-Saxon culture came in direct conflict with a Mongolian one. They can not live side by side and neither will give way to the other without a conflict.

"If you come to Honolulu, . . . you will find the melting-pot really at work."

Asian Americans Are Accepted in Hawaii

Riley H. Allen (1884–1966)

While the people in California and other states were embroiled in debate over Asian Americans, both opponents and proponents of immigrant exclusion laws looked at the experiences of Asians in Hawaii, a group of Pacific islands the United States annexed in 1898 (after decades of U.S. influence and indirect control). By 1920 the population of the original Polynesian inhabitants had been greatly reduced by disease and other causes, and the white population remained relatively small. The majority of Hawaii's inhabitants were farmworkers imported from all parts of the world, with the Japanese, Chinese, and Filipinos coming in greatest numbers. Most of this immigration was directly sponsored by Hawaiian sugar plantation owners seeking labor. The fact that Asians composed a majority of Hawaii's population was often cited by opponents of Asian immigration who feared the "Hawaiianization" of California and other places.

The following viewpoint is taken from an article from the January 1926 issue of *Sunset Magazine* by Riley H. Allen, then editor of the *Honolulu Advertiser*. Allen responds to a question he says is asked by many American visitors: Is the preponderance of Asians in Hawaii a cause of concern? Answering no, he argues that Hawaii provides a stellar example of the American "melting pot" ideal and that the Hawaiian-born children of all ethnic backgrounds are accepted as "fellow-Americans" and are becoming successfully assimilated American citizens.

Abridged from Riley H. Allen, "Americans All—in Hawaii!" *Sunset Magazine*, January 1926. Reprinted with permission from Sunset Publishing Corporation.

A few weeks ago the nationally known editor of an American daily paper sat on the broad lanai of the Moana hotel in Honolulu getting his shoes shined. The industrious little shiner who squatted at the visitor's feet, busily plying his brushes and cloths, was a brown youngster with bright black eyes glinting through slits in his swarthy cheek.

"Son," asked the visitor, "what are you, anyway—Hawaiian or what?"

The youngster glanced up, white teeth flashing, "I'm American," he answered.

"But," said the editor, slightly taken aback, "I mean what's your ancestry, what is your father?"

"Oh," replied the wielder of blacking, bent down to his task, "he's Japanese!"

It was shortly before that time that I heard a girl student at one of Honolulu's many public schools deliver a class address. She took as her subject "Lincoln," and in the course of her very well written speech she referred at least three times to "our forefathers whose toil and sacrifices laid the foundations for this republic."

And she was a girl whose straight black hair, high cheekbones and other racial characteristics showed that she was unmistakably of Chinese blood. Her forefathers came from somewhere in far Kwangtung or Honan—coolies, perhaps, for unnumbered generations, obscure toilers in a land of mandarins and monarchies, and of dynasties which flourished long before and far apart from the republic of the United States.

The Hawaiian "Melting-Pot"

These two incidents will give you a picture of the "racial situation" in Hawaii today, a situation unique and significant.

Nine out of ten visitors to the land of sugar, pineapples, ukuleles, coral beaches, swimming champions and cocoanut palms ask, soon after arrival, a question something like this: "Aren't you people in Hawaii afraid of the future with all these Orientals growing up here?"

And nine times out of ten, if the question is asked of a man or a woman who has been in the islands as long as five years and knows Hawaiian children, the answer will be something like this:

"No, we're not afraid; we're too busy working to be afraid. We have too much hope to be afraid."

In many cities of the United States it has been discovered, according to veracious commentators, that the well-known and far-famed "melting-pot" of Americanization is failing to melt the diverse elements of population thrown into it. You will hear of

Hamtranck, within the city limits of Detroit, where 60,000 Poles are said to be preserving almost intact the characteristics brought from Warsaw and Minsk and Kiev. You will read that after a hundred and fifty years of residence, the Pennsylvania Dutch are far more Dutch than Pennsylvanian or American or anything else; you will read of the Italians of crowded New York, and the Finns of Chicago. And these commentators will draw the conclusion that the "melting-pot" does not work in the United States.

Hawaii and the Japanese

Doremus Scudder, a member of the Federal Council of Commissioners on Friendly Relations with Japan, wrote in the January 1921 issue of the Annals of the American Academy of Political and Social Science *that Hawaii was proof that America could successfully absorb large numbers of Asian immigrants.*

Hawaii is a standing demonstration of America's power to absorb relatively an enormous immigration and yet maintain a dominant Americanism. Because 109,269 of its total population of 255,512 are Japanese it is frequently referred to as Japanese in character and civilization. This is absolutely foreign to the truth.

Having lived for years in Greater Boston, New York, Chicago and San Francisco, I found Hawaii during my fourteen years there as distinctively American as any of these other centers. It behooves our countrymen to have faith in America.

But if you come to Honolulu, a group of islands 2100 miles out in the Pacific from San Francisco, if you will tarry a while in this American territory which geographically is the stepping-stone between Occident and Orient, you will find the melting-pot really at work, fusing and blending and remaking the children of more than a dozen races.

Many successive waves have brought to the surf-washed shores of Hawaii a wide diversity of races. The Hawaiians, original inhabitants of this lovely land, are Polynesians—not negroes, though their remoter ancestry is still a matter of some uncertainty. Anthropologists, students of songs, of languages and customs have for years been endeavoring to trace that ancestry back beyond the days when the brown people of the Pacific islands voyaged from group to group in their outrigger canoes, steering a thousand miles by the stars. Sufficient for us, however, is it to note that the Hawaiians are the original inhabitants of Hawaii, at least insofar as any living race is concerned. . . .

But after the voyages of Cook and Vancouver, came a new era. The "Sandwich Islands" went upon the world map. The tiny port of "Honoruru" was known to trading schooners and to tall clipper ships bound for China with New England goods, to come back presently laden with tea and silk and spices. The halcyon days of whaling brought a great fleet of sailing ships into the Pacific, outfitting at Honolulu or Lahaina. Came, too, naval vessels of every great maritime power, all of which looked with an interested eye at this rich land of such potential strategic value in mid-Pacific.

The era of contact with the world may be said, roughly, to have dawned on the lonely Hawaiian archipelago with the opening of the nineteenth century. In 1820 the first of the missionary ships from New England reached the islands—precursor of a long series of mission bands with devoted American men and women carrying the Gospel to a people which had worshipped idols and been held hard and fast in the bondage of the barbaric *tabu*. Already many white men were coming to the islands, men of both good and evil sorts, from Occident and Orient. Some were intermarrying with the natives and the infusion of alien bloods began.

The Need for Labor

But the great waves of aliens which have come to Hawaii and reduced the Hawaiian people to a numerical minority did not arrive by the routes and circumstances mentioned. A few thousand foreigners voyaged to the islands as traders, whalers, shopkeepers, in various other lines of business, or as missionaries. The great influxes began some decades thereafter, when the possibilities of Hawaii for cane sugar production were realized.

Anywhere and everywhere, cane sugar production requires much manual labor. The very nature of the industry, with its preparation of soil, planting, irrigating, hoeing, harvesting and transportation of cane to the mills for grinding, demands many hands. There are great fortunes waiting for inventors who will find mechanical means to replace, on the average plantation, a thousand or so laborers; inventors who can work out adequate cane-cutters and loaders, thus eliminating some of the most intense and costly manual toil of the industry. These ample rewards are still waiting. The industry still demands a large number of people in the fields, unskilled laborers. And seventy-five years ago there was far less machinery than there is today, so that a much greater proportion of the processes of production had to be hand work.

So the early pioneers of the sugar industry in Hawaii looked about them, saw the possibilities of the islands for growing cane rich in sugar content, and realized the need for labor. It was not to be had in sufficient volume from the islanders. Already, in the 'fifties, less than three-quarters of a century later than Captain Cook's discovery, the islands had begun to lose their native population. Disease swept them off. A thousand causes inseparably connected with the emergence of the islands into modern economic conditions acted adversely on the natives.

The sugar pioneers, therefore, soon had to look beyond the islands as the expanding industry called for more hands in the field and mill. And through this demand for unskilled labor there came the successive waves of aliens which have given to Hawaii its race problems and are responsible for its significant success in handling them.

In any discussion of the "Orientals in Hawaii" it should be remembered and emphasized that, primarily, these Orientals are present by invitation and arrangement—as the result of organized effort by public as well as private organizations to meet the ever-pressing labor shortage. There was no "invasion" in the sense of outsiders streaming in, in defiance either of law or the wishes of the residents. Every new source of supply that was tapped, was tapped by a conscious act of the people of Hawaii. So, to whatever degree there is an "Oriental problem" in Hawaii, it is a problem which goes back fundamentally to the industrial needs of the islands for labor in the mass.

And many such sources of supply were tapped. That is what gives to the Hawaii of today such diversity of colors, aspects, traits, habits, beliefs, backgrounds, in its 306,000 civilian population.

No attempt will be made here to go into detail on the various races brought to Hawaii by hundreds and thousands as laborers. I shall mention only that South Sea islanders were tried, husky natives from the well-peopled and even more barbaric groups far to the south in the flashing Pacific. Russian peasants were brought from Manchuria; Portuguese from Madeira, the Azores and the mainland; Spaniards; small groups of Europeans from more northerly races; Chinese, Japanese, Koreans and Filipinos.

In greatest numbers came Chinese, Japanese and Filipinos.

The Chinese made excellent laborers, but when the United States annexed Hawaii the Chinese exclusion act knocked out the Celestials as labor recruits. The Japanese made excellent workers, but the "gentlemen's agreement" of 1907–08 dried up that source. The Filipinos make good laborers, though needing perhaps more training and building up physically than either of the other two and the Filipinos are still being brought to the islands in large numbers. For the Philippine archipelago is, at this time, the only source of labor supply available for Hawaii.

As the Hawaiian Islands developed industrially, many avenues of employment opened to the laborers recruited for the sugar plantations. The laborers are not in any sense bound to any one master and can easily move from place to place. Moreover, the labor in the fields is hard, no doubt of that, and when laborers, no matter how untutored or unskilled, amass a competence, they are apt to leave the plantations. Many, particularly in earlier days, when immigration laws were not so strict, went to mainland United States. Others drifted into a hundred different lines of employment in the islands. Still others went home—back to Japan or China. Most of the Latin race immigrants stayed but a comparatively short time in the sugar industry. The Russians, though imported for that industry, scarcely entered it at all. And as years grew into decades, death naturally took its toll of all those immigrants who remained on the plantations.

This explains why, after more than forty years of importing labor, the sugar industry in Hawaii still finds it necessary to bring in large numbers of men from the Philippines. Still another factor deals with the children of immigrants. Very few of these stay in plantation work, that is as unskilled labor which constitutes the great bulk of plantation work. They leave it for exactly the same reason that hundreds of thousands of boys brought up on American farms leave those farms—the dislike for toil, manual toil, a degree of monotony, plus the pull of competing attractions of bright lights and white collars to be attained in urban occupations.

I have written thus in detail of the economic history of Hawaii because it is at the root of the racial situation today. What has gone into this mid-Pacific "melting-pot" is the immigrant population from many lands, superimposed upon the native population. And this immigrant population, primarily, is the result of industry's constant and natural demand for labor in masses—labor able to withstand a good deal of heavy toil in the cane-fields.

Hawaii's People

The result of it all may be fairly realized from the latest available figures of population, estimates made by the territorial board of health, a Government institution, as of July 1, 1925. These figures are, by racial ancestry:

> Total population of territory, 323,645.
> Army and navy personnel resident, 17,094.
> Total population exclusive of army and navy, 306,551.
> Americans, British, Germans and Russians, 18,246 citizens, 360 aliens.
> Portuguese, 23,918 citizens, 3652 aliens. Porto Ricans, 6382 citizens (designated as citizens since Porto Rico was taken over by United States).
> Spanish, 1417 citizens, 799 aliens.
> Chinese, 13,075 citizens, 11,776 aliens.
> Filipinos, 4800 citizens, 44,535 aliens.
> Hawaiians, 21,145 citizens. (Upon annexation of Hawaii to the United States, all Hawaiians were given full rights as citizens.)

Japanese, 70,860 citizens, 57,208 aliens.
Koreans, 2916 citizens, 3040 aliens.
Caucasian-Hawaiians, 13,837 citizens.
Asiatic-Hawaiians, 8345 citizens.
All others, 220 citizens, 210 aliens.

This division of citizens and aliens may need a trifle of explanation to readers not closely acquainted with citizenship laws, and in this explanation lies the real reason why the little bootblack on the veranda of the Moana hotel called himself an American though his father was Japanese.

Every child born in Hawaii is an American citizen. His father and mother may be Portuguese or Spanish or German or Swiss or Russian and thus eligible to naturalization. Or they may be Japanese or Chinese or Hindu and thus *in*eligible to naturalization. It does not matter. Born on American soil, the child is American by virtue of the United States Constitution and the law of the land; American by virtue of all the decrees that call this a republic and the battles that have gone to uphold its principles; American by virtue of a hundred and fifty years of struggle and sacrifice.

All the races that have come to Hawaii have been fruitful. Many of the immigrant aliens have become naturalized, but many could not—they were of races ineligible to that privilege. Remaining aliens, they bore children and these children are Americans. Thus we have 70,000 citizens of Japanese ancestry out of a total population of Japanese blood of 128,000.

Summed up, Hawaii has, exclusive of its military and naval personnel, 185,071 citizens and 121,480 aliens. Vastly more than half of the islands' population today is a citizen population.

But acts of Congress or statements in the Constitution do not alone suffice to make real citizens. What proof is there that these Hawaiian Americans are real citizens?

I have given two bits of proof in the illustrations with which I began this article. These are much more than mere anecdotes. They reflect the *feelings* of children, and those feelings are held by certainly the very great majority of Hawaii's 60,000 or 70,000 children of thinking age. They *feel* themselves Americans. The little Chinese girl who spoke of her forefathers fighting to lay the foundations of a republic saw no incongruity in that. Those old colonials who sniped at the Britishers at Lexington, or sailed on the Great Lakes with Perry, or fired from behind cotton-bales at New Orleans, or spoke at Independence Hall in Philadelphia were as real to her as to you or me, who are of a lineage we can trace back to the fighters and statesmen of those days. For all of her life, since she started kindergarten or Sunday school or primary school in Hawaii, she had not merely been *told* she is an American but *treated like an American citizen.*

I do not want to claim for Hawaii any virtues or qualities which Hawaii does not possess, or to compare others unfavorably with Hawaii, or to give any impression that we in Hawaii are "holier than thou" in our treatment of race problems but I do want to say that in Hawaii we accept our young American citizens of alien blood—any alien blood—as fellow-Americans and treat them as such.

We don't start them out in childhood, on the school playground or in the classroom or anywhere else in an atmosphere of discrimination or distrust. They meet everywhere the children of the far-famed and much-lauded Nordics, and meet them on the same plane. There are no race distinctions drawn in school, on streetcars, in the theaters, in business or in politics. They feel no sense of condescension, contempt or condemnation.

American Influences

On the contrary, a thousand American influences constantly play on them. Each morning, all over the territory of Hawaii, from the great stone and concrete structures in the city to the tiny little bungalow-like buildings in the remote villages, 60,000 school children salute the American flag. Their books tell them the inspiring story of great men who served humbly to support and build up the republic. And their daily life teaches them that they have a part in the making of their country.

Every position open to any citizen is open to them. They see men and women of many bloods holding honored public positions and succeeding in private business. This is cogent proof that Hawaii is a land where the equal opportunity declared by law is equal opportunity in fact, subject only to the deficiencies and incapabilities of the individual.

In education, in religion, in recreation, in public service, in sport, in innumerable businesses and professions, the children of immigrant aliens meet the children of Anglo-Saxons and the children of Polynesians. And very often the qualities bred in a long line of indefatigable toilers—the qualities of rigid frugality, persistence, steadiness, commercial acumen—will put the young people of Oriental ancestry up ahead in the competition of island life.

It would be idle to say that there is absolutely no race problem in Hawaii. There are several of them. The alien language school constitutes a real problem into which there is not space here to enter. It is part of a larger problem—that of persistent alien influences at work endeavoring to perpetuate an alien nationalism instead of endeavoring to substitute Americanism to the greatest possible degree. These things are, however, evidences of a passing rather than a coming stage. They are being met partly by legislation, but even more by official and unofficial attitudes and contacts which emphasize and promote friendliness and confidence.

There is no questioning the fact that, economically, the islands tend to become more and more American. One large group of alien businesses is now going through significantly hard times. Locally, this is sometimes ascribed to bad management, but that explanation is inadequate. The fact is that its patronage—always preponderantly alien in character—is falling off. The immigrant people whom it represents, and still more their children, are buying and consuming more strictly American goods.

Children of Orientals, save in a small minority of cases, have no hope or intention of returning to the land of their ancestry. Unless when very young they have been sent to Japan or China for education, they feel slight allegiance to Asia. They know that the land of their fathers offers them almost no economic opportunity, and save in parts of China, no opportunity in public life. Their whole future lies in the United States.

Think of Hawaii, then, not as a land where more than half of the people are Orientals. That is true only as to blood. It is not true as to habits, customs, every-day occupation, education, business, politics or a thousand other factors of contemporary life. It is not true as to citizenship. Far more than half of Hawaii's residents are American citizens, not merely in political status but in thought and feeling.

With all Hawaii's might, its leaders are trying to increase these factors for Americanism. Hawaii never deceives itself as to the necessity for building up so strong a structure of Americanism in this outpost territory that it will be able to withstand an onslaught. We hope, believe and trust that peace will rule on the Pacific, giving us full opportunity to work out here in this land of kindly Nature the logical development of that tolerant and hospitable spirit with which the brown islanders long ago met the first white men. We believe it can be done; not by mere faith but by very practical work which gives to aliens and citizens alike the sort of treatment guaranteed by the Constitution. We believe it can be done in the plain old-fashioned way in which a lot of things have been done in America—keeping everlastingly at it, good-humoredly, patiently, wholeheartedly, determinedly. And up to date there are sufficient encouraging signs to cheer us on the way.

VIEWPOINT 6

"Superficially it would appear that the various races in Hawaii live in perfect harmony. Beneath the surface, however, there is considerable discrimination against the races of color."

Asian Americans Face Discrimination in Hawaii

William C. Smith (dates unknown)

Between 1850 and 1920 more than three hundred thousand Asians were brought to Hawaii to provide a labor force for the islands' sugar plantations. This migration transformed Hawaii's population, which in 1853 was about 97 percent native Hawaiian or part Hawaiian, 2 percent white, and 0.5 percent Chinese. By 1920 Asian Americans accounted for 62 percent of the population in Hawaii, with the Japanese at 42.7 percent, the Chinese at 9.2 percent, the Koreans at 1.9 percent, and the Filipinos at 8.2 percent. Hawaii's other groups included the Hawaiians (16.3 percent); whites or "Haoles" (7.7 percent), who held most of the territory's economic and political power; Puerto Ricans (2.2 percent); and Portuguese (10.6 percent) who, although European, were not considered Haoles.

Some observers extolled Hawaii as a successful example of the American melting pot at work, while opponents of Asian immigration in the United States portrayed Hawaii as a worst-case scenario of Asian takeover. A third perspective can be seen in the following viewpoint, which is excerpted from *Americans in Process*, a sociological study of second-generation Asian Americans by William C. Smith. A sociologist and professor at Linfield College in Oregon, Smith spent years conducting research in Hawaii and the United States before publishing his study in 1937. He in-

Excerpted from William C. Smith, *Americans in Process* (Ann Arbor, MI: Edwards Bros., 1937).

terviewed many Asian Americans and collected more than fifteen hundred personal life histories, many of which were quoted in his book. In the passages excerpted here, Smith compares the treatment of Asian Americans in Hawaii with their treatment in the coastal United States. He concedes that Hawaii has less racial tensions and prejudice against Asian Americans, but argues that people of Asian descent are still not fully accepted by whites in Hawaii and face discrimination in employment, social relations, and other areas. Such discrimination, he writes, presents barriers to their assimilation into American society.

Hawaii differs markedly from the Pacific Coast. The most casual observation will confirm this. In this connection a few of the most striking differences that touch the Americans of oriental ancestry will be considered. . . .

A Striking Contrast

The attitudes of the white people and the treatment they accord members of oriental groups in the two areas stand out in striking contrast. The resultant reactions of the Orientals to these differences in stimuli also vary markedly. Visitors from the Pacific Coast who spend a few days in the Islands often comment on the friendly relations existing between the races. With almost monotonous regularity they tell Honolulu gatherings, usually attended by members of several races, that the people of Hawaii have solved all race problems and have conclusively demonstrated that the different races can live together amicably. But Hawaii is neither California nor Washington, and all too often the tourists do not fully appreciate the real situation. Their eyes are set to recognize behavior characteristic of the Pacific Coast, but since that is not in evidence they are prone to conclude that all is harmonious and there is no prejudice or discrimination. An American sociologist who had spent several years among the Negroes in the southern states said, "Humanly speaking, you have no race prejudice in Hawaii." On the whole, it may be said that in Hawaii the several races are living together in relationships characterized by a high degree of harmony and friendliness. The differences in attitudes in the two areas are disclosed through the experiences and reactions of those who have gone from one area to the other. On his first visit to Honolulu, a California-born Japanese wrote: "The greatest surprise by far was the general cosmopolitan air of the city. Here two cultures meet, the one from the Orient and the other from the Occident. . . . This is one place where the appellation, 'The Land Where Hatred Expires,' may sincerely be applied." On the other hand, persons who have gone to the Pacific Coast have had unpleasant experiences. A Japanese college boy reported the treatment he received.

> The most important thing I learned, while I was in San Francisco, was the attitude of the white people there toward the Japanese. Before I went to San Francisco, I heard various rumors about the treatment of Japanese in California by the Whites. But I didn't realize the true situation until I had personal experience. I went to a barber to get my hair trimmed and on entering the shop, one of the barbers approached me and asked my nationality. I answered that I was Japanese. As soon as he heard that I was of the yellow race, he drove me out of the place as if he were driving away a cat or a dog. I never felt so cheap as when I was treated this way by this animal who wore the face of a man.

In Hawaii this would not happen. We must not conclude, however, that there is no prejudice in Hawaii. In Honolulu the majority of the barbers are Japanese women, while in California the majority are white men. This fact alone changes the situation, because the Orientals are not dependent upon the Occidentals for such service. In Honolulu, however, Orientals are actually served by white barbers. In Hawaii there is, without question, less prejudice than on the Pacific Coast. In many theaters on the Coast Orientals are given none but the most undesirable seats. In Hawaii it is quite the custom for them to attend theaters without differential treatment; to be guests at hotels without discrimination; to participate in formal social events along with Whites, as at the Governor's Reception or the Japanese Consul General's Reception. The fact that there is no prejudice or should be none in Hawaii is a matter of tradition and principle which practically all members of the community feel bound to maintain. This is a creed to which many, especially the leading spokesmen for Hawaii, subscribe, even though in practice they find it difficult. Governor [Wallace R.] Farrington, in season and out of season, proclaimed that there was no race problem in Hawaii. . . .

There is, nevertheless, a certain amount of prejudice against the Japanese in Hawaii, but it is against them as a *class* rather than as a *race*. It seems that all who have come to Hawaii as plantation laborers, no matter what their origin, encounter a certain amount of prejudice. . . .

A Solution to the Labor Problem

The sugar industry in Hawaii is responsible for the high percentage of Orientals in the population. In the early days the sugar growers depended upon the native Hawaiians for their labor supply. Very soon it became evident that they must draw their man power from some other source, for the continuous hard work in the cane fields did not appeal to the easy-going Hawaiians. Furthermore, the Hawaiians were not sufficient in numbers to supply the demand. Attempts were made to secure South Sea Islanders as well as Europeans but with limited success, except for a considerable number of Portuguese. After exploring various possibilities and trying several experiments, the Orient was found to offer the best solution to the labor problem.

Racial Antagonism

In a personal account excerpted in William C. Smith's study Americans in Process, *a Korean college student in Hawaii describes an environment of underlying racial tensions.*

I have had contact with other racial groups such as the Filipinos, the Japanese, Chinese, Hawaiians, Haoles, Portuguese, etc., but I have never been very intimate with them. When I see them I do not ignore them, I laugh, joke, and associate with them, but still I am not intimate with them. We different races may be said to be living in harmony, in brotherliness with one another, but still I feel the racial antagonism. Even in our University, there is racial antagonism veiled behind smiles and friendship. We are mere acquaintances, not friends. The Haoles do not care a bit for the Orientals. The Hawaiians on the other hand do not like the Whites. Every day, I hear remarks about racial antagonism. We try to mix socially, but always the same crowd gathers for a real good time. The great majority stays away and sneers at such gatherings.

Chinese and Japanese came in large numbers to work on the sugar plantations, but for a number of years they have been dwindling. In 1897 the Chinese were at their peak with 8,114, but in 1934 there were only 618 of their men left on the plantations. The peak year of the Japanese was in 1908 with 32,771, but in 1930 their numbers had been reduced to 8,956 men. From this point the Japanese gradually increased until they reached 10,717 in 1934. This was due to an increase in the number of American-born workers. In 1905 the Koreans had 4,946, but in 1932 only 442 of their men were in the sugar industry. The Koreans likewise increased to 522 in 1934. . . .

The American-born generation is a complicating factor in race relationships. The Chinese and Japanese immigrants to America have been given a status of inferiority and have been required to do the drudgery. Because of differences in language and cultural background, comparatively few of the immigrant generation have been able to rise very far. But the second generation is coming to be rather thoroughly Americanized, ambitious, and desirous of acquiring a status superior to that held by their parents; they are not following in the footsteps of the older generation. The dominant white group, in large measure, is unwilling to accede to the demands of this younger group which has the inescapable racial marks of the older generation. As these ambitious and hopeful young Americans endeavor to make a place for themselves, what will be the outcome? Will they become assimilated and gradually become lost in the American group or will they become a sort of racial caste, in America but not of America? . . .

Younger Asian Americans Face Discrimination

The vocational problems of the younger generation in Hawaii are not easy of solution. The range of opportunities is limited. There has been considerable discrimination against them, enough to justify the views they have held. When a certain high school teacher was asked to recommend a chemist with certain qualifications, he suggested a Chinese. The mere mention of an oriental name, however, ruled him out, although the boy was far superior to any white boy in the class. An elderly Chinese business man stated that a number of Chinese in a certain bank were doing work of a more or less mechanical nature. They had no opportunity for advancement, while white boys came in and were advanced over them. In several instances white men have been imported from the mainland and placed in positions over competent Orientals who knew the business and were acquainted with Island conditions. Some employers have declared that since the Chinese lacked initiative they could be used only for the more or less mechanical work. A manager of an industrial establishment, who called his employees in the higher positions his "cabinet," declared that he was determined to keep it white. Another business man said that he would not have an Oriental if he could get a white man. An executive reported that a man was being considered for a certain position, but when the budget committee decided to drop the salary to $75.00 they frankly said, "We'll have to get an Oriental." A letter from a young Japanese is typical of the situation in which many find themselves.

> I am employed in a position where I must have a fairly accurate knowledge of the English language. I will say that while I speak Japanese, I know very little about the written language of that country. The position pays me fairly well—enough to live on decently with a little left over every month for the savings bank. Employed on exactly the same work I am doing is a Caucasian who is paid ten dollars a week more than I receive. Why? Are we not both Americans? I know that I do my work as well as he does, and there are times—when he is away on vacations, for

instance—when I do his work as well as my own, which would indicate that I am as capable as he. The reason I do not receive as much as the white American is because I'm a "Jap." I am not complaining. I know the custom and do not rail against it.

Superficially it would appear that the various races in Hawaii live in perfect harmony. Beneath the surface, however, there is considerable discrimination against the races of color in the occupational field. The Orientals are not promoted to the more responsible positions. In the spring of 1927, the manager of one of the large business houses in Honolulu addressed a group of college Y.M.C.A. boys on the occupational outlook in Hawaii for college-trained men of oriental ancestry. He said that it depended on the individual how far he could go and that he would be given opportunity for advancement in accordance with his own abilities. But he went on to say that he could not employ Orientals to wait on the public in his office because that would result in a loss of business. It has been quite common for speakers representing the sugar industry to talk about the opportunities open to the college-trained man of oriental ancestry who would be willing to begin at the bottom and work up, but when specific questions were directed at them the replies would be more or less evasive.

Executives, however, are not always free to do as they please. The manager of a sugar plantation said that he would like to promote an Oriental to a skilled job which would carry with it a promotion to the skilled workers' residential area. "Then," he said, "I'll have to invite him to my home on Sunday afternoons to play tennis with the other upper-grade employees. But the chemist's wife may object to this and dissensions may arise. The upshot of it all is that I cannot promote him." Many point to the building trades and say that the Orientals have crowded the white men out so that on the large construction jobs it becomes necessary to bring skilled workers from the mainland. Because of this they are giving preferential treatment to white men in order to keep them in the Territory. . . .

Inferior Status of Plantation Workers

The inferior status of the plantation laborers was recognized even by children and came to be a line of division between different groups.

> We fellows of the village considered ourselves better than the laborers of the plantation and the boys of the village used to have gang fights with the plantation boys. We were outnumbered so that all we could do was to tell them and tease them about their fathers' and mothers' cane-field jobs.

That this inferiority in status is not a racial matter but one that is inherent in the occupational situation becomes evident when we consider the Portuguese. Even though they belong to the Caucasoid group, they are not included with the other Caucasians in the popular classification of "Haole" which is used in Hawaii. Because they came to work on the sugar plantations, they have been accorded a status of inferiority. The Portuguese resent this imputation of inferiority. They are trying to throw off this stigma and to decrease the social distance between themselves and the Anglo-Saxons. This has a marked effect upon their behavior; many become loud and noisy in order to attract attention. They do and say things to belittle the Orientals in order to appear superior. Many Portuguese call attention very pointedly to the color differences, using such expressions as "slant-eyed Chink" and "yellow belly." A Chinese college girl wrote:

> I have often wondered how I would enjoy being a member of some other language group, but I have never regretted the fact that I am Chinese. When I first went to school, I felt that I was different from persons of other language groups. Whenever there was a fight, we were sure to hear conversation of this nature: "You old Kanaka [Hawaiian]!" "I can lick all the 'Japs' in the world." All this, however, did not make as much of an impression upon me as did one certain incident. I was in town when a Portuguese girl unconsciously bumped into a Chinese girl. Instead of helping her pick up her packages she walked straight ahead. The Chinese girl said, "The idea!" "I said, 'Excuse me,' didn't I?" shouted the Portuguese girl angrily. "Well, say it loud enough so I can hear it next time," answered the other. Then the Portuguese girl, with a toss of her head said, "Shut up you Pake [Chinese]; I'm white!"
>
> I cannot see anything *white* in a person who can say things so much below her dignity.

Some Portuguese women will not permit their children to play with Orientals. With many it is a serious matter; they cannot afford to endanger their status by permitting such association. The Anglo-Saxons are in less danger of losing status by such intermingling.

The Orientals are aware of the situation and react accordingly. Many of them dislike the dominant Anglo-Saxons but, nevertheless, they envy them and would gladly exchange positions with them. The Portuguese, however, are not objects of envy in the eyes of the Orientals. The behavior of the Anglo-Saxon is unlike that of the Portuguese: he enjoys a superior status and does not have to belittle the Oriental to convince others of his superiority. A few who find it difficult to compete with the Orientals on the basis of merit, resort to such tactics.

The solution of the occupational problems of the younger generation in Hawaii is not merely a matter of technical training to make them more efficient in sugar production. That will not go to the bottom of things; it is a matter of social status. These young people will not be satisfied with a classification of inferiors, as men of the lowest social stratum; they will not respond enthusiastically to one planter's characterization of "human mules." They must be given an honorable status; they must be treated as persons of dignity. It will take more than wages to attract them. Most of the young people of Hawaii prefer to work in some more dignified occupation, even though the monetary return may be less than the wage scale on the plantations. . . .

Education and Racial Prejudice

In their early years, children of diverse racial inheritance mingle freely. If left to themselves, children know no race distinctions; that is, they do not know them as a basis for social discrimination. Blond Nordic children play happily with children of oriental ancestry, no matter whether it be in San Francisco or in Laupahoehoe. . . .

There have been many instances where children of north-European and oriental ancestry have formed close friendships. A white high-school boy in Hawaii had become so friendly toward the Orientals that he was lonesome for them when on a visit to the mainland. He was happy only when he visited a city which had a cosmopolitan population that reminded him of Honolulu.

Gradually, however, changes have come. Many persons of oriental ancestry have unfortunate experiences; bars are raised against them. Furthermore, they observe the treatment others receive. They become sensitive and often magnify trifles. When a person is ignored because of his own individual peculiarities, it is often construed to be a racial matter. Thus the rift between the two groups is widened. A statement by a Japanese high-school boy in Hawaii is typical not only of a large number in his own group, but of the Chinese, Hawaiians, Filipinos, Porto Ricans, and Portuguese as well.

> I began to realize that I was different from other races when I really awoke to this world. I would like to cite some examples. A judge would let off a Haole with an easy term, but is it so with an Oriental? A policeman would be very easy with a Haole, but is it so with an Oriental? One day I was standing on the corner of King and Fort Streets, waiting for my car. A Haole lady, one of the many passers-by, suddenly shoved me with one of her large arms and said, "Get out of my way." It is a fact that many Japanese are ignorant and greedy for money which is earned in a crooked way. I, too, hate those people. I wish they were back in Japan, but there is no reason why some people should loathe all the Japanese people.

After mingling freely with white children in their childhood years, many in their early teens have come to a realization that they were no longer to be accepted. In many instances this awakening has come as a rude shock bringing heartaches and bitter feelings. . . .

In Hawaii, students of oriental ancestry are in the majority in practically all public schools. Because of this, many white people send their children to private schools where the line can be drawn against non-Caucasians. This, however, is an added expense and some have favored the reservation of certain public schools for white children only. In 1920 a movement was inaugurated for an English Standard School in which pupils would be selected on the basis of proficiency in English. Some advocated openly that it be made a "white" school. This, however, aroused considerable opposition. When a public high school was opened on one island, the white group attempted to restrict it to their own children. When a number of Japanese pupils enrolled, the white people objected. The principal maintained that a school supported by public funds was open to all. The white people, nevertheless, continued their objections until the principal was transferred to another island. Pupils of all races, however, are still admitted. A high school was built in a rural district of another island a considerable distance from the population centers. The underlying idea was that the white pupils would commute on the railway line, while the Japanese would be debarred by the added expense. This, however, was not a sufficient barrier. On December 21, 1928, there was a total registration of 411 of which number 237 were Japanese and only twenty-eight were of north-European ancestry. . . .

Other Areas of Discrimination

Labor unions and other organizations usually have drawn the line against Orientals and their American-born descendants, but a more favorable attitude is in process of development. . . .

In 1927 the carpenter's union of Hawaii invited them in. Not all labor unions in Hawaii have let down the bars. The plasterers' union of Honolulu does not admit them and does not take any apprentices from the group. In October, 1928, the Y.M.C.A. school in Honolulu made plans for conducting a class in plastering to which those of oriental ancestry would be admitted but they encountered strong opposition on the part of the union. A white instructor had been engaged for the course but before actual instruction had begun he informed the administration that he would be unable to conduct the class.

Discriminations in the occupational field have been far-reaching. In civil service positions, on the mainland in particular, Chinese and Japanese have not been accepted on an equal footing with white men. Not even in the army during the World War, when so much was said about democracy, were they accepted on an equality with others.

Many white people object to side-by-side working relations with those of oriental lineage. Consequently many employers cannot hire them because of the other workers. . . .

There are considerable differences in the industrial conditions in different areas of the Hawaiian Islands and these diversities result in variant attitudes. In the coffee belt of Kona, where Japanese farmers operate their own leaseholds, there is no anti-plantation or anti-Haole attitude; prejudice is at a minimum and the young men of that district can go to other places and associate more naturally and normally with white people. In striking contrast, on the Hamakua Coast of the same island, which is jocularly called the "Scottish Coast," the lines are sharply drawn. This is in the cane belt. On the sugar plantations a small group of north-European lineage is in a position of dominance and directs the enterprise. Immigrants have been brought from several regions to do the manual labor on the plantations and these laborers, no matter what their origin, are always accorded a status of inferiority. Even the Portuguese are given a status much inferior to the Anglo-Saxons and only a little above the Orientals. Between the management and the workers there is an all but unbridgeable chasm.

The tourist traffic, now rated as the third industry of the Territory next to sugar and pineapples, is a factor of some significance. Since large numbers of visitors come from the Coast they bring their prejudices with them. This is reacting in particular upon those who depend largely on the tourist business for their livelihood. . . .

In Honolulu several areas are almost exclusively white. Several Orientals tried to buy homes in one of these areas but without success. They are excluded by a "Gentlemen's Agreement" among the real estate men. Furthermore, it would be considered unneighborly to sell to an Oriental. There are two Japanese families in the area who secured their property because the white owners wanted to "get even" with their neighbors. . . .

The Military in Hawaii

The military group in Hawaii, a garrison of some 16,000 men, is a factor of considerable importance in connection with race prejudice. The military men talk much about an inevitable war with Japan and discriminate against the Japanese, be they alien or citizen. A secretary of the Y.M.C.A. in Honolulu, who went to the Pearl Harbor Naval Station on a matter of business, had with him his assistant, an American-born Japanese who had served in the army during the World War. The marine at the gate informed them that he had orders from the commandant to exclude all "Japs" from the reservation. When the United States fleet visited Hawaii in April, 1928, the writer went aboard the U.S.S. *California* at the dock in Honolulu. After walking about the ship for some time, he asked a sailor for permission to go to a lower deck when he received the reply: "No! there are too many 'Japs' around and we can't permit them to go below, so we have to refuse everybody." The Intelligence Department of the Army keeps a careful check on anything that is said or written about the Japanese. The military group, however, is rather inconsistent, for many officers have Japanese servants within the military reservations. An advertisement in a Honolulu paper in 1928 read as follows: "Wanted—Two first-class car washers. Japanese preferred. No others need apply. The Post Exchange Service Station, Schofield Barracks.". . .

Cultural Hybridism

Because of the barriers raised against the oriental group, the young Americans of oriental lineage are not given full entree into the white man's world. They have, nevertheless, taken over much of the occidental culture—customs, habits, ideas, ideals, and, in some measure, attitudes. In this way they differ markedly from their parents, but in spite of the differences between the generations, the younger group has not been able to eliminate all influences of the Orient. They have acquired many cultural elements from this source. In a measure, the American-born group is developing a culture of its own which is a syncretism of the Orient and the Occident. This cultural hybridism is exemplified in the marriage ceremonies in which there is oftentimes a mixture of oriental and occidental elements. It is not unusual to read in a Honolulu newspaper an account of the marriage of a young Chinese couple as follows:

> Last Friday cakes were distributed by the bride-to-be to all relatives and friends, which is in accordance with the Chinese custom of announcing one's marriage. Tonight the bride-to-be will spend her last evening as a miss in the company of a few of her intimate friends, which is also in conformity with the Chinese custom. Tomorrow night, at eight o'clock, the marriage ceremony will take place at the Chinese Christian Church.

The younger Japanese generation has also introduced western elements into the marriage ceremony, in spite of the fact that the parental group has clung quite tenaciously to the old-country practice and has tried to impose it upon their American-reared children. . . .

The cultural hybridism is revealed not only in such externalities as marriage ceremonies, but in deeper ideas, attitudes, and outlook upon life. This is illustrated by the writing of poetry. Hiss Kimi Gengo, an Hawaiian-born Japanese girl, has recently issued a book of verse. A reviewer commented that her verses are unique, a blend of two cultures.

Many of the younger generation are in sympathy neither with their ancestral group nor with the Americans. They are no longer oriental; neither are they completely occidental. A Japanese social worker reveals this cultural hybridism.

> I wanted to know about proper relationships with girls, but my friends knew very little about it. I hated to tell my parents about my feelings relative to girls or even ask their opinion of my going with a girl. Yet I wanted to be friendly with girls, but ignorance did not help me to become a good associate with them. Social gatherings began to appeal to me and I attended several, but the inability to make myself feel at home gave me little chance to know or learn much. The inconsistencies of American conduct when compared with that set forth in books began to raise questions in my mind. I feared to break away from my parents' religion, still I was a regular attendant at a Christian church. I questioned my standing in a Japanese society as well as in the American society. I considered myself an American citizen but at the same time I retained some Japanese characteristics, such as loyalty to my parents, obedience, etc.

Many of the younger group live in two worlds—in their oriental homes and in the American school and community. At times this clash of cultures has resolved itself into a conflict of loyalties. To which group shall they give their allegiance? There is confusion, for they do not fully understand the culture of either group. Furthermore, they are understood neither by Occidentals nor by Orientals. This often results in grave inner conflicts. A college girl in Hawaii presents the situation.

> At the end of my second school year I went home for a vacation and there I met the problem of my life—the racial problem. I am afraid I will be called a hypocrite, but when you finish reading this you will understand. I am proud of what I am, but there is a constant conflict within me that I can't control. I am an American of Chinese parentage and I have been educated in American schools, lived with the Americans, and worked with them in social groups. Consequently I am Americanized. How much of the Chinese custom could I follow when I didn't even know enough of it to make myself sociable? I was lost in a crowd of Chinese-speaking people. I couldn't understand their ideas or customs. I could not speak Chinese except baby talk; every time I started to say something I was laughed at. The Chinese friends of my parents thought that my brother deserved an education more than I, in spite of what I was sacrificing to obtain it. Because I was unable to explain my point of view in Chinese, these people would take advantage of me by jeering at me in the presence of my brother. Many quarrels had taken place between us simply because of the perpetual talking of those old-customed Chinese. Oh, I hated Chinese then. I wished I was something other than a Chinese. I thought that I could never

live with a Chinese unless he were thoroughly Americanized, although I admired them in their moral aspects. I loved to hear the tales and stories of the great men of China, but I never had the notion of calling China my own and of being loyal to her. I had played Miss Liberty for America, but I couldn't play that for China—not that I wanted to be a hypocrite but merely because the training in the schools had developed and strengthened American ideas in me.

. . . In the main the younger generation is more occidental than oriental. This becomes evident when they go to the Orient. Many who go there feel lost because everything is so confusingly different. They cannot realize that their own grandparents and other relatives are in any way related to themselves. . . .

Eager to Become American

The children of oriental parentage, in the main, are eager to become thoroughgoing Americans, but this is not entirely possible because of the homes in which they live. The culture systems of the parental groups inevitably leave their impressions. On the other hand, because of skin color Americans classify them with their immigrant parents. So far as outward appearances are concerned that is correct. This judgment, however, is superficial. An older Japanese in California said to one of the younger group, "You look like a Japanese, but you are not one; you do not think as we do." They are oriental in appearance, but not in reality. It is more accurate to say that they belong to both groups and yet to neither; they are neither fully oriental nor yet fully occidental. A Japanese college girl wrote:

> We belong to two groups, the Japanese and the American. In ancestry and in physical appearance we are Japanese, while in birth, in education, in ideals, and in ways of thinking we are Americans. Nevertheless, the older Japanese will not accept us into their group because, as they see us, we are too independent, too pert, and too self-confident, and the Americans bar us from their group because we retain the yellow skin and flat nose of the Oriental. Thus we stand on the border line that separates the Orient from the Occident. Though on each side of us flow the streams of two great civilizations—the old Japanese culture with its formal traditions and customs and the newer American civilization with its freedom and individualism—the chance to perceive and to imbibe the best things from each has been withheld from us.

VIEWPOINT 7

"We petition you as President of the United States of America, that steps be taken immediately for our repatriation to our native land."

A Plea for Filipino Repatriation

Filipino Petitioners

Following the Chinese and the Japanese, the third group of Asians to begin immigrating to the United States in large numbers were the Filipinos (immigrants from other Asian countries came in smaller numbers). While some Filipino immigrants were students sponsored by the U.S. government, most were workers employed at Hawaii's sugar plantations and California's farms. After the Gentleman's Agreement between the United States and Japan effectively ended the flow of Japanese workers to Hawaii, the Hawaiian Sugar Planters' Association turned to Filipinos to replace the Japanese. Many Filipinos migrated to Hawaii and, when their original labor contracts expired, continued to the United States. Between 1910 and 1930 the population of Filipinos grew from around 2,000 to more than 60,000 in Hawaii, and from less than 500 to more than 45,000 in the continental United States.

Moving from job to job and state to state, and confined to low-paying employment in farms, fish canneries, and hotels, many Filipinos found their goals of attaining wealth in America impossible to achieve. Like the Chinese and Japanese before them, the Filipinos also found themselves the victims of violence and racial prejudice.

The legal status of Filipino immigrants in the United States differed from that of their Asian counterparts. The Philippine Islands, under Spanish colonial rule for three centuries, were acquired by the United States in 1898 following the Spanish-American War. As

From "Petition to President Roosevelt," *Philippines Mail*, October 8, 1934.

residents of a U.S. colony, Filipinos were classified as "nationals" and, unlike other Asians, were not subject to alien land laws and immigration restrictions. They lost this status in 1934, when Congress voted to grant independence to the Philippines in ten years, to reclassify Filipinos in the United States as aliens, and to curtail further immigration.

The following viewpoint is a 1934 petition signed by Filipino farm laborers in Salinas, California, and sent to President Franklin D. Roosevelt. Salinas had been the site of a bitter and violent strike by Filipino farmworkers. The petitioners argue that they are being abused and exploited by others, in part because they lack U.S. citizenship. They demand repatriation and transportation to the Philippines at U.S. government expense.

Honorable Franklin D. Roosevelt
President of the United States of America
Washington, D.C.
Your Excellency:

We, the undersigned natives of the Philippine Islands, residing on the Pacific Coast and engaged in agricultural work, respectfully petition as follows:

Due to the fact that we are Nationals of the United States of America, but not entitled to the rights of full citizenship and not having representation through consular agencies or other duly authorized officials, we find ourselves, in the case of social or economic difficulties, without the facilities of protest or protection afforded to citizens of a foreign country, and though we owe allegiance to the United States government, we have no means through which our rights as a non-citizen group may be protected.

We find ourselves accused by the general public of lowering the wage scale by working for lower wages and yet forced by the growers to accept a lower scale than corresponding white labor. With the alternative of being subject to mob violence, the destruction of our homes by fire and to unwarranted arrest, if any action is taken to unite for the purpose of maintaining a higher wage scale.

We find ourselves losing thousands of dollars a year in unpaid wages for employment by citizens of foreign nations, who are well organized and duly represented and who take advantage of the fact that we, as a National group, have no representation.

We find ourselves subject to racial prejudice and discrimination

132

in all social relationships, after having been educated in Americanized schools in the Philippine Islands and encouraged to esteem and strive for the civilization typified by Americans.

We have all emigrated to the United States, stimulated by the high ideals of Americanism and desirous of finding a higher and more worthy means of expression, only to be disillusioned on every hand by the experiences of our unsatisfactory social status.

A Violent Encounter

The fear and anger many Americans felt toward Filipinos, often revolving around the dread of intermarriage, is vividly described in this passage from America Is in the Heart, *the autobiography of noted Filipino writer Carlos Bulosan.*

One day a Filipino came to Holtville with his American wife and their child. It was blazing noon and the child was hungry. The strangers went to a little restaurant and sat down at a table. When they were refused service, they stayed on, hoping for some consideration. But it was no use. Bewildered, they walked outside; suddenly the child began to cry with hunger. The Filipino went back to the restaurant and asked if he could buy a bottle of milk for his child.

"It is only for my baby," he said humbly.

The proprietor came out from behind the counter. "For *your* baby?" he shouted.

"Yes, sir," said the Filipino.

The proprietor pushed him violently outside. "If you say *that* again in my place, I'll bash in your head!" he shouted aloud so that he would attract attention. "You goddamn brown monkeys have your nerve, marrying our women. Now get out of this town! "

"I love my wife and my child," said the Filipino desperately.

"*Goddamn* you!" The white man struck the Filipino viciously between the eyes with his fist.

Years of degradation came into the Filipino's face. All the fears of his life were here—in the white hand against his face. Was there no place where he could escape? Crouching like a leopard, he hurled his whole weight upon the white man, knocking him down instantly. He seized a stone the size of his fist and began smashing it into the man's face. Then the white men in the restaurant seized the small Filipino, beating him unconscious with pieces of wood and with their fists.

He lay inert on the road. When two deputy sheriffs came to take him away, he looked tearfully back at his wife and child.

We find ourselves, for the most part, forced to live in barns and outbuildings in direct violation of the State housing laws and when we secure camps of the most modern type, having such buildings subject to destruction by incendiary fires, because an attempt is made to demand higher wages through orderly and approved methods.

We therefore ask and beg of you, as President of the United States of America, to take the necessary steps through the proper agencies to set up means by which our interests may be represented and protection to our rights afforded.

Repatriation Alternative

If this is not possible, we petition you as President of the United States of America, that steps be taken immediately for our repatriation to our native land in the Philippine Islands at government expense, so that we may work out our destiny and future among our own people, where we hope and trust, that even though it may not afford all the seeming advantages of Western Civilization, it may be more conducive to our future happiness.

It is with the greatest esteem and respect for you, our Chief Executive, that we herewith attach our signatures.

VIEWPOINT 8

"The Filipinos that I have talked to have no desire or intention to take advantage of the [repatriation] act."

Most Filipino Immigrants Do Not Want Repatriation

Carey McWilliams (1906–1980)

The Tydings-McDuffie Act of 1934 granted independence to the Philippines, America's Asian colony, to take effect in ten years. Congress passed the act in large part to control Filipino immigration. Unlike other Asian immigrants, who were aliens, Filipinos were "nationals" not subject to prior immigration restriction laws. By granting independence to the Philippines, the United States was able to reclassify Filipinos as aliens (making them ineligible for public relief programs) and to limit immigration by setting a small Filipino quota of fifty immigrants per year. However, some opponents of Filipino immigrants thought such measures did not go far enough, and sought a way to rid the United States of the thousands of Filipinos remaining in the country. In 1935 Congress passed and President Franklin D. Roosevelt signed the Filipino Repatriation Act, offering government-paid transportation for Filipinos to return to the Philippines.

The following viewpoint on the Filipino Repatriation Act is by Carey McWilliams, a noted writer on American minorities. McWilliams was California's state commissioner on housing and immigration from 1938 to 1942, and editor of the *Nation* magazine from 1955 to 1975. His 1939 book *Factories in the Fields* examined the plight of migrant farmworkers in California, many of whom were Filipino. In this essay, originally published in the *Nation* on September 4, 1935, he reviews the history of Filipino immigra-

Carey McWilliams, "Exit the Filipino," *Nation*, September 4, 1935. Reprinted with permission from the *Nation* magazine; ©The Nation Company, L.P.

tion, arguing that Filipinos were actively recruited to the United States by California farm interests. He contends that the Repatriation Act, coupled with the new immigration restrictions, is essentially a deportation measure, and he predicts that few Filipinos will leave America. Ultimately, only 2,190 Filipinos took advantage of government-paid repatriation during the five years the law was in effect.

President Roosevelt on July 11 signed HR 6464, a measure to provide free transportation to the Philippine Islands for Filipinos residing in the United States. The publicity which the measure received did not, however, make mention of Section 4 of the act: "No Filipino who receives the benefits of this act shall be entitled to return to the continental United States." In other words, the bill is in effect an exclusion act, for no Filipino who takes advantage of the act can reenter the continental United States except within the quota established in the Philippine Island Independence Act of March 24, 1934—which is tantamount to permanent exclusion. It is impossible to understand the motivation back of the transportation measure without having in mind the real story of the Filipino in the United States, which is to say, the Filipino in California.

A Recruited Labor Force

At the time of the passage of the Japanese Exclusion Act of 1924, the farm industrialists intended to use Mexican labor. Mexican labor had been recruited in ever-increasing volume since 1914. It was cheap, plentiful, and docile. But suddenly the Box bill and the Harris bill [proposals to use quotas to limit Mexican immigration] threatened the supply. It was at this point that the farmers beckoned in the Filipino. In fact, the first marked increase in the number of Filipinos entering continental United States occurred in 1923, in anticipation of the exclusion act. In 1923 2,426 Filipinos entered California, whereas in the three preceding years the average annual number of arrivals had been only 618. During the years from 1923 to 1929, the average annual number of Filipinos entering the United States was 4,177. Figures compiled by the State of California, in an official report of 1930, indicate that there were about 34,000 Filipinos in the state at that time. The purpose for which this supply of "cheap" Filipino labor was recruited is conceded. The Commonwealth Club of California, on November 5, 1929, issued a report on Filipino immigration in which it was stated that "threat of Mexican exclusion has created an artificial demand for Filipino laborers. They are regarded as the only remaining substitute in the cheap labor field. . . . The large agricultural interests are acting as a conduit transmitting numbers of such immigrants."

Strike in Salinas

In a letter in the October 17, 1934, issue of the New Republic, *writer Ella Winter provides more details of the farm laborers strike described by Carey McWilliams.*

Last week the Filipinos went on the picket line again. They had been off it for about three weeks. The first day, large details of deputy sheriffs and police were called and there was a fracas in which one Filipino wounded an officer in the forearm and another hit a deputy with a sugar beet. That night a machine gun was set up outside the Filipino union headquarters and fifteen officers entered, clubbing sleeping men to left and right. Sixty-nine were arrested for "inciting to riot." The next day both the local newspapers, The Monterey Peninsula Herald and The Salinas Index-Journal, received anonymous notices that "something would happen that night." It did. Four houses of Filipinos were burned to the ground, being fired with "tracer" bullets. Several shots were fired at gasoline tanks near by so that the gasoline would spray the bunk houses and they would burn more easily. At the same time a fire was started in the town so that the fire engines would be busy there and would be unable to come out to the camp some three miles out of Salinas. The next day the leader of the Filipino Labor Union, Rufo Canete—who had taken the place of the deposed leader Marcuelo who signed the arbitration agreement—was arrested and jailed. He is now out on $500 bail. The day after, the Filipinos called off their strike and went back to work in the fields at thirty cents.

One man, Barsatan, was not allowed medical aid for twenty days and has now been removed to an insane asylum. (The same thing happened to a young Chinese in Sacramento, who was beaten into a state of gibbering terror and then carted off to Stockton insane asylum. He wouldn't say he was foreign born. He wasn't.)

The Arbitration Board (Monterey County Industrial Relations Board) has been meeting spasmodically. The growers refused to allow the item from their books revealing the profits they made this year to be read into the record. Their profits are known to be enormous, on account of the drought in the Middle West.

But it was soon discovered that the Mexicans would not be placed on a quota basis. This circumstance, coupled with the discovery of the militancy of Filipino labor, prompted the farm industrialists to start a movement to exclude the Filipino. In 1927 Congressman [Richard J.] Welch of California, who is the sponsor for HR 6464, and Senator Hiram Johnson introduced legislation in Congress which had as its aim the exclusion of the Filipino. This plot was scotched when it was pointed out that the Filipino probably could not be excluded under his status as a national, and the plan to get rid of him had to wait until the passage of the Philippine Island Independence Act created a situation which made exclusion legally feasible.

The Filipino, militantly race-conscious, began to protest against his exploitation in California at an early date, and has grown increasingly rebellious. The Filipino Labor Union, restricted to agricultural workers, has seven locals with a membership of about 2,000 in California today. The Filipino is a real fighter and his strikes have been dangerous. In August, 1934, about 3,000 Filipino workers went on strike in the valuable lettuce fields near Salinas, California. On September 3 a union of white workers employed in the packing sheds returned to work under an agreement to arbitrate. In fact, they were told to return to work by Joseph Casey, A.F. of L. official. But the Filipino field workers refused to call off the strike. State highway patrolmen were summoned and, aided by special deputies and a local vigilante group, they formed a small army which went the round of the lettuce fields "suggesting to idle Filipino field hands that they move." Approximately 700 Filipinos, among those who refused to return to work, were driven out of the Salinas fields by force. The camp of Rufo Canete, a popular Filipino labor contractor, was raided by vigilantes and burned to the ground, at a loss to Canete of approximately $16,000. Many Filipinos were corraled and held incommunicado; and of course the strike was broken.

With the exception of the Mexican, the Filipino has been the most viciously exploited of any of the various races recruited by the California agriculturists to make up their vast army of "cheap labor." Practically all Filipino agricultural labor is supplied by contract, the contractor charging for board and transportation and a fee for his services besides. It is impossible to verify just how much the average Filipino field worker is bilked by the contractor, so closely is he "protected" from investigators. The very sociability of the Filipino has been exploited. For example, the Filipinos like to work in large numbers. The use of large numbers of Filipinos in the asparagus beds of the Delta region near Stockton, California, has enabled the growers to increase productivity per acre—as it makes possible a more thorough picking—while at the same time it has decreased the average wage of the workers. In 1929, as compared with 1925, there was an increase of 16.2 per cent in the number of Filipino workers in this district, but a decrease of 38.5 per cent in the average daily earnings. Admittedly the Filipinos are excellent workers: "They are willing to work under all sorts of weather conditions, even when it is raining and the fields are wet," reads one report.

A Trick

Today, after his brief but strenuous period of service to American capital, the Filipino faces deportation, as a fitting reward for his efforts. The acute Commissioner of Immigration, in reporting on HR 6464, pointed out that "the Filipino cannot be removed unless he makes application for the benefits of the act." But the Filipino lives in California, and he applies to Washington for free transportation. There is a great distance intervening and doubtless many forces can be applied in California that would not echo too loudly in Washington. It is estimated that about 15,000 Filipinos will "avail" themselves of the offer to return. But the Filipinos that I have talked to have no desire or intention to take advantage of the act. They regard it as a trick, and not a very clever trick, to get them out of this country.

CHAPTER 3

The World War II Internment of Japanese Americans

Chapter Preface

World War II marked a significant turning point for Asian Americans, in part because the conflict involved the United States and several Asian countries. Chinese and Filipino Americans benefited from the fact that China and the Philippines fought with America in its war against Japan. In 1943, the Chinese Exclusion Act was repealed in favor of an annual quota of 105 Chinese immigrants, and Chinese Americans were allowed to become naturalized U.S. citizens. President Franklin D. Roosevelt and others defended these moves as gestures of solidarity with China, America's wartime ally. Similar legislation was passed for Filipino Americans in 1946.

For Japanese Americans, however, the war had disastrous results. Japanese community leaders were arrested, many Japanese Americans were harassed and vilified, and those who attempted to enlist in the U.S. armed forces were initially turned away. In one of America's most controversial acts of World War II, 110,000 Japanese Americans—two-thirds of them American citizens—were exiled from their homes in California, Washington, and Oregon, and held in detention camps. Their relocation and internment resulted in divided families, lost property, and disrupted and shattered lives. The wartime detention, write historians Harry H. L. Kitano and Roger Daniels,

> was and remains the central event of Japanese American history. It makes that history unique, setting off the Japanese American experience from that of not just other ethnic groups from Asia but from all other immigrant ethnic groups.

Military and political leaders defended this internment as a necessary wartime measure to prevent spying and sabotage. Past and present critics of internment have argued that such fears were overblown and that actions against Japanese Americans were instead the result of political pressures from local leaders and newspapers and were the culmination of longstanding anti-Asian sentiment in the United States. To support this contention they point to the fact that such blanket detentions did not take place in Hawaii, the site of the Pearl Harbor attack and the only American territory where Japanese Americans composed a significant portion (one-third) of the population.

The viewpoints in this chapter examine arguments about whether the Japanese internment was justified as well as controversies within the Japanese American community on whether or not to cooperate with the U.S. government before and during detention.

VIEWPOINT 1

"Both the alien Japanese and the Japanese-American citizen should be removed from the entire Pacific coast for the proper defense of our Nation."

All Japanese Americans Should Be Evacuated from the West Coast

San Benito County Chamber of Commerce

When America and Japan went to war in December 1941, approximately 150,000 people of Japanese descent lived in Hawaii, then a U.S. territory. In addition, approximately 127,000 lived in the rest of the United States, of which 90 percent resided in California, Washington, and Oregon. Two-thirds of the Japanese in the United States were American-born U.S. citizens; the remainder were Japanese immigrants who as nonwhite aliens were barred from U.S. citizenship. Following Japan's attack on Pearl Harbor and the commencement of war between the United States and Japan, some newspaper columnists, radio commentators, and political leaders began to express fear over the presence of Japanese Americans in their communities. Much of this fear was based on the belief that Japanese Americans had sabotaged American defenses or in some other way contributed to the Pearl Harbor attack—an assertion frequently made during World War II although official investigations did not uncover evidence of such activity.

The following viewpoint consists of a resolution made on February 11, 1942, by the chamber of commerce of San Benito County (a western inland county of California). The members of the chamber of commerce, citing fears of Japanese sabotage and

From the "Resolution of the San Benito County Chamber of Commerce," during hearings before the House Select Committee Investigating Defense Migration, 77th Cong., 2nd sess. (1942), p. 11238.

arguing that the loyalty of all Japanese is suspect, call for the mass removal of both Japanese aliens and citizens from the Pacific Coast. Many towns, communities, and organizations (such as the American Legion) issued similar resolutions and statements, putting substantial political pressure on the federal and military authorities to respond. On February 19, 1942, President Franklin D. Roosevelt issued Executive Order 9066, which authorized the U.S. Army to exclude "any or all persons" from vital "military areas." The West Coast was deemed such a vital area, and in late March the U.S. Army began mass evacuations of all Japanese to "relocation centers" in eastern California and other western states.

Whereas the cowardly and dastardly attack by Japan on the armed forces of the United States at Pearl Harbor and the subsequent declaration of war by the United States on Japan and the Axis Powers has made the citizens of San Benito County aware of the presence of enemy aliens, particularly Japanese, and un-American Japanese citizens holding dual citizenship with the Japanese Empire; and

Whereas raids conducted by the Federal Bureau of Investigation in the adjoining counties of Monterey and Santa Cruz within the past few days disclosed the indisputable fact that enemy aliens, particularly Japanese, had in their possession an appalling quantity of contraband articles including firearms, weapons, ammunition, cameras, short-wave radios, and like apparatus, in defiance of rules and regulations established by the Federal Government when this region was designated as a combat zone; and

Whereas it is well known to the citizens of San Benito County that resident enemy aliens, particularly Japanese, and their descendants known as Japanese-American citizens, suspected of holding dual citizenship with the Empire of Japan, have in their possession and control in this county, farm equipment consisting of heavy and light trucks, tractors, tools, and other equipment which could be used by said aliens most effectively destroying and damaging highways, bridges, railroads, and communication, water, power, gas, and oil lines within this county as effectively as was the case at Pearl Harbor, in event of an invasion by our wartime enemies or as a separate act of sabotage which might be committed at any time; and

Whereas it is noticeable that the actions of most enemy aliens, particularly Japanese and their descendants, are not now, nor

Military Justification

John L. DeWitt, commanding general of the Western Defense Command, recommended mass evacuation of all Japanese from the West Coast of the United States. The passage below is from his February 14, 1942, report for Secretary of War Henry L. Stimson.

The Japanese race is an enemy race and while many second and third generation Japanese born on United States soil, possessed of United States citizenship, have become "Americanized," the racial strains are undiluted. . . . That Japan is allied with Germany and Italy in this struggle is no ground for assuming that any Japanese, barred from assimilation by convention as he is, though born and raised in the United States, will not turn against this nation when the final test of loyalty comes. It, therefore, follows that along the vital Pacific Coast over 112,000 potential enemies, of Japanese extraction, are at large today. There are indications that these are organized and ready for concerted action at a favorable opportunity. The very fact that no sabotage has taken place to date is a disturbing and confirming indication that such action will be taken. . . . As the term is used herein, the word "Japanese" includes alien Japanese and American citizens of Japanese ancestry. . . .

I now recommend the following: That the Secretary of War procure from the President direction and authority to designate military areas . . . from which, in his discretion, he may exclude all Japanese, all alien enemies, and all other persons suspected for any reason by the administering military authorities of being actual or potential saboteurs, espionage agents, or fifth columnists.

have they ever been, such as would lead us to believe that in event of an emergency, or at a given opportunity, they would maintain strict neutrality or be loyal to the United States of America; and

Whereas a large part of this county is devoted to agricultural crops and grazing lands which become highly inflammable during the early summer, which is fast approaching, and would afford a most favorable opportunity for these enemy aliens and disloyal citizens to stage a disastrous and widespread conflagration, and

Whereas numerous requests have been made to this body that it take immediate action in urging and requesting the proper authorities to take immediate action to prevent the repetition of the Pearl Harbor incident or a worse disaster, and

Whereas it is well known that the American people do not wish to be unfair or unjust to the loyal American-born Japanese-American citizens but do wish to be protected against any and all disloyal Japanese-American citizens, and

Whereas it appears to this body that in view of the seriousness of the present war with the Japanese Government and the lack of time in which to carefully evaluate the standing and loyalty of the American-born Japanese-American citizens that both the alien Japanese and the Japanese-American citizen should be removed from the entire Pacific coast for the proper defense of our Nation; therefore, be it

Resolved, That the San Benito County Chamber of Commerce does and it hereby urges that the proper civil and military authorities take immediate action to cause the removal of all enemy alien citizens and Japanese-American citizens from the entire Pacific coast area; and be it further

Resolved, That copies of this resolution be sent to commanding officers of the Army and Navy, the Federal Bureau of Investigation, to each Senator and Representative from California in the Congress of the United States, to the Governor of California, the Adjutant General, and the Attorney General.

VIEWPOINT 2

"I fully accept as our paramount aim: Win the war—maintain national security. . . . But I am convinced that the sweeping evacuation of Japanese residents, whether aliens or citizens, would hinder, not help, the attainment of these ends."

Japanese Americans Should Not Be Subject to Mass Evacuation

Galen M. Fisher (1873–1955)

In late February and early March 1942, a special committee of the House of Representatives investigating "National Defense Migration" (commonly called the Tolan Committee after its chairman, Democrat John H. Tolan of Oakland, California) held public hearings in Los Angeles, San Francisco, Portland, and Seattle on the "Problems of Evacuating Enemy Aliens and Others from Prohibited Military Zones." The hearings took place shortly after President Franklin D. Roosevelt issued Executive Order 9066, which authorized the U.S. Army to exclude "any or all persons" from vital "military areas," but before the army began to carry out such evacuations. Many of the witnesses, including California attorney general (and future Supreme Court justice) Earl Warren testified in favor of mass evacuation of all Japanese citizens and noncitizens for security reasons.

The following viewpoint is taken from the prepared statement of one of the minority of witnesses testifying in opposition to the mass evacuation of Japanese Americans. Galen M. Fisher was senior secretary in Japan for the Young Men's Christian Association (YMCA) for twenty-one years. Later he was executive secretary

From Galen M. Fisher's statement during hearings before the House Select Committee Investigating Defense Migration, 77th Cong., 2nd sess. (1942), p. 11199.

for the Rockefeller Institute of Social and Religious Research in New York. In 1942 he was a research associate in the political science department at the University of California, adviser to the Institute for Pacific Relations, and secretary of the Northern California Committee on Fair Play for Citizens and Aliens of Japanese Descent. In his statement before the Tolan Committee, Fisher argues that most Japanese American citizens are loyal to America and that mass evacuation is both impractical and undemocratic.

I fully accept as our paramount aim: Win the war—maintain national security. Therefore, I approve any measures for control of either aliens or citizens that may be required to achieve these ends, in line with the President's proclamation of February 20.

But I am convinced that the sweeping evacuation of Japanese residents, whether aliens or citizens, would hinder, not help, the attainment of these ends. Removal of persons of any race or nationality should be confined to such as special investigation shows to be dangerous or decidedly suspicious. Identification cards, fingerprinting and photographs are all desirable.

Reasons for Opposing Mass Evacuation

1. The huge numbers involved make sweeping evacuation impracticable. . . . There are in California over 90,000 Japanese residents alone, not to mention the much larger numbers of Germans and Italians.

2. No definite plans have been made by any Government department for settling or supervising large numbers of evacuees. The most specific plan I have heard of is that proposed by several Japanese-American citizens, graduates in agriculture, for establishing farm cooperatives, but that would require huge Government loans to accommodate the 50,000 rural Japanese resident population, and would not care for the many city dwellers who are unsuited to agriculture.

3. Some two-thirds—over 60,000—of the Japanese in California are American citizens. Very few of them are dangerous, if we may judge by the fact that during December only 2 or 3 of them were detained by the Federal Bureau of Investigation, and I have not heard of many more being detained since them. Evidently, the few who are found to be dangerous can be interned, without disturbing the large majority.

4. Several thousand citizens of Japanese parentage are serving in our armed forces. Keeping their morale high is desirable for

147

military efficiency; but to evacuate their families, or even their alien parents alone, would impair their morale and breed disaffection among the whole body of Japanese-American citizens.

5. Any organized and extensive fifth-column activity by residents of Japanese stock would presumably have to be led by experienced alien Japanese. Most of the natural leaders have already been detained, and others can be, without evacuating the thousands of rank and file Japanese.

National Archives

This child was one of more than 110,000 Japanese Americans to be detained in internment camps during World War II.

6. Harsh treatment of the Japanese residents will give the military rulers of Japan the finest sort of propaganda to support their claim to be "the protectors and deliverers of the colored races of Asia from the arrogant and race-biased white nations." The Nazis have already made much of our maltreatment of the Negro. If we violate in any degree the equal rights of our fellow citizens of Japanese stock, we mock our pretensions of fighting to defend democracy.

7. Since we are confident of winning the war, the Japanese residents are a possible menace to our national security only during

the war. Upon the coming of peace, we shall presumably wish them to continue as heretofore to take their place in our general life. If, however, we isolate them and give them cause to resent unnecessary discriminations imposed during the war, then they will not fit smoothly into our national life, but will present another acute race problem.

8. Our citizens of Japanese parentage are just as trustworthy now as they were a few weeks ago when Governor [Cuthbert] Olson and other publicists paid tribute to their loyalty and civic devotion. Has the set-back given to the Allied arms by the military machine of Japan made our political leaders in State, county, and municipality play the bully and turn against our Japanese citizens as scapegoats for the remote culprits, in Japan, whom our Japanese-American citizens have repeatedly denounced? Like many other Americans who have long known hundreds of Japanese, I would testify that among their most marked traits are loyalty and gratitude. I strongly believe that the Nisei citizens [second generation Japanese Americans] will, with few exceptions, be as loyal to the United States as any other group of citizens. The exceptions are likely to be found chiefly among the Kibei, or American-born Japanese who are sent to Japan for their schooling, especially those who go before they have finished grammar and high school here. The Kibei, however, are reliably estimated to number less than a quarter of the total of the Nisei.

9. In connection with the whole question of citizens of Japanese stock, I wish to testify to the great service to our Nation already rendered by the Japanese-American Citizens' League. It is the only inclusive organization touching the Nisei and it can be of great value in maintaining their undivided loyalty to the United States.

10. Little evidence pointing to fifth-column activity seems yet to have been discovered by the Federal Bureau of Investigation or the naval and military intelligence, although they have been hunting hard to find it. A high military authority recently told me that he took no stock in the alarmist predictions that fifth-columnists in California were only waiting for the ides of March. I hope that our intelligence services will not relax for a moment their vigilance, but I also hope that a panicky public will not try to stampede our military and judicial authorities into evacuating thousands or tens of thousands of people, in order to avert a possible danger that can probably be averted by evacuating a few hundreds. In all the clamor about the Japanese residents, it may be that we are overlooking a greater menace in the form of the Nazi partisans in our midst. The Japanese spies and saboteurs can be much more easily spotted because of their color and physiognomy than can Nazi or Italian plotters.

"With any policy of evacuation definitely arising from reasons of military necessity and national safety, we are in complete agreement."

Japanese Americans Should Cooperate with Government Evacuation Plans

Mike Masaoka (1915–1991)

In 1942, Mike Masaoka was the national secretary for the Japanese American Citizens League. Formed in 1930, with membership limited to American-born citizens (thus excluding the first generation of Japanese immigrants), the JACL's main thrust prior to World War II was promoting American values. Its creed, adopted in 1940, began, "I am proud that I am an American citizen of Japanese ancestry, for my very background makes me appreciate more fully the wonderful advantages of this nation." Masaoka and other JACL leaders made the decision in 1942 to cooperate fully with U.S. government and military authorities during World War II.

Masaoka's cooperative stance can be seen in the following viewpoint, taken from his February 1942 statement before the Tolan Committee, a committee of the House of Representatives considering the proposal to evacuate Japanese Americans and other suspected internal wartime enemies. Masaoka argues against mass evacuation of Japanese Americans, but he pledges full cooperation if such evacuation is ordered, and offers suggestions as to how it could be peacefully accomplished.

From Mike Masaoka's statement during hearings before the House Select Committee Investigating Defense Migration, 77th Cong., 2nd sess. (1942), p. 11137.

Masaoka and his family were eventually transported to a relocation camp, where he continued to cooperate with authorities. He was involved in the decision by the U.S. Army to create a segregated Japanese American regiment (the 442nd Regimental Combat Team), which received acclaim for its combat record in Europe (Masaoka and two of his brothers served and were wounded in the war). Following World War II Masaoka became a Washington lobbyist for the JACL and was instrumental in passing legislation compensating internees for "damage to or loss of real or personal property" and in ending the ban on Japanese immigration.

On behalf of the 20,000 American citizen members of the 62 chapters of the Japanese American Citizens League in some 300 communities throughout the United States, I wish to thank the Tolan committee for the opportunity given me to appear at this hearing. The fair and impartial presentation of all aspects of a problem is a democratic procedure which we deeply appreciate. That this procedure is being followed in the present matter, which is of particularly vital significance to us, we look upon as a heartening demonstration of the American tradition of fair play.

We have been invited by you to make clear our stand regarding the proposed evacuation of all Japanese from the West coast. When the President's recent Executive order was issued, we welcomed it as definitely centralizing and coordinating defense efforts relative to the evacuation problem. Later interpretations of the order, however, seem to indicate that it is aimed primarily at the Japanese, American citizens as well as alien nationals. As your committee continues its investigations in this and subsequent hearings, we hope and trust that you will recommend to the proper authorities that no undue discrimination be shown to American citizens of Japanese descent.

Our frank and reasoned opinion on the matter of evacuation revolves around certain considerations of which we feel both your committee and the general public should be apprised. With any policy of evacuation definitely arising from reasons of military necessity and national safety, we are in complete agreement. As American citizens, we cannot and should not take any other stand. But, also, as American citizens believing in the integrity of our citizenship, we feel that any evacuation enforced on grounds violating that integrity should be opposed.

If, in the judgment of military and Federal authorities, evacuation of Japanese residents from the West coast is a primary step toward assuring the safety of this Nation, we will have no hesitation in complying with the necessities implicit in that judgment. But, if, on the other hand, such evacuation is primarily a measure whose surface urgency cloaks the desires of political or other pressure groups who want us to leave merely from motives of self-interest, we feel that we have every right to protest and to demand equitable judgment on our merits as American citizens.

Recommendations

In any case, we feel that the whole problem of evacuation, once its necessity is militarily established, should be met strictly according to that need. Only these areas in which strategic and military considerations make the removal of Japanese residents necessary should be evacuated. Regarding policy and procedure in such areas, we submit the following recommendations:

1. That the actual evacuation from designated areas be conducted by military authorities in a manner which is consistent with the requirements of national defense, human welfare, and constructive community relations in the future;

2. That, in view of the alarming developments in Tulare County

---

Against Test Cases

Minoru Yasui, a Japanese American attorney in Portland, Oregon, deliberately violated military curfew orders in 1942 in order to test the constitutionality of Japanese American mass evacuation. On April 7, 1942, Mike Masaoka wrote a bulletin to local chapters of the Japanese American Citizens League explaining JACL policy on such legal challenges.

National Headquarters is unalterably opposed to test cases to determine the constitutionality of military regulations at this time. We have reached this decision unanimously after examining all the facts in light of our national policy of: "the greatest good for the greatest number."

We recognize that self-styled martyrs who are willing to be jailed in order that they might fight for the rights of citizenship, as many of them allege, capture the headlines and the imaginations of many more persons than our seemingly indifferent stand. We realize that many Japanese and others who are interested in our welfare have condemned the JACL for its apparent lackadaisical attitude on the matter of defending the rights and privileges of American citizens with Japanese features. . . .

Since our motives are too often misunderstood . . . we believe that test cases should not be made. We do not intend to create any unnecessary excuses for denouncing the Japanese as disloyal and dangerous.

---

and other communities against incoming Japanese evacuees all plans for voluntary evacuations be discouraged;

3. That transportation, food, and shelter be provided for all evacuees from prohibited areas, as provided in the Presidential order;

4. That thoroughly competent, responsible, and bonded property custodians be appointed and their services made available immediately to all Japanese whose business and property interests are affected by orders and regulations;

5. That all problems incidental to resettlement be administered by a special board created for this purpose under the direction of the Federal Security Agencies;

6. That the resettlement of evacuees from prohibited areas should be within the State in which they now reside;

7. That ample protection against mob violence be given to the evacuees both in transit and in the new communities to which they are assigned;

8. That effort be made to provide suitable and productive work for all evacuees;

9. That resettlement aims be directed toward the restoration, as far as possible, of normal community life in the future when we have won the war;

10. That competent tribunals be created to deal with the so-called hardship cases and that flexible policies be applicable to such cases.

Although these suggestions seem to include only the Japanese, may I urge that these same recommendations be adapted to the needs of other nationals and citizens who may be similarly affected.

We Cherish Our American Citizenship

I now make an earnest plea that you seriously consider and recognize our American citizenship status which we have been taught to cherish as our most priceless heritage.

At this hearing, we Americans of Japanese descent have been accused of being disloyal to these United States. As an American citizen, I resent these accusations and deny their validity.

We American-born Japanese are fighting militarist Japan today with our total energies. Four thousand of us are with the armed forces of the United States, the remainder on the home front in the battle of production. We ask a chance to prove to the rest of the American people what we ourselves already know: That we are loyal to the country of our birth and that we will fight to the death to defend it against any and all aggressors.

We think, feel, act like Americans. We, too, remember Pearl Harbor and know that our right to live as free men in a free Nation is in peril as long as the brutal forces of enslavement walk the earth. We know that the Axis aggressors must be crushed and we are anxious to participate fully in that struggle.

The history of our group speaks for itself. It stands favorable comparison with that of any other group of second generation Americans. There is reliable authority to show that the proportion of delinquency and crime within our ranks is negligible. Throughout the long years of the depression, we have been able to stay off the relief rolls better, by far, than any other group. These are but two of the many examples which might be cited as proof of our civic responsibility and pride.

In this emergency, as in the past, we are not asking for special privileges or concessions. We ask only for the opportunity and the right of sharing the common lot of all Americans, whether it be in peace or in war.

This is the American way for which our boys are fighting.

VIEWPOINT 4

"The forceful evacuation of citizen Americans on the synthetic theory of racial fidelity—"Once a Jap, always a Jap"—would be an indictment against every racial minority in the United States."

Japanese Americans Should Not Cooperate with Government Evacuation Plans

James M. Omura (b. 1912)

James M. Omura was one of several Japanese American citizens to testify before a congressional committee (the Tolan Committee) regarding proposals to evacuate people of Japanese descent from the West Coast of the United States. A florist by vocation, Omura and his wife published *Current Life*, a small-circulation magazine on Japanese American affairs. In his testimony for the committee, excerpted below, Omura criticizes the Japanese American Citizens League (JACL) and its decision to cooperate with the U.S. government. Omura argues that Japanese Americans should resist any plans for their mass evacuation.

Omura's confrontational stance continued during the war. When the Selective Service System reinstated the draft for Japanese Americans in 1944 (it had previously excluded Japanese from military service, in violation of federal law), Omura's editorials for the Denver newspaper *Rocky Shimpo* helped inspire internees at the concentration camp in Heart Mountain, Wyoming, to defy draft orders.

From James M. Omura's statement during hearings before the House Select Committee Investigating Defense Migration, 77th Cong., 2nd sess. (1942), p. 11229.

155

I requested to be heard here due largely to the fact that I am strongly opposed to mass evacuation of American-born Japanese. It is my honest belief that such an action would not solve the question of Nisei loyalty. If any such action is taken I believe that we would be only procrastinating on the question of loyalty, that we are afraid to deal with it, and that at this, our first opportunity, we are trying to strip the Nisei of their opportunity to prove their loyalty.

I do not believe there has ever been, or ever could be again, a situation of this kind where the Nisei can prove their loyalty.

I suppose you understand that I am in some measure opposed to what some of the other representatives of the Japanese community have said here before this committee. Unfortunately, I wasn't here, and I have no report on it, so I do not know actually what was said, but I do know generally what they are promoting.

I specifically refer to the J. A. C. L. It is a matter of public record among the Japanese community that I have been consistently opposed to the Japanese-American Citizen League. I have not been opposed to that organization primarily in regards to its principles, but I have felt that the leaders were leading the American-born Japanese along the wrong channels, and I have not minced words in saying so publicly.

I do not know what else I could say, except that I desire to have an unpublished editorial of *Current Life* read into this record. . . .

In Spirit, We Are Americans

Promoters of racialism—the gulf which seems to eternally divide oriental Americans from fellow Americans of Caucasian ancestry—have enjoyed a virtual field day to date in their vigorous campaign to oust resident Japanese, including bona fide citizens, from their hard-won economic niche. . . . The theory of racial "divine creation" is a theory which gains greater and more ominous impetus with the progress of war in the Pacific, especially intensified at the current hour by virtue of repeated Allied losses in the Far East.

The Nisei Americans, the unfortunate children of destiny in this Pacific war, are mere stepping stones for political aspirants and self-seekers. They are being utilized today as political footballs for ambitious officeholders and aspiring demagogs who find it quite opportune to grind their personal axes on the fate of these oft-vilified and persecuted voiceless Americans. The extent to which bigotry and racial antipathy can go in denying civil liberties—a vital cornerstone of democracy—to a segment of the population is witnessed in the summary dismissal of Nisei civil-service employees in the city and county of Los Angeles.

Racialism doubtlessly will play a significant and important role in the war over the Pacific. And the brunt of the guilt for the criminal act of December 7, at Pearl Harbor seems destined to fall upon the guiltless brow of the poor, hapless Nisei—merely because they wear the outward features of the race whose people committed the now historic crime. For that act, the Caucasian population on the Pacific coast will find fiendish glee in exacting punishment upon citizen Americans with Japanese faces. What could be more unjust and un-American?

The future of Nisei Americans is indeed dark. They walk through life in fear, dreading that with each passing moment new restrictions and edicts, disrupting the normal conduct of their daily lives will be adopted. They have watched with saddening brows the pathos and confusion of their alien parents being uprooted forcefully from the homes which took some of the best years of their oppressed lives to build commanded by the stern measures of a nation at war to go elsewhere in some distant alien surroundings to build anew. Will the hour arrive when they, too, must unwillingly follow after?

Should that hour come, the history of our American Republic will never again stand high in the council chambers of justice and tolerance. Democracy will suffer deeply by it. The forceful evacuation of citizen Americans on the synthetic theory of racial fidelity—"Once a Jap, always a Jap"—would be an indictment against every racial minority in the United States. It would usher in the bigoted and misguided belief that Americanism is a racial attribute and not a national symbol. The scar that will be left will be broad and deep—a stigma of eternal shame.

We must stand shoulder to shoulder in these critical hours. National unity is not best served by discriminating against a segment of the citizenry merely because of physical differences. It would be well to remember that the Nisei Americans and their alien parents have contributed generously and are continuing to contribute in like fashion to the cause of national defense. In spirit, we are Americans. . . .

It is doubtlessly rather difficult for Caucasian Americans to properly comprehend and believe in what we say. Our citizenship has even been attacked as an evil cloak under which we expect immunity for the nefarious purpose of conspiring to destroy the American way of life. To us—who have been born, raised, and educated in American institutions and in our system of public schools, knowing and owing no other allegiance than to the United States—such a thought is manifestly unfair and ambiguous.

I would like to ask the committee: Has the Gestapo come to America? Have we not risen in righteous anger at Hitler's mistreatments of the Jews? Then, is it not incongruous that citizen Americans of Japanese descent should be similarly mistreated and persecuted? I speak from a humanitarian standpoint and from a realistic and not a theoretical point of view. This view, I be-

157

lieve, does not endanger the national security of this country nor jeopardize our war efforts. . . .

Are we to be condemned merely on the basis of our racial origin? Is citizenship such a light and transient thing that that which is our inalienable right in normal times can be torn from us in times of war? We in America are intensely proud of our individual rights and willing, I am sure, to defend those rights with our very lives. I venture to say that the great majority of Nisei Americans, too, will do the same against any aggressor nation—though that nation be Japan. Citizenship to us is no small heritage; it is a very precious and jealous right. You have only to look back on our records in social welfare and community contributions to understand that.

The Spineless JACL

Joseph Yoshisuke Kurihara, a Hawaiian-born Nisei, served in the U.S. Army during World War I and was a successful California businessman. He felt betrayed by the military evacuation orders and disappointed in the response of the Japanese American Citizens League (JACL). The following passage is excerpted from an autobiographical account he wrote in 1945 for a group of social scientists studying Japanese American internment during World War II (parts of which were reprinted in the 1946 book The Spoilage).

Truly it was my intention to fight this evacuation. On the night of my return to Los Angeles from San Diego was the second meeting which the Citizens Federation of Southern California held to discuss evacuation. I attended it with a firm determination to join the committee representing the Nisei and carry the fight to the bitter end. I found the goose was already cooked. The Field Secretary of the JACL instead of reporting what actually transpired at a meeting they had had with General [John L.] DeWitt just tried to intimidate the Nisei to comply with evacuation by stories of threats he claimed to have received from various parts of the State.

I felt sick at the result. They'd accomplished not a thing. All they did was to meet General DeWitt and be told what to do. These boys claiming to be the leaders of the Nisei were a bunch of spineless Americans. Here I decided to fight them and crush them in whatever camp I happened to find them. I vowed that they would never again be permitted to disgrace the name of the Nisei as long as I was about.

May I ask the committee members if any or all of you are acquainted with the Nisei? I believe that much of this distrust of citizen Japanese is based on ignorance. It would seem more compatible in the sense of fair play and justice that we should not be prejudged and that racialism should not be the yardstick by which our loyalty is measured. Our words, in current times, have no meaning, and so I ask you to examine our records, for there I believe that to a large measure, if not necessarily so, lies the true determination of our oft-questioned loyalty.

It seems to me that we are less fortunate than our alien parents. They, at least, are subjects of Japan and are entitled to recourse and redress through the Japanese Government. Not so is our case. We are but children of destiny—citizens by birth but citizens in virtually name only.

"The fear and enmity instilled through years of anti-Oriental campaigns has not disappeared overnight."

A Pessimistic Look at the Postwar Future for Japanese Americans

Ina Sugihara (dates unknown)

On December 18, 1944, the Supreme Court in separate rulings upheld the legality of military exclusion areas but decreed that citizens could not be indefinitely detained once their loyalty was established. The U.S. Army revoked its 1942 exclusion orders and told Japanese American internees that they were free to return to their homes as of January 2, 1945. Some internees, however, many of them elderly or young, remained in the detention camps because of economic uncertainties and fears of local prejudice. As World War II drew to a close and the relocation centers were slated for closure, Japanese Americans both within and outside the camps faced fundamental choices on their future in America. Some, bitter about the treatment during the war, were repatriated to Japan (renouncing their American citizenship if necessary). Others sought to return to their homes or to resettle in other parts of America.

The following viewpoint by Ina Sugihara was written during this time of transition. Sugihara was one of several thousand Japanese Americans who, by moving or residing outside the proscribed military areas of the West Coast prior to April 1942, avoided internment during World War II. During the war she studied at the New School for Social Research in New York and worked for the Religious News Service. In a 1945 article for the *Commonweal*, excerpted here, she explains why she does not in-

Ina Sugihara, "I Don't Want to Go Back," *Commonweal*, July 20, 1945. Copyright Commonweal Foundation. Reprinted with permission.

tend to return to California, where she lived from 1933 to 1942. She argues that the evacuation and internment of Japanese Americans was the latest example of an ongoing history of anti-Asian prejudice in that state, and she expresses pessimism for the future of Japanese Americans and other Asians in that part of the country.

This war's creation, concentration camps, have in part been removed with the capitulation of Germany, but we still have America's "concentration camps"—those nine Relocation Centers in which Americans of Japanese descent, evacuated from the West Coast three years ago, continue to live.

Official announcement has been made that these camps will be disbanded by January 2, 1946, when the present Congressional appropriation runs out. This means that 65,000 men, women, and children—equivalent to one-half of Kansas City—must be absorbed by communities either in the West or in other parts of the country within six months. Each of the 65,000 faces three possibilities: go back to California, Washington, Oregon, or Arizona; start anew in the Middle West or the East; stay in camp until forced to leave.

Going back to the Pacific Coast, the only familiar territory these people know, would mean returning to that area where the very groups who initiated the evacuation, and other discriminatory measures, hold power. These forces now have a stronger weapon than that of public prejudice; they have a Supreme Court decision in their favor. That decision, in the Korematsu case last December, upholding the constitutionality of the evacuation, was a serious blow to civil liberties for everyone. By comparison, the revocation of evacuation orders by the Western Defense Command, effective January 2 of this year, permitting "loyal" Japanese Americans to return to the Coast, was not a real consolation.

Sanctioning Racism

The high court ruling gave federal sanction to the activities of Pacific Coast racists who originally wanted the Japanese Americans out of California because they were its chief independent farmers, producing 85 percent of the state's fruits and vegetables. Their competition was felt strongly by the Associated Farmers and the State Grange, California's monopoly and industrial agriculturists. The long-time campaign of these groups, together with that of the American Legion, the Native Sons and Daughters of the Golden West, the California State Committee on Naturalization and Immigration, the Asiatic Exclusion League, the Mc-Clatchy newspapers, and others, culminated in the evacuation.

These forces revealed their objectives when, following the mass removal, they advocated that evacuees be returned to the state during the war as tenant farmers and migrant laborers, thus reducing them again to the status of contract laborers from which the Japanese Americans had risen during past decades. They proved that "military necessity" had been an excuse.

The Decision to Renounce Citizenship

Joseph Yoshisuke Kurihara, a World War I veteran who was interned at the relocation center in Manzanar, California, was arrested on December 7, 1942, for agitating against camp authorities and for his role in instigating a riot at the detention camp. He renounced his U.S. citizenship and left for Japan in 1946. In the following passage from an autobiographical account written for social scientists studying Japanese American internment (reprinted in an appendix of the 1946 book The Spoilage), *he expresses his disillusionment with America.*

My American friends . . . no doubt must have wondered why I renounced my citizenship. This decision was not that of today or yesterday. It dates back the day when General [John L.] DeWitt ordered evacuation. It was confirmed when he flatly refused to listen even to the voices of the former World War Veterans and it was doubly confirmed when I entered Manzanar. We who already had proven our loyalty by serving in the last World War should have been spared. The veterans asked for special consideration but their requests were denied. They too had to evacuate like the rest of the Japanese people, as if they were aliens.

I did not expect this of the Army. When the Western Defense Command assumed the responsibilities of the West Coast, I expected that at least the Nisei would be allowed to remain. But to General DeWitt, we were all alike. "A Jap's a Jap. Once a Jap, always a Jap.". . . I swore to become a Jap 100 percent, and never to do another day's work to help this country fight this war. My decision to renounce my citizenship there and then was absolute.

Going back to California now to me would be like jumping into a witches' cauldron that had been bubbling for centuries. I would be powerless to stop the bubbling.

Students of Pacific Coast history are familiar with the long-standing organized discrimination which hovered over Oriental people almost from the time of their arrival, starting with the Chinese Exclusion Act in 1882 (now repealed), then the San Francisco school segregation campaign in 1908, the California Alien Land Act of 1921, and the general Asiatic Exclusion Acts of 1924. To this series we can now add the evacuation of 1942 and other bad measures in 1950, 1965, et cetera, unless a nationwide movement is organized to prohibit any brand of "manufactured prejudice" against any group of people.

Because of this background of planned discrimination, an insidious prejudice exists in all Pacific Coast communities. A minority is free from it, but the vast majority follow biased thinking with regard to "Oriental" people. Scarcely a person in that region believed that the evacuation was not necessary.

Whenever I think of California, I see blue-green hills behind wavy roads, towering eucalypti, and the Campanile on the Berkeley campus, the magnificent, swinging San Francisco Bay Bridge, a string of lights reaching out into the night, the miles and miles of white sandy beaches stretching from San Diego to Santa Barbara, and the love and kindness of many good people whose hearts have no room for hate. But the moment the California I loved comes to mind, the state that initiated and promoted the evacuation of thousands of innocent men, women and children overshadows pleasant memories. I know that the fear and enmity instilled through years of anti-Oriental campaigns has not disappeared overnight. Residence ordinances stating, "Orientals can't live here," are still in effect. I could have few jobs outside of housework and selling apples. Living in that social climate as an individual, rather than as a social guinea pig, would be well-nigh impossible.

Personal Rebuffs

I can't forget the multitude of insults one met as an "Oriental" in the "Golden State." Every year hundreds of Japanese Americans and Chinese Americans were graduated from West Coast colleges. The following year they were doing housework, farming, selling fruits and vegetables in Los Angeles, or displaying curios in San Francisco's Chinatown.

The rebuffs I met from landlords, when entering the University of California as a junior and looking for a place to live, will forever stay in my mind. The people were courteous, but firm. Either the "vacancy" sign did not mean anything, or the rent was obviously too high for a student to afford. One particular incident, later in my college life, remains as a vivid example of the anomaly of prejudice. A girl friend, not an "Oriental," and I decided to move into an apartment together. I went to a renting agent who called a landlord about a listed vacancy. While she was talking on the phone, she asked me, "Are you Chinese or Japanese?"

"I am an American of Japanese descent," I said.

"And your friend. . . ?"

163

"She is an American, too."

"Not Oriental?"

"No."

She repeated this information to the landlord and then gave the verdict: "Your friend can live there, but you can't—the apartment is suitable for two. Do you think your friend would be interested?"

My friend, being loyal to me and ideals, was not interested.

During my student boarding house days, the Berkeley city council almost passed a residential ordinance prohibiting "Orientals" from living in a wide area extending from the northern campus border to the city limits. If that ordinance had been passed, not only would I have had to move, but the Japanese American Men's and Women's Student Clubs would have had to transfer elsewhere their residential and social centers used by 400 to 500 people. . . .

Stories to tell my grandchildren will include the months of waiting I encountered after finishing at the university in 1941, when defense plants had drained most of California's available labor supply. I canvassed all employment agencies for miles around—and there were many in the San Francisco Bay region—including the segregated "Oriental Division" of the US Employment Service in San Francisco. I was never sent on an interview once during the ten months that I was around, except for housekeeping jobs and one offer from a labor union who wanted to use me to organize Oriental workers in its field.

This story will continue with the drudgery and incongruity of mopping floors, washing dishes, and cooking other people's meals for a living, which I did for several months, while plenty of more creative jobs were going begging.

I was not quite old enough to have to fly to Reno to get married while I was in the West, but that was what I would have had to do if I had chosen a mate not an "Oriental," for California has a miscegenation law affecting "Orientals."

Because of California's Alien Land Act (1921), my parents, who are not allowed to become citizens, cannot own real estate there, not even a home in which to live during their declining years.

Theodore Roosevelt stopped segregation of "Oriental" children in San Francisco's schools in 1908, but this practice existed as late as 1940 in other communities. I met people who had been trained in "Oriental" sections of school districts, and their handicap through lack of cultural contact was apparent even when they had reached the university. It is true that I have met employment and housing discrimination in the East, but this to my mind is mostly a temporary ailment caused by war hysteria. Of course, some of it is not, but it at least is not a part of an organized campaign. That on the West Coast is a chronic sickness growing worse each year.

The East has proved its sincerity by opposing most of the West's anti-Oriental measures. Organizations in New York and elsewhere objected to both the Chinese and Asiatic Exclusion Acts. The only vocal opposition to the evacuation came from the East. Individuals and groups three years ago prevented the Eastern Defense Command from evacuating individuals, following the West Coast example.

Just as the Negro American who ventured North will not go back to Georgia, so the Japanese American who wants to live a normal life does not want to go back to California. The right to do so is important, but the practicality of the step is another matter.

The Future

I cannot see a brighter life for Japanese Americans on the West Coast than in earlier years. The American Legion and others are again on the march. Already they have voiced opposition to return of the "Japs." Mayor Fletcher Bowron of Los Angeles predicts clashes in former "Lil' Tokio" between returning Japanese Americans and the Mexican Americans, Negro Americans, and Chinese Americans who have moved in since the evacuation. He will be the last to prevent these conflicts, as demonstrated in the Zoot Suit Riot of 1943, when police arrested Mexican Americans and no others.

If Japanese Americans return in large numbers to Los Angeles's international ghetto, it will be the center of a multiple discrimination and "bigger and better" riots. No one will know who is directly at fault, but tighter restrictions in the rest of the community against all minority groups will crowd them into an extremely limited territory, and lack of privacy, together with the search for a scapegoat, will cause bloodshed.

Economic boycotts against farm produce of Japanese Americans are now effective in various parts of Oregon and California. We have heard of the many outbreaks of violence against returning evacuees and the "sleight of hand" justice given offenders. No, I don't want to go back to California. If doing so would mean a chance effectively to fight the industrial agriculturists who are determined to fan the breath of prejudice, I would be glad to start back today. But I know that a group as strong as theirs can be beaten only through an uncompromising national movement to eliminate their practices—a sincere effort by people who are not poisoned by the prejudice so prevalent in that area.

The "Oriental problem" is not a Pacific Coast one; though the West initiated it. It is now bigger and far more destructive than the evils existing in any one region alone. It is an American problem.

Viewpoint 6

"The Evacuation has opened new vistas of opportunity for the Nisei."

An Optimistic Look at the Postwar Future for Japanese Americans

Bill Hosokawa (b. 1915)

Born and raised in Seattle, Washington, the son of Japanese immigrant parents, Bill Hosokawa's experiences during World War II mirrored those of many Japanese Americans. In 1942 he and his wife and son were evacuated to a detention camp in Puyallup, Washington, and later that year they were relocated to Heart Mountain War Relocation camp in Wyoming (his parents were sent to Idaho). After bleak months spent in the "black tarpaper-sheathed barracks" in Wyoming, in October 1943 he and his family moved to Des Moines, Iowa, where he worked for the *Des Moines Register*. Hosokawa was one of thousands of Japanese Americans who left the camps during the war as part of the War Relocation Authority's (WRA) campaign to resettle and find employment for Japanese Americans (after first screening them for loyalty through interviews and questionnaires).

In 1942, while still in Puyallup, Hosokawa began writing a column called "From the Frying Pan," which appeared in the *Pacific Citizen*, a newspaper published by the Japanese American Citizens League (JACL) from their wartime headquarters in Salt Lake City, Utah. The *Pacific Citizen* was one of only a few Japanese American newspapers to serve the internees. Hosokawa's column featured both personal and political observations of Japanese American life, and frequently took issue with the anti-Japanese opinions expressed by political leaders and by other newspapers.

Bill Hosokawa, From the Frying Pan column, December 30, 1944, as reprinted in *Thirty-five Years in the Frying Pan* by Bill Hosokawa (New York: McGraw-Hill, 1978). Reprinted with permission of the author and McGraw-Hill.

(The column's title, Hosokawa explains in a 1978 compilation of his writings, refers to his experience of working as a journalist in Shanghai, China, and returning to the United States six weeks prior to Pearl Harbor, thus leaping "from the fire of the Pacific war into the frying pan of evacuation.")

The following viewpoint is taken from a column written on December 30, 1944. While calling the mass evacuation of Japanese Americans a "tragic experience" that should never be repeated, Hosokawa nevertheless takes an optimistic view of the future. He argues that through their wartime experiences, especially resettlement in communities throughout the United States, Japanese Americans and other Americans have learned much about each other, and that such exposure will help Japanese Americans succeed in America. In 1946 Hosokawa joined the *Denver Post*, where he eventually became editor of its editorial page. The author of several books, including *Nisei: The Quiet Americans*, he continued to write his "From the Frying Pan" column for Japanese American newspapers for many years.

The three-year exile of Japanese Americans from their homes is about to end. It has been a period of toil and tears, of fear and gnawing uncertainty, of doubts that shook men's faith in democracy. It has been a period of raw emotions when bigots stood unashamed to trumpet their bigotry, and others made light of the Constitution in efforts to promote their economic self-interest.

It is too early, even now, to assess accurately the full, long-term significance of the Evacuation. It would seem a dangerous precedent has been set in the exile, solely on a racial basis, of an American minority. . . .

Results of Evacuation

But two tangible, constructive results of the Evacuation already are evident. The first is the effect on the Nisei themselves; the second the effect the Evacuation has had on the people of the United States.

The Evacuation has opened new vistas of opportunity for the Nisei. It has accomplished in a sudden, revolutionary and oftentimes cruel manner something that would have come to pass in a generation or two. And the Nisei and their offspring will profit when the pain of being wrenched from their homes is forgotten.

The story of the prewar Japanese communities is too well known to need much repetition. There the talents of eager young

Nisei were stifled for lack of opportunity. There were not jobs enough to go around, and prejudice kept the Nisei from finding opportunities in the cities which surrounded these colonies.

The War Has Removed Barriers

Carey McWilliams's books include Factories in the Fields, *which documents the conditions of migrant farm workers in California, and* Prejudice, *a book on Japanese Americans. In the following passage from* Brothers Under the Skin, *a study of American ethnic groups published in 1943, he argues that Japanese Americans have a better future before them because of World War II.*

In most of the areas where they are working at the present time, the [relocated] Japanese are being well received despite a rhetorically violent opposition at the outset. When an economic reality (labor shortage) collides with a subjective emotion (prejudice), the economic reality usually emerges triumphant. But the real test will come, of course, when the war is over. Whatever barriers it may raise in the future, the war will certainly have removed some barriers that, in the past, have retarded assimilation. Until Japanese militarism had been liquidated, until the Far Eastern crisis had been settled, it was chimerical to have expected a satisfactory solution to the Japanese problem. With these issues settled by the war, then the Japanese would seem to face a tolerably hopeful future. A few may decide to return to Japan (1250 evacués have signed up with WRA [War Relocation Authority] for repatriation), but the majority will unquestionably want to stick it out. This majority has already demonstrated its patriotism and loyalty. "I would say," testified Mr. Milton Eisenhower (formerly director of WRA) before a Congressional committee, "that from 80 per cent to 85 per cent of the *Nisei* are loyal to the United States. I just cannot say things too favorable about the way they have co-operated under the most adverse circumstances." When coupled with the fine effort they are making in relocation centers, this kind of assurance should go a long way toward winning for the Japanese a much wider range of acceptance after the war. The war has, also, forever broken the dominance of the *Issei*; it has shattered the isolation of Little Tokyo; and, violently and crudely, it is bringing the Japanese into the main current of American life. If American democracy overcomes its *laissez faire* attitude toward race problems and demonstrates an ability to cope with such questions, then it is likely that some of our fixations on race may be profoundly modified.

The bonds of family and habit kept all but a few of the Nisei from leaving the West Coast in search of a livelihood elsewhere.

The prewar plight of the Nisei well could be epitomized in the youth who wore a Phi Beta Kappa key on his watch chain and stacked oranges in a fruit stand for a living.

Now, thanks to the Evacuation, the Nisei are scattered in forty-seven of the forty-eight states. They have found, on a large scale, job opportunities undreamed of before the war. In spite of occasional local prejudices they have found the chance to compete for jobs and advancement on the basis of merit. And they are making good.

The Nisei have lost their narrow provincial outlook. California no longer is the limit of their interests. They speak more casually of traveling 2,000 miles across the country than they did before the war about making a trip from Los Angeles to San Francisco.

Discovering the Real America

The Nisei have discovered the real America. They have seen for the first time its towering mountains and its broad plains, its wheatfields and cornfields and the forests of industrial smokestacks. They have found the heart of America, and they know now that they no longer need be a group of marginal citizens of questioned loyalty.

And perhaps unconsciously, America is the stronger for having undergone the difficulties of the Evacuation. Thinking Americans have had it brought home as never before that this is a war of ideals and not of races. They are more cognizant of America's racial minority problems. They understand better the meaning of democracy.

In the once-upon-a-time of prewar days the so-called "Jap" problem was thought to be solely California's concern. Outside of the Pacific Coast the Japanese American had his prototype in the grinning gardener and truck farmer, or the domestic who spoke in Hashimura Togo English.

Now the Nisei are a curiosity no longer. The American public has found through the dispersal of the Nisei that they are thoroughly American with valuable skills to be contributed to the war effort. Americans have discovered that Nisei make good neighbors and are of credit to the communities in which they have resettled.

Nisei soldiers have brought home dramatically the lesson that the color of one's skin and the shape of one's facial features do not preclude loyalty or disloyalty. . . .

Unmasking the Patriots

And finally, the super-patriots have been unmasked. Their argument that American citizens should be punished because their forefathers were Japanese always had a phony ring. Now, by their own actions they have revealed themselves as of the lunatic fringe, not hesitant about denying Constitutional rights or inciting to riot and violence in order to satisfy their pettish prejudices or to fatten their pocketbooks.

Because the facts were little known, it was not difficult at one time for many Americans to believe the charges that West Coast hate-mongers leveled against the Nisei. So skillfully were the lies and half-truths interwoven with the truth by paid propagandists that it was well nigh impossible for anyone to distinguish the facts for certain.

Thanks to national publicity in newspapers, magazines and the radio, the truth has come out. When organizations continue to beat the drums of hatred, to warn of violence against returning Japanese Americans and then go out of their way to arouse unrest, it is obvious that there is more than patriotism behind their efforts. It is only too obvious that covetous eyes are being cast on the verdant fields— most of them developed out of wasteland by Japanese Americans—which evacuation forced their tenants to leave behind. Americans will not be fooled so easily hereafter by cries of wolf on this or other issues.

The Evacuation has been a tragic experience both for those who were affected directly and the nation as a whole. It is the duty of evacuees as Americans to see that an evacuation is never repeated on a racial or any other basis.

CHAPTER 4

The "Model Minority": Asian Americans After 1965

Chapter Preface

The years since 1965 constitute a new era in the history of Asian Americans, one with several distinguishing characteristics. The legal reforms of the 1950s and 1960s removed barriers to both immigration and naturalization for Asians. Because of these reforms, immigration from Asian countries increased greatly, both among ethnic groups already in the United States (Chinese, Filipinos, Koreans) as well as ethnic groups not previously well represented (Vietnamese, Asian Indians, and others). For the first time Asia surpassed Europe as a source of U.S. immigrants and refugees. This new era was also a time when the popular public image of Asian immigrants underwent a transformation from one of a threatening alien presence to that of a "model minority" characterized by intelligence, hard work, and economic success. The viewpoints in this chapter examine some of the debates surrounding these developments among Asian Americans.

Legislative reforms following World War II helped pave the way for the post-1965 era. The first step toward major immigration reform was the passage of the McCarran-Walter Act. The 1952 law removed racial barriers to naturalization, giving the right of citizenship to all immigrants. However, it maintained strict annual quotas on Asian immigration (generally one hundred immigrants per Asian country). The Immigration Act of 1965 went further, abolishing the national origins quota system entirely and giving high priority to the reunification of families and to skilled workers.

Asians proved to be the biggest beneficiaries of these reforms. The population of Asian Americans grew from 900,000 in 1960 to 3.5 million in 1980, and to almost 7.3 million in 1990. After Mexico, the leading sources of U.S. immigrants became the Philippines, Korea, China, and Vietnam. Beginning in 1975 a new wave of Asian refugees (people escaping from political persecution and war in their homeland) came to the United States. Most were from Vietnam and neighboring countries in Southeast Asia and were fleeing the aftermath of the Vietnam War.

While California is still home to more than a third of all Asian Americans, Asian immigrants have settled throughout the United States. They have become much more diverse in ethnic background, American acculturation, and degree of economic success. Chinese Americans, for example, have become an increasingly bifurcated group split between "ABCs" (American-born Chinese), many of whom are college-educated and live outside traditional China-towns, and "FOBs" (fresh off the boat), who are often poor and une-ducated and who live in Chinatowns and toil at low-wage jobs.

The social climate facing Asian Americans, be they newly ar-rived refugees or third- or fourth-generation Americans, has also significantly changed over the past few decades. In 1966, sociolo-gist William Petersen published an article on Japanese Americans in the *New York Times Magazine* in which he originated the term "model minority." Petersen argued that by hard work, cultural assimilation, family stability, and thrift, Japanese Americans had succeeded where other American minority groups had failed. During the 1970s and 1980s, the model minority label was ap-plied to Asian Americans in general in numerous studies and ar-ticles that highlighted the high median family incomes among Asian Americans, the exploits of Asian students in schools and colleges, and the growth of retail markets and businesses owned by Korean and other Asian Americans.

While some Asian Americans have embraced the model minor-ity label, others have criticized it and its implications. Some have objected to what historian Sucheng Chan has described as the un-derlying political agenda of "telling Black and Chicano activists that they should follow the example set by Asian Americans who work hard to pull themselves up by the bootstraps instead of us-ing militant protests to obtain their rights." Chan and others ar-gue that racism and discrimination still hamper the progress of even the most successful Asian Americans, that Asian Americans are still clustered in low-paying occupations such as janitorial and food service, and that they trail white Americans in personal income (as opposed to family income). Some Asian American ac-tivists assert that the model minority label is a stereotype that is as misleading to others and as confining to individual develop-ment as any other stereotype.

The anti-Asian sentiment that has been a large part of American politics since the nineteenth century plays a much smaller role to-day; exclusion of all Asians is no longer debated in Congress. The debates in this chapter reflect this shift in American thinking. However, whether Asian Americans are yet fully accepted within American society remains, for some, an open question. The 1982 brutal killing in Detroit of Vincent Chin, a Chinese American, by two unemployed white auto workers who thought he was Japanese, aroused much anger and frustration in many Asian Americans. The incident and the legal system's response (the two assailants were allowed to plea to manslaughter and avoid prison) were viewed by many as an indictment of a society that, despite all the notable changes of recent years, still has not fully accepted Asian Americans as equals.

VIEWPOINT 1

"A quiet, little-noted American success story [is] the almost total disappearance of discrimination against . . . Chinese- and . . . Japanese-Americans since the end of World War II."

Asian Americans No Longer Face Significant Discrimination

Fox Butterfield (b. 1939)

Beginning in the late 1960s and early 1970s, a number of American newspapers and magazines ran articles on the economic and social successes of Chinese and Japanese Americans. Typical of these articles is one by *New York Times* reporter Fox Butterfield, first published in December 1970 and reprinted here. (Butterfield later wrote the book *China: Alive in the Bitter Sea,* based on his experiences as a reporter in that country.)

Using personal interviews and other sources, Butterfield argues that the rampant discrimination Asian Americans faced in the past has largely vanished. Although vestiges of discrimination remain and some residents of the Chinese communities in New York and San Francisco remain isolated and impoverished, he writes, impressive numbers of Chinese and Japanese Americans have successfully assimilated into "the mainstream of American life."

When J. Chuan Chu came to the United States as a student at the end of World War II from his home in North China he had trouble finding a place to live. Having an Oriental face, he discovered, was a liability.

But Mr. Chu, with an engineering degree from the University of Pennsylvania, has now risen to become a vice-president of Honeywell Information Systems. He lives today in the wealthy Boston suburb of Wellesley, near his concern's headquarters. "If you have ability and can adapt to the American way of speaking, dressing, and doing things," Mr. Chu said recently, "then it doesn't matter anymore if you are Chinese."

His story reflects a quiet, little-noted American success story—the almost total disappearance of discrimination against the 400,000 Chinese- and 500,000 Japanese-Americans since the end of World War II and their assimilation into the mainstream of American life.

Some Chinese have been left behind in the nation's depressed Chinatown ghettos, unable to speak English or too old, too poorly educated, or too fixed in their traditional ways to be assimilated.

And some younger Asian-Americans have become increasingly sensitive, like blacks and Indians, to what they consider white Americans' patronizing attitude toward them. They resent the tourists in Chinatown who politely ask if they can speak English. They indignantly reject the old Oriental stereotype of the slant-eyed, pig-tailed Chinaman, eating chop suey and mumbling "Ah-so." And they insist that many whites, behind a façade of believing in equality, are still prejudiced.

But the great majority of Chinese- and Japanese-Americans, whose humble parents had to iron the laundry and garden the lawns of white Americans, no longer find any artificial barriers to becoming doctors, lawyers, architects, and professors.

Some have achieved national reputations, a feat unimaginable twenty years ago: I.M. Pei and Minoru Yamasaki as architects, Gerald Tsai as head of the Manhattan Fund; Tsung Dao Lee and Chen Ning Yang as Nobel Prize winners in physics; S.I. Hayakawa as president of San Francisco State College, and Daniel Inouye as Senator from Hawaii.

With one Senator and two Representatives, the Japanese may well be the nation's most overrepresented minority.

Few Complaints of Discrimination

In interviews with dozens of Chinese- and Japanese-Americans, from executives like Mr. Chu to militant students in Chinatown, very few complaints of discrimination in jobs, housing, or education could be found.

Many people below thirty could not recall a single personal instance of discrimination. The Los Angeles Housing Opportunities Center, which helps people who feel discriminated against, reports that it has had only one complaint from an Oriental in the last three years.

Some prejudice still exists. Mr. Chu, for example, was told last year that he would not be allowed to join the Wellesley Country Club.

A spokesman for the club, in a telephone interview, denied that the club discriminates against people of any race. He said that he could not recall Mr. Chu's case. However, he also said that the club at present had no members of Oriental ancestry.

The Model Minority

One of the earliest articles praising the Asian American work ethic appeared in U.S. News & World Report *on December 26, 1966.*

Visit "Chinatown U.S.A." and you find an important racial minority pulling itself up from hardship and discrimination to become a model of self-respect and achievement in today's America.

At a time when it is being proposed that hundreds of billions be spent to uplift Negroes and other minorities, the nation's 300,000 Chinese-Americans are moving ahead on their own—with no help from anyone else. . . .

Not all Chinese-Americans are rich. Many, especially recent arrivals from Hong Kong, are poor and cannot speak English. But the large majority are moving ahead by applying the traditional virtues of hard work, thrift and morality.

Most of the problems confronting Asian-Americans today are more subtle. Dr. Ai-li Chin, a Chinese sociologist at the Massachusetts Institute of Technology, who is doing a study of the Chinese experience in the United States, feels that "discrimination against Orientals has definitely diminished." "In any statement you make about prejudice you must be very careful," she feels. "But for most Chinese the problem is not so much physical barriers, as it is for blacks, as it is the question of identity. Who are you as a Chinese in the United States." This is particularly true, Dr. Chin believes, for the younger people who have grown up in the United States and have an Oriental face but do not speak their parents' language.

"Ironically, at the same time as prejudice has diminished, some of these younger people have now begun to become concerned about white Americans' attitudes toward them," Dr. Chin, a diminutive, soft-spoken woman points out. "They refuse to accept, as their parents did, the old humiliating Oriental stereotype."

Under the influence of the Black Panthers and Young Lords, some young Chinese have organized radical groups with names like the Boxers and the Red Guards to try to stop tourists from visiting New York's and San Francisco's Chinatowns. "This is our community, it is not a zoo" reads one sign in the Boxers' dingy store-front headquarters in New York.

Even the old stereotype, however, has undergone a metamorphosis. The pig-tailed coolie has been replaced in the imagination of many Americans by the earnest, bespectacled young scholar.

"My teachers have always helped me because they had such a good image of Chinese students," recalled Elaine Yuehy, a junior at Hunter College whose father used to run a laundry. "'Good little Chinese kid,' they said, 'so bright and so well behaved and hard-working.'" Her comment was echoed by many of those interviewed.

Past Discrimination

For many years, from the time the first Chinese came to California in the 1850s, prejudice and discrimination against Orientals were very real indeed. Many were barred from obtaining citizenship. In California, where the great majority settled, none born outside the United States were allowed to own land.

A report written by the San Francisco Board of Aldermen in 1854 typified the nineteenth-century American view. "The Chinese live in a manner similar to our savage Indians," the report said. "Their women are the most degraded prostitutes and the sole enjoyment of the male population is gambling." The aldermen recommended "the immediate expulsion of the whole Chinese race from the city."

The ultimate indignity came during World War II when thousands of Japanese on the West Coast were interned in concentration camps and their property sold for 10 cents on the dollar. Many Japanese-Americans feel that white Americans' guilt over the internment has helped lead to their increased acceptance since the end of the war.

Another factor, cited by Dr. Chin, "is the general growth in awareness of racial problems since the end of World War II." Dr. Chin points to the beneficial effect of the Negro civil rights movement, with its fair housing laws. The old California law barring foreign-born Orientals from owning land was ruled unconstitutional by the California State Supreme Court in 1952 after a test case brought by a Japanese lawyer. And the McCarran Act of 1952 made foreign-born Orientals eligible for citizenship.

177

Dr. Chin also feels that the respect Chinese and Japanese have gained by their recent achievements in the professions has helped ease discrimination. Where before the war San Francisco's Chinese were all crowded into Chinatown and Los Angeles' Japanese were confined to a small area in west Los Angeles, today they have spread out over all parts of their cities.

According to Jeffrey Matsui of the Japanese American Citizens League, Los Angeles, 150,000 Japanese have been able to move into exclusive communities like Bel Air, Beverly Hills, and Pacific Palisades. Two judges and the county coroner are Japanese. Mr. Matsui reported that although Japanese on the West Coast still have some difficulty finding executive or sales jobs, which require large amounts of personal contact, they have no trouble getting jobs as secretaries, accountants, doctors, or engineers. Before the war they were largely restricted to working as gardeners or small farmers.

The situation is much the same across the country. Chicago's 14,000 Japanese live in every section of the city and its suburbs. "There used to be discrimination here," said the Rev. Shinei Shigefuji, minister of the Midwest Buddhist Church, "but I don't think there's much now."

In the South, Orientals are now considered whites rather than Negroes. Young Chinese and Japanese growing up in such widely scattered areas as Richmond, Durham, N.C., and Atlanta remember attending white schools and going in the white entrance to movie theaters.

In Augusta, Georgia, where a group of Chinese laborers was brought in 1910 to dig the Augusta Canal, their descendants have gone to college and become pharmacists, doctors, and insurance salesmen: in its small way, a typical American immigrant success story.

Chinatown

But for the minority of Chinese who have not been assimilated, Chinatown, behind the glitter of its red-tile store fronts and pagodalike roofs is a slum. In San Francisco's Chinatown, with 50,000 people the nation's largest, 45 percent of the families live below the federal poverty level of a $3,700 annual income; 15 percent are unemployed; 60 percent share a bathroom with another family or have none at all.

Half of the people cannot speak or read English in the heart of Chinatown, nearly half have never been to school. Employment for many means long hours sewing dresses in backroom sweatshops at wages below the legal minimum.

Control in Chinatown rests as it always has with the mysterious family and district associations, ruled by elders who see no need to change their old patterns. Some younger Chinese radicals, like those in the Boxers and Red Guards, blame white racism for the situation. But discrimination appears to be much less of a factor than old age, preference for Chinese tradition, and difficulty with English. Japanese-Americans, who have not clung so closely to their traditional ways, have not encountered the Chinatown problem.

"We resent ignorant Americans coming in here and staring at us as if we were animals," explained Richard Lee, a twenty-year-old resident of New York's Chinatown. "But we're not really discriminated against. If you can speak English you can get through school and get a job like any American."

"We still have problems," said Mr. Lee, who wears blue jeans and lets his straight black hair grow long over his ears, "but they are more internal problems, problems of what you are, than of discrimination."

Looking around his tiny, cramped room at a picture of Raquel Welch, he said: "Our parents suppressed this identity problem for themselves, but we think about it a lot. Chinese have always considered that they are Chinese no matter where they are. Now we have to figure out what this means for us."

VIEWPOINT 2

"Prejudice against the Orientals in America . . . is still ubiquitous although now couched in very sophisticated, subtle forms."

Asian Americans Still Face Significant Discrimination

James W. Chin (dates unknown)

The 1965 repeal of Asian immigration exclusion laws and quotas, the federal civil rights legislation passed in the 1960s, and the success of many Chinese and Japanese Americans in achieving middle-class American lifestyles led several observers in the 1970s to conclude that Asian Americans no longer faced significant discrimination. In the following viewpoint, taken from a 1971 article in *East/West, the Chinese American Journal*, James W. Chin takes issue with this conclusion. Discrimination against Asian Americans has become more subtle, he argues, but it still remains a major problem. Asian Americans, he writes, should not be expected to shed their ethnic identity in order to fit into American society. Chin contends that, unlike their elders, younger generations of Asian Americans have refused to accept second-class citizenship and are increasingly demanding their civil rights.

Prejudice against the Orientals in America is no longer gross or blatant as in the past. Nevertheless, it is still ubiquitous although now couched in very sophisticated, subtle forms. Unfortunately,

James W. Chin, "The Subtlety of Prejudice," *East/West: The Chinese American Journal*, January 6, 1971.

to many observers not sensitive to the new nuances of prejudice, there is the frequent misinterpretation that there is no longer any discrimination against Orientals.

The *New York Times* article of December 13, 1970, by Fox Butterfield, is an example of such misinterpretation. There is no question that the racial milieu was more oppressive in the 1940s and 1950s, when many Chinese-Americans with bachelor's degrees and even advanced university degrees could not find work in white companies, and when they could not purchase homes in the "nicer" residential areas. But this improvement has not been achieved solely by "chance." Due to the civil rights legislation of 1964, reinforced by Executive Order 11246 of September 25, 1965, companies with government contracts (including Honeywell Information Systems and virtually all other major corporations) must now pursue an affirmative action program to hire, recruit, train, and promote minority group members.

Barriers Remain

Younger Asian-Americans—in contrast to their elders who were grateful just to be in America and who were also silent for fear of deportation—expect the full rights and privilege of citizenship, not second-class status. True, many Chinese, "whose humble parents had to iron the laundry and garden the lawns of white Americans," encounter fewer barriers to becoming doctors, lawyers, architects, and professors, but it is also true these same professionals have not been able to become members of the San Francisco Board of Supervisors, Board of Education, or any other key commissions. From private industry to government agencies, Orientals in San Francisco (despite their reputed superior educational qualifications and 14 percent population) still are underrepresented in executive, managerial, supervisory, sales, personnel, and highly paid craft positions such as ironworkers, operating engineers, plumbers, and electricians.

Like the Blacks and Chicanos, conditions have improved substantially within the last two decades and it is now easier to cite a few "success" stories. But a few cases, whether they be Willie Mays, Mayor Carl Stokes, Wilson Riles, S.I. Hayakawa, or Gerald Tsai, do not prove barriers are no longer in existence. More appropriately, the question should be posed, "Why is it that so few minorities have been able to 'make it' in the system?"

The *New York Times* article states, "It is interesting that in interviews with dozens of Chinese- and Japanese-Americans from executives . . . to militant students in Chinatown, very few complaints of discrimination in jobs, housing, or education could be found." Perhaps if the *New York Times* would have sent a representative to the FEPC [Fair Employment Practices Commission]

181

hearing in San Francisco on December 10 [, 1970], when over twenty individuals testified for three hours on problems of discrimination faced by Chinese-Americans, the conclusion drawn would have been a different one.

Racial Violence

Washington, D.C.-based writer Karl Zinsmeister wrote of increasing incidents of violence and prejudice against Asian Americans in the July/August 1987 issue of Public Opinion.

Figures from the Justice Department show a 62 percent increase in anti-Asian incidents from 1984 to 1985. In Los Angeles County, Asians were targets of an astounding 50 percent of the racial incidents in 1986 (versus 15 percent in 1985). In Boston, a city where Asian-Americans make up a small fraction of the population, 29 percent of racial crimes recorded by police were committed against Asian-Americans in the latest year, compared to just 2 percent five years earlier. Given their low numbers, inner-city Asian-Americans have been exposed to relatively high rates of racial harassment.

On Christmas Eve 1986 in Revere, Massachusetts, arsonists burned down a house sheltering twenty-eight Cambodian immigrants. The incident was one in a dramatic series of anti-Asian attacks in Revere, a working-class suburb of Boston. Rock and brick throwing at Southeast Asian immigrants are everyday occurrences in the town. A long string of beatings, vandalism, and attacks on property, carried out mostly by white teenagers, dates back several years. A neighbor of one Southeast Asian family complained to a *Wall Street Journal* reporter, "Immigrants used to come from countries nearly as civilized as the United States. These people come from jungle communities." His street, he says, "looks like a refugee camp." A former Revere city councilor whispers that, "The rumor, strictly a rumor, is that they eat dogs."

It is indeed unfortunate that many Orientals, who have been the direct beneficiaries of state-federal programs for equal employment opportunities, are not aware of the forces which have opened up the doors to job opportunity. It is not simply a case of, "If you have ability and can adapt to the American way of speaking, dressing, and doing things, then it doesn't matter any more if you are Chinese." Quite the contrary. Equal Employment Opportunity programs have stressed to corporations the obligation to be more tolerant of the cultural diversity presented by the various ethnic groups and subcultures of the society whether it be a Black with an Afro (hairdo) or an Oriental with an accent. For example, corporations are required to eliminate culturally biased tests such as the Wonderlic unless the tests can be demonstrated to be directly related to actual performance required on the job. In addition, minority group members have frequently been added to recruitment and promotional panels to ensure greater objectivity and to reduce the chances of racial or cultural bias. Most importantly, corporations must now set goals and timetables to consciously and deliberately seek out minority group applicants in areas where there is a current underutilization.

Issues of Identity and
Discrimination Are Inseparable

The *New York Times* notes that many Chinese may unknowingly perceive a crisis of identity rather than prejudice. In reality, however, the issues of discrimination, identity, and alienation are closely interconnected and in many ways inseparable. Identity crises exist because Orientals are told that if they just act white, they will be treated accordingly, but subconsciously they know that being Chinese still means they will not be allowed to join the Elks Club, "Wellesley Country Club," etc. Even if they should live in a wealthy, exclusive suburb armed with a university degree, professional licence, and great hope, the question persists whether they will be treated and accepted as equals.

We all know of many Orientals who in their quest for acceptance have rejected their Oriental identity and heritage. It is indeed a heavy price to pay for admission to a group that one must reject one's own background since this is a form of self-hatred. Even more vital and critical, Orientals are distinguished by certain physical traits and characteristics unique to Orientals. Even if an Oriental should go to the extreme of changing his name from Wong to Wright, and have surgery performed to make his eyes more oval in conformity to Western ideals of beauty, there will always be some Caucasian who will remind him that "all Orientals look alike."

VIEWPOINT 3

"The American dream is real and can come true."

Korean American Entrepreneurship Is an Indication of Economic Success

Elizabeth Mehren (dates unknown)

Korean immigrants first came to the United States in 1903, when a small number were imported to work the sugar plantations in Hawaii (then a U.S. territory). A second influx of Koreans immigrated to America following the Korean War. However, Koreans did not enter the United States in significant numbers until after immigration laws were liberalized in 1965. Between 1960 and 1985 the Korean American population grew from ten thousand to half a million. Much of this immigration wave consisted of college-educated professionals and middle-class families.

Beginning in the 1970s, Korean Americans became highly visible in several cities, including New York and Los Angeles, as owners of family businesses, such as liquor stores, wig shops, and especially fruit and vegetable markets. Numerous articles in the 1970s and 1980s held up Korean Americans as examples of how new immigrants enrich American society and achieve economic success through frugality and hard work. In the following viewpoint, taken from a 1987 newspaper article, *Los Angeles Times* staff writer Elizabeth Mehren profiles one such Korean entrepreneur who successfully established a grocery store in New York.

Elizabeth Mehren, "Success Saga in America: Korean Style," *Los Angeles Times*, August 12, 1987. Copyright, 1987, Los Angeles Times. Reprinted with permission.

As a boy in Korea, Chung U Chon dreamed of the good life, the life he knew he would find in America. He dreamed of big houses, cars, an important job and many people working for him. Someday, he told his parents and his six brothers, he would move to America and make that dream a reality.

The day he moved his wife and three children into their $75-a-month, fifth-floor walkup apartment in Brooklyn 11 years ago, that dream played over and over in Chung's head. There was no hot water, and only a large vat to bathe in. The walls were filthy, and at any moment, the ceiling threatened a cave-in. Chung's wife, Sun, burst into tears. "You made us sell our house in Korea for this?" she accused him. "For this life?"

Late that night, when Chung finally prepared to fall asleep, mice scampered across the pillow.

Now, surveying his corner kingdom in Manhattan's Washington Heights neighborhood, greengrocer Chung can smile at the irony of those memories.

His days still begin with a trip to the big wholesale produce center in the Bronx at 3:30 a.m., and each day Chung is still in his store, the California Fruit Market, when it closes at 7 o'clock at night.

But now Chung oversees six employees. From the 18-hour days she worked when they first entered the produce business, his wife has cut back to a less grueling schedule, sometimes even taking days off at midweek. They have a four-bedroom house in Norwood, N.J., and an assortment of shiny cars. Two children are in college; the third recently completed nursing school. Chung, 49, has become an American citizen, still debating how he will register for his first presidential election in 1988. Not long ago, he took up golf.

These days Chung presides over a lush cornucopia lining the sidewalk at 183rd Street and St. Nicholas Avenue: corn, cucumbers, cabbage, beets, broccoli, bananas—his inventory reads like the produce section in Eden.

Pausing one recent morning after straightening a box of nectarines, Chung tossed a peach in the air, caught it, and bit into it with wicked delight. From under his blue baseball cap, a grin spread across his face.

"In this country, you still got a lot of chances," Chung said. "You want to make money here, you can make money. You can do anything in this country."

Then he added what might have been an endorsement for the ethic on which America was founded.

"If you work hard," he said. "Work *very* hard."

In New York, the prospect of round-the-clock shifts selling

foodstuffs that are often foreign to their own culture has not deterred thousands of Chung's countrymen from taking over the leases of small groceries and delicatessens that fall idle with an owner's death or retirement.

In the space of a decade, at least 1,300 such stores in New York's five boroughs have been turned over to Korean ownership. All around the city, entire families of Koreans make tending them a group experience: Grandmother on the sidewalk, peeling vegetables for the salad bar; wife at the cash register; husband loading boxes; children straightening the displays; grandfather watching over the buckets of flowers. In Manhattan, "the Koreans'" has come to be the short name for the corner fruit-and-vegetable store.

©Rafael Macia/Photo Researchers, Inc.

During the 1970s and 1980s immigrants from Korea and other Asian countries established a large presence in several American cities, including Flushing, Queens, New York City.

Almost no one spoke Korean when Chung U Chon began haunting the Bronx's wholesale produce center 11 years ago. His own English was so shaky then, and his familiarity with American taste in produce so limited, that he had friends write down the names of particular items in English so he could show the list to the wholesalers.

"Navel oranges," he said. "I never knew there was more than one kind of orange. Peppers. I never knew there were so many varieties."

Now Chung estimates that 70% of the merchants who pull up to the warehouses at 3 and 3:30 in the morning are Koreans. "All around you, what you hear spoken is Korean," he said.

New Korean immigrants gravitated to the fruit and vegetable business because they are "labor-oriented and very hard-working," Eugene Kang, executive director of the Korean Produce Assn. Inc., said.

"Before the Korean immigrants landed in this city, who were the greengrocers?" Kang asked. "Most likely, they were Jewish and Italian, along with Greeks."

But those ethnic groups fell prey to the third-generation syndrome, Kang said, where sons-of-sons of immigrants were not willing to labor long hours in a business decidedly lacking in glamour.

"The Jews and Italians and Greeks, they are third generation now," Kang said. "They want to go to law school. They are no longer taking care of father's business, which was greengrocer."

Like Chung U Chon, many of the Koreans who set up as greengrocers are college-educated. As Chung did in 1974, they often arrive carrying their life's savings, sometimes tens of thousands of dollars or more. Because so many Korean emigrants send generous amounts of money to their relatives at home, South Korea's government encourages the tide of its citizens to this country by offering free language lessons, job training and orientation programs.

Coming to America

For Chung, no such opportunities existed when he uprooted his family and headed to the United States. Once a language student at the University of Seoul, he had supplanted his schoolboy's English by palling around with GIs in Korea. But Sun spoke no English, not one word.

Chung first chose to settle in Washington, where he had friends. Having worked in hotel management in Korea, he quickly landed a job at Washington's Statler Hilton Hotel, earning "$160, $170 a week, about the same as in Korea." Sun, a housewife in Korea, went to work as a busgirl in a cafeteria in the mornings, and as a housemaid in the afternoons, earning half as much.

Expenses were high. They had to buy a car, and rent, clothes and food cost far more than they had expected.

"We thought it would be cheaper here," Chung said. "But surprise, much more expensive."

In a year and a half they watched the $20,000 life's savings they had brought from Korea dwindle to $6,000.

Panicked, Chung flew to California to visit a Korean friend who had a 7-Eleven franchise in San Jose. The whole family worked in the store, his friend told him, spreading their shifts through the

187

day. Chung was impressed; he submitted his own application for a California fast-food-store franchise.

But on a last-minute whim after he returned to Washington, Chung decided that before he left, he wanted to see New York. One Sunday, he and a friend climbed in the car and headed up Route 95.

"We came out the Holland Tunnel, right into Chinatown," Chung said, eyes widening at the recollection. Chung thought he was home at last. "It looked just like Seoul at that time."

In 24 hours, Chung changed his mind. He would move the family to New York, not California.

"All the people here, in New York, they told me it was better here than in California," he said. "They said you don't need a car, they got a subway. Apartments are cheap. You can take the bus. All this kind of story I hear from people here."

Yet another Korean friend knew a woman who wanted to sell her corner fruit-and-vegetable store in Brooklyn. Chung negotiated, and for $5,000, the place was his.

"I didn't look around, I didn't know where was Brooklyn, where was Manhattan, where was the highway," Chung said.

"I felt like I had no more chances, like 'this is it. This is my last chance.' I'd given up my job, I'd canceled California. I couldn't go back to Korea, not like that.

"At that time," Chung said, looking prosperous now in his La-Coste shirt and pleated chino pants, "I was maybe a little crazy."

Hard Beginnings

But he was also determined. On his first day of work, Chung learned that the workday of a greengrocer starts with choosing the merchandise and hauling the merchandise—three hours after midnight. By 7 a.m., he and his wife were opening their doors in a neighborhood where Spanish was as likely to be spoken as English.

Sun Y Chon had never worked a cash register, and neither she nor her husband knew how to use a scale. Sun's English was nonexistent. To explain a price, she would point to the figure on the cash register. In rapid-fire English and Spanish, impatient customers demanded fruits and vegetables the couple had never heard of in either language.

"One month later, I could not move my fingers," Chung said. "I could not pick up my pants and put them on. I never worked so hard in my life."

Exhausted each night after they closed, the pair retreated to their apartment, the awful fifth-floor walkup with the mice. They fed the children, enrolled by now in a nearby parochial school, put them to bed and contemplated the feeble family finances.

"During the day, we worked so hard we don't know how much

money we were making, how much we were losing," Chung said. "We just kept running the store."

For three years, they worked that pace, day in, day out.

"Never a day off. Only Sundays, we went to church. That was it," Chung said. "No movies, no restaurants. We were just too tired to do anything."

Koreatown

A May 26, 1975, article in Newsweek *describes the burgeoning Korean community in Los Angeles, California.*

It's called Koreatown, a 2-mile stretch along Los Angeles's busy Olympic Boulevard, where 45,000 Korean immigrants have settled into new lives during the last five years. What used to be Mexican-American, Japanese and Jewish stores and businesses are now mostly Korean, with giant Oriental letters spread across their low-slung storefronts. Packed into the houses and apartments just off Olympic is a complicated Oriental society driven by a mix of aspirations as American as Coca-Cola. Here dozens of Asian visions of the American dream are being played out, and here too may be some clues as to what will ultimately happen to the newest Americans, the Vietnamese refugees. . . .

Today, there are about 1,400 Korean-owned businesses in Los Angeles, including gas stations, insurance agencies and travel companies. There are 58 restaurants serving Korean food, 150 grocery stores, 26 martial-arts schools, two Korean hospitals, exchange banks, nightclubs, academies that teach traditional Korean dance, and the Korean Philharmonic Orchestra. The community has five newspapers, two radio stations and even two UHF television stations that operate on weekends.

Chung vowed he would make some changes the minute things turned around.

"As soon as I made some money, I was going to move to California," he said. "California had to be a better life."

Changing Fortunes

But Chung's fortunes did begin to change. The family amassed savings of nearly $40,000. Chung began looking for a house, and finally bought a $130,000 place in New Jersey, about 15 miles from the George Washington Bridge. For Christmas that year, 1979, he gave his wife a key to the still-unfinished house.

"All my friends in church, they were very surprised because I was making money so fast," Chung said. "They knew that store. Three or four owners before me, nobody had made any money in that store." He smiled. "Maybe they did not work so hard."

"Every time they see me," Chung said of his acquaintances from their Korean-speaking Catholic church in Queens, "they call me the Hard Work Man."

Eventually Chung sold the Brooklyn store for $15,000 more than he had paid for it and bought a larger one in the Bronx. Then he began to set his eye on his current property, the California Fruit Market, in a Manhattan neighborhood composed largely of older Jewish residents and younger Spanish-speaking people.

Three years ago, Chung sold the Bronx store to concentrate his time and energy on the market in Manhattan. He does not like to talk about how much money he actually makes, and insists that high rent, salaries for his six employees and other expenses gobble up the profits. Even the 35% markup he charges over wholesale price barely covers his costs, he says.

"Right now, we save no money," he said. "You're lucky to break even now."

Eugene Kang, of the Korean Produce Assn., agrees that hefty profits are not necessarily a byproduct of the business. "I don't think it is so profitable," Kang said. "Believe me, it is not easy. They work very, very hard."

"That is the main thing," Chung concurred. "You've got to work so many hours. All the Korean grocers here, they all work 15-, 16-, 17-hour days, with their families. But employees, they don't want to work that hard, that long."

Chung even advised his own brothers not to follow in his path and move to America. "I tell them they have to work too hard," he said.

For Chung the day is a constant barrage of questions. "Where are the rutabagas?" "How much are the leeks?" "Do you have cilantro?" "Where's the fresh basil?" There are boxes to be filled, displays to be arranged, bruised produce to be disposed of.

Some customers haggle over prices. Others plead for free food. From a steady client, Chung will trade a ripe plum for the promise of a quarter.

Now Chung converses comfortably in Spanish, speaking easily to customers and his four Latino employees alike. Working the cash register, Sun Y Chon is less uncomfortable speaking English now.

The Next Generation

When they are in town, all three Chung children will sometimes work in the family store. Christine, 19, is studying international business at the University of Chicago. Clara, 24, has just finished nursing school. At 22, Augustine (also known by his Korean name, Jin-soo, or by his American nickname, Jake), is majoring in business at a small college on Staten Island, and studying for his real estate license.

Chung jokes that his children speak Korean with a Bronx accent. Last summer, he sent them all to their home country for a long visit, their first since they left 13 years ago. They found it interesting, Chung said, but showed no interest in remaining.

"I'm just more comfortable here," said Jake, a strapping youth with gel-treated hair and hopes of becoming a New York real estate tycoon. "This is home."

Chung, lord of his small urban empire of mangoes and melons, grapefruits and green beans, would be hard pressed to disagree. America has been good to him, he said, and the American dream is real and can come true.

"Right now I am happy here," Chung said. "I've had no trouble until—" abruptly he brightened, "until last month when I got one speeding ticket."

Chung laughed hard. All those years of endless toil, mice on the pillowcases, fingers that went on strike. All those trips to the Bronx produce warehouse in the middle of the night. All the confusion, the strange fruits, learning to count in Spanish. All that, and his one complaint is a speeding ticket?

There was a big smile on Chung's face as he calmly helped himself to a strawberry. He had earned it, after all.

VIEWPOINT 4

"Small businesses of Asian Americans must be viewed as what they really are—a form of underemployment and a source of cheap labor."

Korean American Entrepreneurship Is an Indication of Economic Exploitation

Joseph S. Chung (b. 1929)

Korean Americans, one of America's fastest growing ethnic groups, have acquired a reputation as successful small-business entrepreneurs. A 1984 survey by the Korean Chamber of Commerce of Southern California counted seven thousand Korean–owned businesses in Los Angeles County alone. Whether these small businesses represent a path to success (and a model for other American minority groups) is a matter of dispute, however.

The following viewpoint is excerpted from a paper that Joseph S. Chung, a professor emeritus of economics at Illinois Institute of Technology at Chicago, first presented at a 1979 conference on the civil rights of Asian and Pacific Americans, which was sponsored by the United States Commission on Civil Rights. Chung argues that, far from being a symbol of success, small-business entrepreneurship is instead often a form of underemployment for Korean immigrants. Many of the Korean immigrants who end up working as shopowners or greengrocers are highly educated doctors, professors, and pharmacists who, Chung asserts, cannot find employment in their professions because of discrimination. These small-business owners often work long hours for relatively low pay, he maintains.

Abridged from Joseph S. Chung, "Small Ethnic Business as a Form of Disguised Unemployment and Cheap Labor," in *Civil Rights Issues of Asian and Pacific Americans: Myths and Realities* (Washington, DC: U.S. Commission on Civil Rights, 1979). Reprinted by permission of the author.

Exclusion of Asian/Pacific Americans from full participation in the economic, social, and political life in the United States has been attributable to various forms of discrimination against them. Discrimination, in turn, has often been the byproduct of myths and stereotypes, both negative and positive. Further, these stereotypes have acted as obstacles in dealing effectively with the problems and needs of the Asian ethnic communities. The magnitude and complexity of their needs have multiplied since the large influx of Asian immigrants resulting from the 1965 amendments to the Immigration and Naturalization Act and the 1975 inflow of Indochinese refugees. Ironically, it is frequently the positive public image of typecasting Asians as successful minorities who have no serious problems and hence require no special assistance that does no less harm.

A particular example of problems created by positive stereotyping of Asian Americans is found in the area of Asian ethnic business. It deals with the public image of Asians as successful businessmen. The public points to the size and number of little Tokyos, Chinatowns, little Manilas, and Koreatowns in major cities around the U.S. as evidence. In recent years, for example, the growing small ethnic enterprises in Koreatowns, particularly in and around Olympic Avenue in Los Angeles, have often been cited in the news media and in popular magazines as symbols of the success of new immigrants from Asia. Going further, some even suggest that Korean immigrants serve as models for other newcomers such as Vietnamese refugees.

It is the contention of this testimony that the so-called success of Asian business is only a myth, and that in reality the preponderance of small business among the Asian Americans represents symptoms of underlying fundamental problems that the new Asian immigrants face in their newly adopted country. Further, small businesses of Asian Americans must be viewed as what they really are—a form of underemployment and a source of cheap labor. . . .

Asian Businesses

Asian business enterprises are very small in scale, concentrated in retail trade dealing with a narrow range of products and services requiring small amount of capital. The most popular Asian family enterprises are ethnic grocery stores and restaurants, short order and fast food restaurants, wig shops, laundries, insurance and travel agencies, gas stations, establishments teaching martial arts, liquor stores, TV and appliance repair shops, and the like. Most of these show a high degree of ethnic homogeneity, that is, their business transactions are chiefly confined to people who are coethnics. The owner/managers of Asian business establishments tend to be very highly educated.

According to a survey conducted in 1972 by the U.S. Bureau of the Census, of a total of 1,201 business enterprises owned by Koreans, 45.0 percent were located in California which led all other States. The Los Angeles–Long Beach area had the most concentration of Korean firms with 33.1 percent of the 1,201 total located in the areas. The small scale of the Korean ethnic enterprise can be surmised by the fact that only 249 firms employed paid workers and that the average number of employees per firm was six. Average gross receipts per year was $64,839. There were more retail stores than any other type of business. Of the total 736 firms reported by the 9 standard metropolitan statistical areas (SMSA), 335 firms (45.5 percent) were engaged in the retail business.

Overrepresentation of Korean business by retail trade is confirmed in a survey of Korean business firms in Los Angeles County in 1975–76 by Ivan Light. Out of a total of 1,142 firms listed in the Korean business directory, 550 firms were engaged in retail trade, showing a margin of Korean overrepresentation in retail trade of 193.1 percent (of the expected number based on industrial distribution of the base business population in Los Angeles County).

The 1975 survey by [Hyung-Chan] Kim of 52 Korean retail business enterprises in Chicago, Honolulu, Los Angeles, and the San Francisco Bay Area also confirms findings by the Census Bureau and offers significant new information on the nature of Asian business in the U.S. Sizes of the retail stores in the survey are small with an average of 2.46 paid workers. Twenty enterprises out of 52, or 38.5 percent, had no paid workers. A majority of the enterprises in the sample started with a small amount of initial capital. Out of 50 firms reporting the information, 23 (46.0 percent) started with less than $10,000 and 34 firms representing 62.0 percent started with an initial capital of less than $15,000. Only 7 firms reported an initial capital of more than $30,000.

H. Kim's survey reveals that the owner/managers of Korean retail stores are a very highly educated group. An overwhelming majority, 71.2 percent of them finished 4 or more years of college. Reflecting their high educational background, most had professional and managerial positions before they immigrated to the U.S. All respondents, with the exception of one person, switched professions since arriving in the U.S. Eight former teachers in Korea represented the largest single group for professionals in Korea. Most of them were high school teachers or college instructors. One, a former college professor, now operates a service station. An overwhelming proportion of the total, 71.2 percent, resided in the U.S. 3 years or less before they started their business. They were rather young: 61.5 percent were between the age bracket of 36–45.

Koreans and Blacks

One important aspect of the experiences of Korean immigrants has been their relationship with African Americans. Many of the small stores owned by Korean Americans are located in black communities, and tension has often arisen between the two ethnic groups. Historian Gary H. Okihiro recounts some representative incidents in his 1994 book Margins and Mainstreams.

Between 1985 and 1990 in New York City, there were three major protests against Korean storeowners in African communities, while in Los Angeles, as one boycott ended in the summer of 1991, another began, and within a six-month period, five Korean grocery stores were firebombed. In a Los Angeles courtroom, the television monitors showed fifteen-year-old Latasha Harlins punch Soon Ja Du and turn to leave the store, when Du lifts a gun and fires point-blank at Harlins's head, killing her. On December 15, 1991, Yong Tae Park died of bullet wounds received during a robbery on his liquor store the previous day; Park was the seventh Korean storeowner killed in Los Angeles by African male suspects that year. "Black Power. No Justice, No Peace! Boycott Korean Stores! The Battle for Brooklyn," the poster read. "Crack, the 'housing crisis,' and Korean merchants is a conspiracy to destabilize our community. . . . The Korean merchants are agents of the U.S. government in their conspiracy to destabilize the economy of our community. They are rewarded by the government and financed by big business." In south central Los Angeles in April and May 1992, following the acquittal of police officers in the beating of African American Rodney G. King, Koreatown was besieged, eighteen-year-old Edward Song Lee died in a hail of bullets, nearly fifty Korean merchants were injured, and damage to about 2,000 Korean stores topped $400 million.

Light's study also indicates a high degree of ethnic homogeneity of business. He found, for example, in the case of transactions dealing with liquor licenses, 79.0 percent of Korean sellers of liquor licenses found Korean buyers even though Koreans represented only 15.0 percent of all buyers. Light's explanation of high ethnic homogeneity are: enhanced trust resulting from the mutual sympathy of coethnics, convenience arising from the propensity of ethnics, to associate with one another, and advertisement in the ethnic press. Whatever the reasons, a high level of ethnic homogeneity must be regarded as a growth-limiting factor for Asian businesses beyond the initial stage of development. High ethnic homogeneity is particularly severe for the Korean group as compared to the Chinese and Japanese, as Light points out.

Ethnic homogeneity is even higher within the Koreatowns. There most business establishments are geared for retailing of immediate daily necessities of the Koreans and related services. For this reason the growth of Koreatowns is highly positively correlated to the growth of the Korean immigrant population.

A Form of Cheap Labor

While the undocumented workers, particularly from Mexico, have received national attention as a potential source of cheap labor, a new form of imported cheap labor has emerged. This arises from a high propensity on the part of new immigrants from Asia to enter small ethnic business. Edna Bonacich hypothesizes that such small business is a disguised form of cheap labor for the following reasons. To begin with, the owner/operator tends to work long hours, often under poor working conditions. In addition, his profit margin and, hence, his equivalent wage is low. Further, he is helped by unpaid family labor—his spouse and children. Even those few businesses large enough to employ nonfamily paid workers often maintain paternalistic relations with these employees, resulting in long hours of work and low pay. The low profit margin, no doubt, is attributable to the small scale, limited market, concentration in retail and service trade, severe competition, lack of managerial know-how, and the like. To be sure, these characteristics apply to small business in general whether they are operated by the native Americans or by new immigrants. But it is the unusually high propensity of Asian Americans who enter small business that poses special problems for the new group particularly in view of their higher-than-national-average educational and professional/managerial background.

Why Koreans Enter Small Business

In a recent [1979] survey of Koreans in Los Angeles, [Changsoo] Lee and [Hiroshi] Wagatsuma found that out of 23,908 Koreans in the labor force, 10,796, or 45 percent, were self-employed. The comparable figure for the national average is a mere 9 percent.

What explains this high rate of Korean immigrants who enter small business? The following are typically mentioned as responsible for the trend. All these factors act as handicaps in the labor markets, and, as a result, conspire against the new immigrants' efforts to obtain jobs commensurate with their education and employment experiences. First, there is the severe language barrier which most Asian immigrants face. For example, in the 1970 census 76 percent of all Koreans in the U.S. listed Korean as their mother tongue. The proportion was even higher, naturally, for the foreign-born Korean Americans. These figures are much higher than those of other Asian groups with the exception of the Chinese. The linguistic handicap of Koreans has been worsening since 1970 due to the increasing number of Korean immigrants. . . . Kim's sample of Korean retail businessmen listed poor English as one of the most difficult problems they faced, followed by severe competition among Korean fellow retail traders and lack of capital.

The second factor is job discrimination. Although the covert nature of its practice makes discrimination difficult to prove, many Asians, nevertheless, feel they have been subjected to it. Often discrimination takes the subtle form of requiring from Asian applicants more credentials than the job normally requires. Few Asians ever reach the supervisory and management level positions, and they feel this is due to discrimination. The [Bok-Lim C.] Kim-[Margaret E.] Condon field survey of Chicago showed that Korean and Filipino respondents both felt they experienced job-related discrimination. Being passed over for promotion seems to be an important facet of discrimination as 27.3 percent of Korean respondents in the study stated they experienced this form of discrimination while 14.5 percent of the sample said they were discriminated against in housing. . . . A questionnaire administered in 1971 at the meeting of Korean Residents Association of Southern California revealed that the sense of discrimination was positively correlated with the length of residence in the U.S. Thus, more oldtimers felt discrimination than did newcomers. This may partially be due to the newcomers' relative satisfaction with their standard of living in comparison with that which they left behind in Korea. Thus, in the beginning, their reference is to Koreans in Korea. As time goes on they begin to compare themselves with the mainstream of American life. This tends to create feelings of general discontent which, in turn, lead to an awareness of an income-education-occupation gap.

The fourth is the refusal by the appropriate agencies in the U.S. to recognize Asian education and training. This is particularly true of health-related professionals such as physicians, dentists, nurses, and pharmacists. Although they are given preference by immigration laws, once in the country their educational credentials are questioned, their training is unaccepted, and their certifications are not recognized. The fifth factor is the low cost of wives and, particularly, children. A labor intensive family business is an easy and readymade source for employment for everyone in the family whose employability outside the family business is severely limited.

Faced with these overwhelming handicaps in the labor market and the ready availability of family labor, many a newcomer turns to small business as an alternative in spite of their high educational and professional qualifications. No wonder the recurrent and persistent aspiration of many Asian immigrants is to start a business of their own.

Disguised Poverty

It is clear that the public image of Asian success in business is only a myth. Owing to severe handicaps in obtaining jobs consistent with their qualifications, the majority of Asian immigrants enter into business simply because there are few other alternatives. An unusually high propensity of new Asian immigrants entering business must be regarded as a form of underemployment and a source of cheap labor. These businesses are mostly small in scale, dealing with ethnic and labor-intensive products, buying and selling principally with coethnics, and demand long and arduous hours from both the owner/managers and family members. Some community leaders claim that many of these ventures fail because too many go into business without the prior experience or management training necessary to run a business of their own. In the haste to escape low paying jobs, many start business with inadequate planning. Moreover, competition from fellow ethnic businessmen is severe.

The preponderance of small business, in reality [, writes Hyong-Chan Kim], is "more a symbol of disguised poverty than of marked success." In the words of [Ivan Light,] a longtime student of Asian enterprises in the U.S., "Koreans have not struck it rich in business or demonstrated a rags-to-riches success story in the Alger tradition. They have, however, developed nearly twice as many retail stores in proportion to their number as have other Los Angeles residents."

Corrective Measures

The first corrective measure to rectify the employment difficulties of Asian/Pacific Americans is to educate the general public and government agencies with regard to the Asian image. Any programs dealing with assisting the Asians must start from a full realization of the problems they face. In this particular case, the myth surrounding the success of Asian Americans in business must be destroyed. Asian businesses in the U.S. must be seen for what they really are. For this reason I recommend that appropriate Federal agencies publish, for wide general public consumption, literature concerning the real story of Asian business. Next, appropriate Federal agencies should take immediate steps to collect data to appraise the specific needs of the Asian communities. Third, Federal agencies concerned must take special notice and actions to remedy factors that limit accessibility of Asians to the labor market such as job discrimination. Funds must be provided to make English classes widely and easily available to new immigrants in order to reduce language as a labor market handicap. Fourth, I recommend that the appropriate Federal agencies provide funding and programs to assist Asian businessmen in the area of management training for the purpose of reducing business failures and increasing profitability. These programs must be given bilingually if they are to be effective. They must be staffed by experts who know the special problems faced by Asians. Federal agencies concerned must increase funding to collect data and analyze the pattern of employment, underemployment, and unemployment of Asian Americans as well as their pattern of income distribution.

Lastly, I recommend that the appropriate Federal agencies collect data and study the pattern of ethnic Asian business enterprises. Such a study must deal with tracing the process by which Asians enter business and accumulate savings as well as analyzing the causes of successes and failure in their business ventures, the commodity structure and size distribution, and educational and other background of the ethnic entrepreneurs.

VIEWPOINT 5

"In light of . . . history, the current problems of the Asian-American community seem relatively minor, and its success appears even more remarkable."

Asian Americans Represent an American Success Story

David A. Bell (dates unknown)

Emigration from Asian countries greatly increased following the lifting of immigration restrictions in 1965. By the 1980s it was apparent to many observers that the Asian American population in the United States was growing fast both in numbers and in educational and economic advancement. The following viewpoint is taken from "The Triumph of Asian-Americans," a 1985 article published in the *New Republic*. David A. Bell, a former reporter-researcher for the journal, examines Asian immigration and its effects on the United States over the previous two decades. He argues that Asian Americans have built an astonishing record of achievement in education, economics, and politics. Bell draws a sharp contrast between Asian Americans' recent success and America's prior record of racial discrimination against Asians. While Bell concedes that some Asian ethnic groups suffer from poverty and cultural disorientation and that all Asian Americans must cope with problems of assimilation, he concludes that developments since 1965 have been positive overall for both Asian Americans and the nation as a whole.

David A. Bell, "The Triumph of Asian-Americans," *New Republic*, July 15 & 22, 1985.
Reprinted by permission of the *New Republic*, ©1985, The New Republic, Inc.

It is the year 2019. In the heart of downtown Los Angeles, massive electronic billboards feature a model in a kimono hawking products labeled in Japanese. In the streets below, figures clad in traditional East Asian peasant garb hurry by, speaking to each other in an English made unrecognizable by the addition of hundreds of Spanish and Asian words. A rough-mannered policeman leaves an incongruously graceful calling card on a doorstep: a delicate origami paper sculpture.

This is, of course, a scene from a science-fiction movie, Ridley Scott's 1982 *Blade Runner*. It is also a vision that Asian-Americans dislike intensely. Hysterical warnings of an imminent Asian "takeover" of the United States stained a whole century of their 140-year history in this country, providing the backdrop for racial violence, legal segregation, and the internment of 110,000 Japanese-Americans in concentration camps during World War II. Today integration into American society, not transformation of American society, is the goal of an overwhelming majority. So why did the critics praise *Blade Runner* for its "realism"? The answer is easy to see.

The Asian-American population is exploding. According to the Census Bureau, it grew an astounding 125 percent between 1970 and 1980, and now stands at 4.1 million, or 1.8 percent of all Americans. Most of the increase is the result of immigration, which accounted for 1.8 million people between 1973 and 1983, the last year for which the Immigration and Naturalization Service has accurate figures (710,000 of these arrived as refugees from Southeast Asia). And the wave shows little sign of subsiding. Ever since the Immigration Act of 1965 permitted large-scale immigration by Asians, they have made up over 40 percent of all newcomers to the United States. Indeed, the arbitrary quota of 20,000 immigrants per country per year established by the act has produced huge backlogs of future Asian-Americans in several countries, including 120,000 in South Korea and 336,000 in the Philippines, some of whom, according to the State Department, have been waiting for their visas since 1970.

The numbers are astonishing. But even more astonishing is the extent to which Asian-Americans have become prominent out of all proportion to their share of the population. It now seems likely that their influx will have as important an effect on American society as the migrations from Europe of 100 years ago. Most remarkable of all, it is taking place with relatively little trouble.

The new immigration from Asia is a radical development in several ways. First, it has not simply enlarged an existing Asian-American community, but created an entirely new one. Before

1965, and the passage of the Immigration Act, the term "Oriental-American" (which was then the vogue) generally denoted people living on the West Coast, in Hawaii, or in the Chinatowns of a few large cities. Generally they traced their ancestry either to one small part of China, the Toishan district of Kwantung province, or to a small number of communities in Japan (one of the largest of which, ironically, was Hiroshima). Today more than a third of all Asian-Americans live outside Chinatowns in the East, South, and Midwest, and their origins are as diverse as those of "European-Americans." The term "Asian-American" now refers to over 900,000 Chinese from all parts of China and also Vietnam, 800,000 Filipinos, 700,000 Japanese, 500,000 Koreans, 400,000 East Indians, and a huge assortment of everything else from Moslem Cambodians to Catholic Hawaiians. It can mean an illiterate Hmong tribesman or a fully assimilated graduate of the Harvard Business School.

Asian-Americans have also attracted attention by their new prominence in several professions and trades. In New York City, for example, where the Asian-American population jumped from 94,500 in 1970 to 231,500 in 1980, Korean-Americans run an estimated 900 of the city's 1,600 corner grocery stores. Filipino doctors—who outnumber black doctors—have become general practitioners in thousands of rural communities that previously lacked physicians. East Indian–Americans own 800 of California's 6,000 motels. And in parts of Texas, Vietnamese-Americans now control 85 percent of the shrimp-fishing industry, though they only reached this position after considerable strife (now the subject of a film, *Alamo Bay*).

Individual Asian-Americans have become quite prominent as well. I.M. Pei and Minoru Yamasaki have helped transform American architecture. Seiji Ozawa and Yo Yo Ma are giant figures in American music. An Wang created one of the nation's largest computer firms, and Rocky Aoki founded one of its largest restaurant chains (Benihana). Samuel C.C. Ting won a Nobel prize in physics.

Most spectacular of all, and most significant for the future, is the entry of Asian-Americans into the universities. At Harvard, for example, Asian-Americans ten years ago made up barely three percent of the freshman class. The figure is now ten percent—five times their share of the population. At Brown, Asian-American applications more than tripled over the same period, and at Berkeley they increased from 3,408 in 1982 to 4,235 only three years later. The Berkeley student body is now 22 percent Asian-American, UCLA's is 21 percent, and MIT's 19 percent. The Julliard School of Music in New York is currently 30 percent Asian and Asian-American. American medical schools had only

571 Asian-American students in 1970, but in 1980 they had 1,924, and last year 3,763, or 5.6 percent of total enrollment. What is more, nearly all of these figures are certain to increase. In the current, largely foreign-born Asian-American community, 32.9 percent of people over 25 graduated from college (as opposed to 16.2 percent in the general population). For third-generation Japanese-Americans, the figure is 88 percent.

The Super Minority

Anthony Ramirez, writing in the November 24, 1986, issue of Fortune *magazine, extols the achievements of Asian Americans.*

Asian Americans are rising in corporate America faster than any other minority group. . . . Asian Americans have won top posts at companies not only in Hawaii and California, where most Asians first settle, but across America's heartland from Memphis to Kalamazoo. They have high-powered jobs at some of the best-known firms of Wall Street and Madison Avenue as well.

Asian immigrants, their children, and their grandchildren also crowd America's top universities: While a scant 2% of the U.S. population are Asian American, they account for 12% of this year's freshman class at Harvard, for example, and 20% at the University of California at Berkeley. This year the Westinghouse Science Talent Search, one of the country's most prestigious high school academic contests, awarded all five of its top scholarships to Asians. Some 35% of Asian Americans graduate from college, twice the percentage among whites.

All that education pays off spectacularly. Even though Asian Americans are generally newcomers—the majority are not descendants of immigrants but immigrants themselves—they are already way ahead of the rest of the nation at the bank. According to the 1980 census, the median annual income for Asian American families was $23,600. It exceeded the level not only for the overall population ($19,900) but for whites in particular ($20,800). Of the various ethnic groups that make up the Asian American population, only Vietnamese families, with meager annual incomes of $12,840, fell below white and national levels.

Why is it that Asian Americans tower above the rest of the population in both dollars and sense? Their speeded-up realization of the American dream is due in great measure to hard work, dedication to education, a willingness to adapt to a predominantly white culture—and, not least, to brains.

By any measure these Asian-American students are outstanding. In California only the top 12.5 percent of high school students qualify for admission to the uppermost tier of the state university system, but 39 percent of Asian-American high school students do. On the SATs, Asian-Americans score an average of 519 in math, surpassing whites, the next highest group, by 32 points. Among Japanese-Americans, the most heavily native-born Asian-American group, 68 percent of those taking the math SAT scored above 600—high enough to qualify for admission to almost any university in the country. The Westinghouse Science Talent search, which each year identifies 40 top high school science students, picked 12 Asian-Americans in 1983, nine last year, and seven this year. And at Harvard the Phi Beta Kappa chapter last April named as its elite "Junior Twelve" students five Asian-Americans and seven Jews.

Some Problems of Adjustment

Faced with these statistics, the understandable reflex of many non-Asian-Americans is adulation. President Reagan has called Asian-Americans "our exemplars of hope and inspiration." *Parade* magazine recently featured an article on Asian-Americans titled "The Promise of America," and *Time* and *Newsweek* stories have boasted headlines like "A Formula for Success," "The Drive to Excel," and "A 'Model Minority.'" However, not all of these stories come to grips with the fact that Asian-Americans, like all immigrants, have to deal with a great many problems of adjustment, ranging from the absurd to the deadly serious.

Who would think, for example, that there is a connection between Asian-American immigration and the decimation of California's black bear population? But Los Angeles, whose Korean population grew by 100,000 in the past decade, now has more than 300 licensed herbal-acupuncture shops. And a key ingredient in traditional Korean herbal medicine is *ungdam*, bear gallbladder. The result is widespread illegal hunting and what *Audubon* magazine soberly calls "a booming trade in bear parts."

As Mark R. Thompson recently pointed out in *The Wall Street Journal*, the clash of cultures produced by Asian immigration can also have vexing legal results. Take the case of Fumiko Kimura, a Japanese-American woman who tried to drown herself and her two children in the Pacific. She survived but the children did not, and she is now on trial for their murder. As a defense, her lawyers are arguing that parent-child suicide is a common occurrence in Japan. In Fresno, California, meanwhile, 30,000 newly arrived Hmong cause a different problem. "Anthropologists call the custom 'marriage by capture,'" Mr. Thompson writes. "Fresno police and prosecutors call it 'rape.'"

A much more serious problem for Asian-Americans is racial violence. In 1982 two unemployed whites in Detroit beat to death a Chinese-American named Vincent Chin, claiming that they wanted revenge on the Japanese for hurting the automobile industry. After pleading guilty to manslaughter, they paid a $3,000 fine and were released. More recently, groups of Cambodians and Vietnamese in Boston were beaten by white youths, and there have been incidents in New York and Los Angeles as well.

Is this violence an aberration, or does it reflect the persistence of anti-Asian prejudice in America? By at least one indicator, it seems hard to believe that Asian-Americans suffer greatly from discrimination. Their median family income, according to the 1980 census, was $22,713, compared to only $19,917 for whites. True, Asians live almost exclusively in urban areas (where incomes are higher), and generally have more people working in each family. They are also better educated than whites. Irene Natividad, a Filipino-American active in the Democratic Party's Asian Caucus, states bluntly that "we are underpaid for the high level of education we have achieved." However, because of language difficulties and differing professional standards in the United States, many new Asian immigrants initially work in jobs for which they are greatly overqualified.

Asian-American Students and Universities

Ironically, charges of discrimination today arise most frequently in the universities, the setting generally cited as the best evidence of Asian-American achievement. For several years Asian student associations at Ivy League universities have cited figures showing that a smaller percentage of Asian-American students than others are accepted. At Harvard this year, 12.5 percent of Asian-American applicants were admitted, as opposed to 16 percent of all applicants; at Princeton, the figures were 14 to 17 percent. Recently a Princeton professor, Uwe Reinhardt, told a *New York Times* reporter that Princeton has an unofficial quota for Asian-American applicants.

The question of university discrimination is a subtle one. For one thing, it only arises at the most prestigious schools, where admissions are the most subjective. At universities like UCLA, where applicants are judged largely by their grades and SAT scores, Asian-Americans have a higher admission rate than other students (80 percent versus 70 percent for all applicants). And at schools that emphasize science, like MIT, the general excellence of Asian-Americans in the field also produces a higher admission rate.

Why are things different at the Ivy League schools? One reason, according to a recent study done at Princeton, is that very few Asian-Americans are alumni children. The children of alumni are accepted at a rate of about 50 percent, and so raise the overall admissions figure. Athletes have a better chance of admission as well, and few Asian-Americans play varsity sports. These arguments, however, leave out another admissions factor: affirmative action. The fact is that if alumni children have a special advantage, at least some Asians do too, because of their race. At Harvard, for instance, partly in response to complaints from the Asian student organization, the admissions office in the late 1970s began to recruit vigorously among two categories of Asian-Americans: the poor, often living in Chinatowns; and recent immigrants. Today, according to the dean of admissions, L. Fred Jewett, roughly a third of Harvard's Asian-American applicants come from these groups, and are included in the university's "affirmative action" efforts. Like black students, who have a 27 percent admission rate, they find it easier to get in. And this means that the *other* Asian-Americans, the ones with no language problem or economic disadvantage, find things correspondingly tougher. Harvard has no statistics on the two groups. But if we assume the first group has an admissions rate of only 20 percent (very low for affirmative action candidates), the second one still slips down to slightly less than nine percent, or roughly half the overall admissions rate.

Dean Jewett offers two explanations for this phenomenon. First, he says, "family pressure makes more marginal students apply." In other words, many Asian students apply regardless of their qualifications, because of the university's prestige. And second, "a terribly high proportion of the Asian students are heading toward the sciences." In the interests of diversity, then, more of them must be left out.

It is true that more Asian-Americans go into the sciences. In Harvard's class of 1985, 57 percent of them did (as opposed to 29 percent of all students) and 71 percent went into either the sciences or economics. It is also true that a great many of Harvard's Asian-American applicants have little on their records except scientific excellence. But there are good reasons for this. In the sciences, complete mastery of English is less important than in other fields, an important fact for immigrants and children of immigrants. And scientific careers allow Asian-Americans to avoid the sort of large, hierarchical organization where their unfamiliarity with America, and management's resistance to putting them into highly visible positions, could hinder their advancement. And so the admissions problem comes down to a problem of clashing cultural standards. Since the values of Asian-American applicants differ from the universities' own, many of those applicants appear narrowly focused and dull. As Linda Matthews, an alumni recruiter for Harvard in Los Angeles, says with regret, "We hold them to the standards of white suburban kids. We want them to be cheerleaders and class presidents and all the rest."

The universities, however, consider their idea of the academic community to be liberal and sound. They are understandably hesitant to change it because of a demographic shift in the admissions pool. So how can they resolve this difficult problem? It is hard to say, except to suggest humility, and to recall that this sort of thing has come up before. At Harvard, the admissions office might do well to remember a memorandum Walter Lippmann prepared for the university in 1922. "I am fully prepared to accept the judgment of the Harvard authorities that a concentration of Jews in excess of fifteen per cent will produce a segregation of cultures rather than a fusion," wrote Lippmann, himself a Jew and a Harvard graduate. "They hand on unconsciously and uncritically from one generation to another many distressing personal and social habits. . . ."

Past Discrimination

The debate over admissions is abstruse. But for Asian-Americans, it has become an extremely sensitive issue. The universities, after all, represent their route to complete integration in American society, and to an equal chance at the advantages that enticed them and their parents to immigrate in the first place. At the same time, discrimination, even very slight discrimination, recalls the bitter prejudice and discrimination that Asian-Americans suffered for their first hundred years in this country.

Few white Americans today realize just how pervasive legal anti-Asian discrimination was before 1945. The tens of thousands of Chinese laborers who arrived in California in the 1850s and 1860s to work in the goldfields and build the Central Pacific Railroad often lived in virtual slavery (the words ku-li, now part of the English language, mean "bitter labor"). Far from having the chance to organize, they were seized on as scapegoats by labor unions, particularly Samuel Gompers's AFL, and often ended up working as strikebreakers instead, thus inviting violent attacks. In 1870 Congress barred Asian immigrants from citizenship, and in 1882 it passed the Chinese Exclusion Act, which summarily prohibited more Chinese from entering the country. Since it did this at a time when 100,600 male Chinese-Americans had the company of only 4,800 females, it effectively sentenced the Chinese community to rapid decline. From 1854 to 1874, California had in effect a law preventing Asian-Americans from testifying in court, leaving them without the protection of the law.

Little changed in the late 19th and early 20th centuries, as large numbers of Japanese and smaller contingents from Korea and the Philippines began to arrive on the West Coast. In 1906 San Francisco made a brief attempt to segregate its school system. In 1910 a California law went so far as to prohibit marriage between Caucasians and "Mongolians," in flagrant defiance of the Fourteenth

Amendment. Two Alien Land Acts in 1913 and 1920 prevented noncitizens in California (in other words, all alien immigrants) from owning or leasing land. These laws, and the Chinese Exclusion Act, remained in effect until the 1940s. And of course during the Second World War, President Franklin Roosevelt signed an Executive Order sending 110,000 ethnic Japanese on the West Coast, 64 percent of whom were American citizens, to internment camps. Estimates of the monetary damage to the Japanese-American community from this action range as high as $400,000,000, and Japanese-American political activists have made reparations one of their most important goals. Only in Hawaii, where Japanese-Americans already outnumbered whites 61,000 to 29,000 at the turn of the century, was discrimination relatively less important. (Indeed, 157,000 Japanese-Americans in Hawaii at the start of the war were *not interned*, although they posed a greater possible threat to the war effort than their cousins in California.)

Self-Sufficiency

In light of this history, the current problems of the Asian-American community seem relatively minor, and its success appears even more remarkable. Social scientists wonder just how this success was possible, and how Asian-Americans have managed to avoid the "second-class citizenship" that has trapped so many blacks and Hispanics. There is no single answer, but all the various explanations of the Asian-Americans' success do tend to fall into one category: self-sufficiency.

The first element of this self-sufficiency is family. Conservative sociologist Thomas Sowell writes that "strong, stable families have been characteristic of . . . successful minorities," and calls Chinese-Americans and Japanese-Americans the most stable he has encountered. This quality contributes to success in at least three ways. First and most obviously, it provides a secure environment for children. Second, it pushes those children to do better than their parents. As former Ohio state demographer William Petersen, author of *Japanese-Americans* (1971), says, "They're like the Jews in that they have the whole family and the whole community pushing them to make the best of themselves." And finally, it is a significant financial advantage. Traditionally, Asian-Americans have headed into family businesses, with all the family members pitching in long hours to make them a success. For the Chinese, it was restaurants and laundries (as late as 1940, half of the Chinese-American labor force worked in one or the other), for the Japanese, groceries and truck farming, and for the Koreans, groceries. Today the proportion of Koreans working without pay in family businesses is nearly three times as high as any other group. A recent *New York* magazine profile of one typical Korean grocery in New York showed that several of the family members running it consistently worked 15 to 18 hours a day. Thomas Sowell points out that in 1970, although Chinese median family income already exceeded white median family income by a third, their median personal income was only ten percent higher, indicating much greater participation per family.

Also contributing to Asian-American self-sufficiency are powerful community organizations. From the beginning of Chinese-American settlement in California, clan organizations, mutual aid societies, and rotating credit associations gave many Japanese-Americans a start in business, at a time when most banks would only lend to whites. Throughout the first half of this century, the strength of community organizations was an important reason why Asian-Americans tended to live in small, closed communities rather than spreading out among the general population. And during the Depression years, they proved vital. In the early 1930s, when nine percent of the population of New York City subsisted on public relief, only one percent of Chinese-Americans did so. The community structure has also helped keep Asian-American crime rates the lowest in the nation, despite recently increasing gang violence among new Chinese and Vietnamese immigrants. According to the 1980 census, the proportion of Asian-Americans in, prison is one-fourth that of the general population.

The more recent immigrants have also developed close communities. In the Washington, D.C., suburb of Arlington, Virginia, there is now a "Little Saigon." Koreans also take advantage of the "ethnic resources" provided by a small community. As Ivan Light writes in an essay in Nathan Glazer's new book, *Clamor at the Gates*, "They help one another with business skills, information, and purchase of ethnic commodities; cluster in particular industries; combine easily in restraint of trade; or utilize rotating credit associations." Light cites a study showing that 34 percent of Korean grocery store owners in Chicago had received financial help from within the Korean community. The immigrants in these communities are self-sufficient in another way as well. Unlike the immigrants of the 19th century, most new Asian-Americans come to the United States with professional skills. Or they come to obtain those skills, and then stay on. Of 16,000 Taiwanese who came to the U.S. as students in the 1960s, only three percent returned to Taiwan.

Some Groups Lag Behind

So what does the future hold for Asian-Americans? With the removal of most discrimination, and with the massive Asian-American influx in the universities, the importance of tightly knit communities is sure to wane. Indeed, among the older Asian-

American groups it already has: since the war, fewer and fewer native-born Chinese-Americans have come to live in Chinatowns. But will complete assimilation follow? One study, at least, seems to indicate that it will, if one can look to the well-established Japanese-Americans for hints as to the future of other Asian groups. According to Professor Harry Kitano of UCLA, 63 percent of Japanese now intermarry.

But can all Asian-Americans follow the prosperous, assimilationist Japanese example? For some, it may not be easy. Hmong tribesmen, for instance, arrived in the United States with little money, few valuable skills, and extreme cultural disorientation. After five years here, they are still heavily dependent on welfare. (When the state of Oregon cut its assistance to refugees, 90 percent of the Hmong there moved to California.) Filipinos, although now the second-largest Asian-American group, make up less than ten percent of the Asian-American population at Harvard, and are the only Asian-Americans to benefit from affirmative action programs at the University of California. Do figures like these point to the emergence of a disadvantaged Asian-American underclass? It is still too early to tell, but the question is not receiving much attention either. As Nathan Glazer says of Asian-Americans, "When they're already above average, it's very hard to pay much attention to those who fall below." Ross Harano, a Chicago businessman active in the Democratic Party's Asian Caucus, argues that the label of "model minority" earned by the most conspicuous Asian-Americans hurts less successful groups. "We need money to help people who can't assimilate as fast as the superstars," he says.

Harano also points out that the stragglers find little help in traditional minority politics. "When blacks talk about a minority agenda, they don't include us," he says. "Most Asians are viewed by blacks as whites." Indeed, in cities with large numbers of Asians and blacks, relations between the communities are tense. In September 1984, for example, *The Los Angeles Sentinel*, a prominent black newspaper, ran a four-part series condemning Koreans for their "takeover" of black businesses, provoking a strong reaction from Asian-American groups. In Harlem some blacks have organized a boycott of Asian-American stores.

Another barrier to complete integration lies in the tendency of many Asian-American students to crowd into a small number of careers, mainly in the sciences. Professor Ronn Takaki of Berkeley is a strong critic of this "maldistribution," and says that universities should make efforts to correct it. The extent of these efforts, he told *The Boston Globe* last December, "will determine whether we have our poets, sociologists, historians, and journalists. If we are all tracked into becoming computer technicians and scientists, this need will not be fulfilled."

Yet it is not clear that the "maldistribution" problem will extend to the next generation. The children of the current immigrants will not share their parents' language difficulties. Nor will they worry as much about joining large institutions where subtle racism might once have barred them from advancement. William Petersen argues, "As the discrimination disappears, as it mostly has already, the self-selection will disappear as well. . . . There's nothing in Chinese or Japanese culture pushing them toward these fields." Professor Kitano of UCLA is not so sure. "The submerging of the individual to the group is another basic Japanese tradition," he wrote in an article for *The Harvard Encyclopedia of American Ethnic Groups*. It is a tradition that causes problems for Japanese-Americans who wish to avoid current career patterns: "It may only be a matter of time before some break out of these middleman jobs, but the structural and cultural restraints may prove difficult to overcome."

A Promising Future

In short, Asian-Americans face undeniable problems of integration. Still, it takes a very narrow mind not to realize that these problems are the envy of every other American racial minority, and of a good number of white ethnic groups as well. Like the Jews, who experienced a similar pattern of discrimination and quotas, and who first crowded into a small range of professions, Asian-Americans have shown an ability to overcome large obstacles in spectacular fashion. In particular, they have done so by taking full advantage of America's greatest civic resource, its schools and universities, just as the Jews did 50 years ago. Now they seem poised to burst out upon American society.

The clearest indication of this course is in politics, a sphere that Asian-Americans traditionally avoided. Now this is changing. And importantly, it is *not* changing just because Asian-Americans want government to solve their particular problems. Yes, there are "Asian" issues: the loosening of immigration restrictions, reparations for the wartime internment, equal opportunity for the Asian disadvantaged. Asian-American Democrats are at present incensed over the way the Democratic National Committee has stripped their caucus of "official" status. But even the most vehement activists on these points still insist that the most important thing for Asian-Americans is not any particular combination of issues, but simply "being part of the process." Unlike blacks or Hispanics, Asian-American politicians have the luxury of not having to devote the bulk of their time to an "Asian-American agenda," and thus escape becoming prisoners of such an agenda. Who thinks of Senator Daniel Inouye or former senator S.I.

Hayakawa primarily in terms of his race? In June a young Chinese-American named Michael Woo won a seat on the Los Angeles City Council, running in a district that is only five percent Asian. According to *The Washington Post*, he attributed his victory to his "links to his fellow young American professionals." This is not typical minority-group politics.

Since Asian-Americans have the luxury of not having to behave like other minority groups, it seems only a matter of time before they, like the Jews, lose their "minority" status altogether, both legally and in the public's perception. And when this occurs, Asian-Americans will have to face the danger not of discrimination but of losing their cultural identity. It is a problem that every immigrant group must eventually come to terms with.

For Americans in general, however, the success of Asian-Americans poses no problems at all. On the contrary, their triumph has done nothing but enrich the United States. Asian-Americans improve every field they enter, for the simple reason that in a free society, a group succeeds by doing something better than it had been done before: Korean grocery stores provide fresher vegetables; Filipino doctors provide better rural health care; Asian science students raise the quality of science in the universities, and go on to provide better medicine, engineering, computer technology, and so on. And by a peculiarly American miracle, the Asian-Americans' success has not been balanced by anyone else's failure. Indeed, as successive waves of immigrants have shown, each new ethnic and racial group adds far more to American society than it takes away. This Fourth of July, that is cause for hope and celebration.

"It is a myth that Asian Americans have proven the American Dream."

Asian American Success Is a Myth

Deborah Woo (dates unknown)

Deborah Woo is a sociology professor at the University of California, Santa Cruz, specializing in cross-cultural issues in mental health and in the politics of culture. The following viewpoint is taken from an essay that was published in 1989 in *Making Waves: An Anthology of Writings By and About Asian American Women*. In the article, Woo argues that the Asian American success story is largely a myth—one that especially overlooks the problems Asian American women face. Asian Americans, she argues, still confront significant discrimination in American society and are not receiving opportunities or income commensurate with their education or efforts.

Much academic research on Asian Americans tends to underscore their success, a success which is attributed almost always to a cultural emphasis on education, hard work, and thrift. Less familiar is the story of potential not fully realized. For example, despite the appearance of being successful and highly educated, Asian American women do not necessarily gain the kind of recognition or rewards they deserve.

The story of unfulfilled dreams remains unwritten for many Asian Americans. It is specifically this story about the gap be-

Deborah Woo, "The Gap Between Striving and Achieving: The Case of Asian American Women," in *Making Waves: An Anthology of Writings by and About Asian American Women* by Asian Women United of California. Copyright ©1989 by Asian Women United of California. Reprinted by permission of Beacon Press, Boston.

tween striving and achieving that I am concerned with here. Conventional wisdom obscures the discrepancy by looking primarily at whether society is adequately rewarding individuals. By comparing how minorities as disadvantaged groups are doing relative to each other, the tendency is to view Asian Americans as a "model minority." This practice programs us to ignore structural barriers and inequities and to insist that any problems are simply due to different cultural values or failure of individual effort.

Myths about the Asian American community derive from many sources. All ethnic groups develop their own cultural myths. Sometimes, however, they create myths out of historical necessity, as a matter of subterfuge and survival. Chinese Americans, for example, were motivated to create new myths because institutional opportunities were closed off to them. Succeeding in America meant they had to invent fake aspects of an "Oriental culture," which became the beginning of the Chinatown tourist industry.

What has been referred to as the "model minority myth," however, essentially originated from without. The idea that Asian Americans have been a successful group has been a popular news media theme for the last twenty years. It has become a basis for cutbacks in governmental support for all ethnic minorities—for Asian Americans because they apparently are already successful as a group; for other ethnic minorities because they are presumably not working as hard as Asian Americans or they would not need assistance. Critics of this view argue that the portrayal of Asian Americans as socially and economically successful ignores fundamental inequities. That is, the question "Why have Asians been successful vis-à-vis other minorities?" has been asked at the expense of another equally important question: "What has kept Asians from *fully* reaping the fruits of their education and hard work?"

The achievements of Asian Americans are part reality, part myth. Part of the reality is that a highly visible group of Asian Americans are college-educated, occupationally well-situated, and earning relatively high incomes. The myth, however, is that hard work reaps commensurate rewards. This essay documents the gap between the level of education and subsequent occupational or income gains.

The Model Minority Myth

Since World War II, social researchers and news media personnel have been quick to assert that Asian Americans excel over other ethnic groups in terms of earnings, education, and occupation. Asian Americans are said to save more, study more, work more, and so achieve more. The reason given: a cultural emphasis on education and hard work. Implicit in this view is a social judgment and moral injunction: if Asian Americans can make it on their own, why can't other minorities?

While the story of Asian American women workers is only beginning to be pieced together, the success theme is already being sung. The image prevails that despite cultural and racial oppression, they are somehow rapidly assimilating into the mainstream. As workers, they participate in the labor force at rates higher than all others, including Anglo women. Those Asian American women who pursue higher education surpass other women, and even men, in this respect. Moreover, they have acquired a reputation for not only being conscientious and industrious but docile, compliant, and uncomplaining as well.

In the last few decades American women in general have been demanding "equal pay for equal work," the legitimation of housework as work that needs to be recompensed, and greater representation in the professional fields. These demands, however, have not usually come from Asian American women. From the perspective of those in power, this reluctance to complain is another feature of the "model minority." But for those who seek to uncover employment abuses, the unwillingness to talk about problems on the job is itself a problem. The garment industry, for example, is a major area of exploitation, yet it is also one that is difficult to investigate and control. In a 1983 report on the Concentrated Employment Program of the California Department of Industrial Relations, it was noted:

> The major problem for investigators in San Francisco is that the Chinese community is very close-knit, and employers and employees cooperate in refusing to speak to investigators. In two years of enforcing the Garment Registration Act, the CEP has never received a complaint from an Asian employee. The few complaints received have been from Anglo or Latin workers.

While many have argued vociferously either for or against the model minority concept, Asian Americans in general have been ambivalent in this regard. Asian Americans experience pride in achievement born of hard work and self-sacrifice, but at the same time, they resist the implication that all is well. Data provided here indicate that Asian Americans have not been successful in terms of benefitting fully, (i.e., monetarily), from their education. It is a myth that Asian Americans have proven the American Dream. How does this myth develop?

The working consumer: income and cost of living. One striking feature about Asian Americans is that they are geographically concentrated in areas where both income and cost of living are very high. In 1970, 80 percent of the total Asian American population resided in five states—California, Hawaii, Illinois, New York, and Washington. Furthermore, 59 percent of Chinese, Filipino, and

Japanese Americans were concentrated in only 5 of the 243 Standard Metropolitan Statistical Areas (SMSA) in the United States—Chicago, Honolulu, Los Angeles/Long Beach, New York, and San Francisco/Oakland. The 1980 census shows that immigration during the intervening decade has not only produced dramatic increases, especially in the Filipino and Chinese populations, but has also continued the overwhelming tendency for these groups to concentrate in the same geographical areas, especially

Rationalizing Racism

Amy Takaki was one of the editors of Roots: An Asian American Anthology, *a 1971 volume produced by the UCLA Asian American Studies Center. In an introductory essay, she writes about the model minority stereotype.*

Like all stereotypes, there is some factual support for the success image of Asian Americans, if success is to be defined along economic, materialistic parameters. A sizable number of Chinese and Japanese Americans have attained higher educational, employment, and income levels—that is, compared to other *non*white groups in the United States. What the mass media selectively overlooks in Asian success are such factors as middle management ranks, de facto segregation, delayed promotion in jobs, and other subtleties of institutional subordination. In addition, the success stereotype does not consider the psychological and cultural costs which have been the price of Asian American success. . . .

Basic to the success story are the means by which Asian Americans have assimilated. They have often adhered to this society's prescribed mode of behavior for minority assimilation: through hard work, education, quietly remaining in the background, inaction in the face of injustice, and blind faith to the American dream of equality and opportunity for all. The danger in upholding this success myth is that it reinforces the underlying value structure that created it. The Asian success story functions to validate the fundamental soundness of this system and to support the "truth" that all deserving people of any color can and should earn a middle-class position and life style within this society. Despite the disadvantaged status of millions in the United States, most Americans cling to the ideal that American democratic capitalism guarantees self-determination for all its people. By accepting the distorted picture of Asian American success, America rationalizes its racist behavior—and fools itself that it is responsive to the people. Furthermore, the Asian model of assimilation frees the white majority from assuming responsibility for its own oppressiveness, since it implies that nonwhite minorities have to *earn* their rights to American society and it shifts the causes for minority problems away from the society and onto minority communities.

those in California. Interestingly enough, the very existence of large Asian communities in the West has stimulated among more recent refugee populations what is now officially referred to as "secondary migration," that is, the movement of refugees away from their sponsoring communities (usually places where there was no sizeable Asian population prior to their own arrival) to those areas where there are well-established Asian communities.

This residential pattern means that while Asian Americans may earn more by living in high-income areas, they also pay more as consumers. The additional earning power gained from living in San Francisco or Los Angeles, say, is absorbed by the high cost of living in such cities. National income averages which compare the income of Asian American women with that of the more broadly dispersed Anglo women systematically distort the picture. Indeed, if we compare women within the same area, Asian American women are frequently less well-off than Anglo American females, and the difference between women pales when compared with Anglo males, whose mean income is much higher than that of any group of women.

When we consider the large immigrant Asian population and the language barriers that restrict women to menial or entry-level jobs, we are talking about a group that not only earns minimum wage or less, but one whose purchasing power is substantially undermined by living in metropolitan areas of states where the cost of living is unusually high.

Another striking pattern about Asian American female employment is the high rate of labor force participation. Asian American women are more likely than Anglo American women to work full time and year round. The model minority interpretation tends to assume that mere high labor force participation is a sign of successful employment. One important factor motivating minority women to enter the work force, however, is the need to supplement family resources. For Anglo American women some of the necessity for working is partly offset by the fact that they often share in the higher incomes of Anglo males, who tend not only to earn more than all other groups but, as noted earlier, also tend to receive higher returns on their education. Moreover, once regional variation is adjusted for, Filipino and Chinese Americans had a median annual income equivalent to black males in four mainland SMSAs—Chicago, Los Angeles/Long Beach, New York, San Francisco/Oakland. Census statistics point to the relatively lower earning capacity of Asian males compared to Anglo males, suggesting that Asian American women enter the work force to help compensate for this inequality. Thus, the mere fact of high employment must be read cautiously and analyzed within a larger context.

The different faces of immigration. Over the last decade immigration has expanded the Chinese population by 85.3 percent, making it the largest Asian group in the country at 806,027, and has swelled the Filipino population by 125.8 percent, making it the second largest at 774,640. Hence at present the majority of Chinese American and Filipino American women are foreign-born. In addition the Asian American "success story" is misleading in part because of a select group of these immigrants: foreign-educated professionals.

Since 1965 U.S. immigration laws have given priority to seven categories of individuals. Two of the seven allow admittance of people with special occupational skills or services needed in the United States. Four categories facilitate family reunification, and the last applies only to refugees. While occupation is estimated to account for no more than 20 percent of all visas, professionals are not precluded from entering under other preference categories. Yet this select group is frequently offered as evidence of the upward mobility possible in America when Asian Americans who are born and raised in the United States are far less likely to reach the doctoral level in their education. Over two-thirds of Asians with doctorates in the United States are trained and educated abroad.

Downward Mobility

Also overlooked in some analyses is a great deal of downward mobility among the foreign-born. For example, while foreign-educated health professionals are given preferential status for entry into this country, restrictive licensing requirements deny them the opportunity to practice or utilize their special skills. They are told that their educational credentials, experience, and certifications are inadequate. Consequently, for many the only alternatives are menial labor or unemployment. Other highly educated immigrants become owner/managers of Asian businesses, which also suggests downward mobility and an inability to find jobs in their field of expertise.

"Professional" obscures more than it reveals. Another major reason for the perception of "model minority" is that the census categories implying success, "professional-managerial" or "executive, administrative, managerial," frequently camouflage important inconsistencies with this image of success. As managers, Asian Americans, usually male, are concentrated in certain occupations. They tend to be self-employed in small-scale wholesale and retail trade and manufacturing. They are rarely buyers, sales managers, administrators, or salaried managers in large-scale retail trade, communications, or public utilities. Among foreign-born Asian women, executive-managerial status is limited primarily to auditors and accountants.

In general, Asian American women with a college education are concentrated in narrow and select, usually less prestigious, rungs of the "professional-managerial" class. In 1970, 27 percent of native-born Japanese women were either elementary or secondary school teachers. Registered nurses made up the next largest group. Foreign-born Filipino women found this to be their single most important area of employment, with 19 percent being nurses. They were least represented in the more prestigious professions—physicians, judges, dentists, law professors, and lawyers. In 1980 foreign-born Asian women with four or more years of college were most likely to find jobs in administrative support or clerical occupations.

Self-help through "taking care of one's own." Much of what is considered ideal or model behavior in American society is based on Anglo-Saxon, Protestant values. Chief among them is an ethic of individual self-help, of doing without outside assistance or governmental support. On the other hand, Asian Americans have historically relied to a large extent on family or community resources. Their tightly-knit communities tend to be fairly closed to the outside world, even when under economic hardship. Many below the poverty level do not receive any form of public assistance. Even if we include social security benefits as a form of supplementary income, the proportion of Asian Americans who use them is again very low, much lower than that for Anglo Americans. Asian American families, in fact, are more likely than Anglo American families to bear economic hardships on their own.

While Asian Americans appear to have been self-sufficient as communities, we need to ask, at what personal cost? Moreover, have they as a group reaped rewards commensurate with their efforts? The following section presents data which document that while Asian American women may be motivated to achieve through education, monetary returns for them are less than for other groups.

The Nature of Inequality

The decision to use white males as the predominant reference group within the United States is a politically charged issue. When women raise and push the issue of "comparable worth," of "equal pay for equal work," they argue that women frequently do work equivalent to men's, but are paid far less for it.

The same argument can be made for Asian American women, and the evidence of inequality is staggering. For example, after adjustments are made for occupational prestige, age, education, weeks worked, hours worked each week, and state of residence in 1975, Chinese American women could be expected to earn only 70 percent of the majority male income. Even among the college-educated, Chinese American women fared least well, making only 42 percent of what majority males earned. As we noted earlier, the mean income of all women, Anglo and Asian, was far below that of Anglo males in 1970 and 1980. This was true for both native-born and foreign-born Asians. In 1970 Anglo women earned only 54 percent of what their male counterparts did. Native-born Asian American women, depending on the particular ethnic group, earned anywhere from 49 to 57 percent of what Anglo males earned. In 1980, this inequity persisted.

Another way of thinking about comparable worth is not to focus only on what individuals do on the job, but on what they bring to the job as well. Because formal education is one measure of merit in American society and because it is most frequently perceived as the means to upward mobility, we would expect greater education to have greater payoffs.

Asian American women tend to be extraordinarily successful in terms of attaining higher education. Filipino American women have the highest college completion rate of all women and graduate at a rate 50 percent greater than that of majority males. Chinese American and Japanese American women follow closely behind, exceeding both the majority male and female rate of college completion. Higher levels of education, however, bring lower returns for Asian American women than they do for other groups.

While education enhances earnings capability, the return on education for Asian American women is not as great as that for other women, and is well below parity with white males. Data on Asian American women in the five SMSAs where they are concentrated bear this out. In 1980 all these women fell far behind Anglo males in what they earned in relation to their college education. Between 8 and 16 percent of native-born women earned $21,200 compared to 50 percent of Anglo males. Similar patterns were found among college-educated foreign-born women.

The fact that Asian American women do not reap the income benefits one might expect given their high levels of educational achievement raises questions about the reasons for such inequality. To what extent is this discrepancy based on outright discrimination? On self-imposed limitations related to cultural modesty? The absence of certain social or interpersonal skills required for upper managerial positions? Or institutional factors beyond their control? It is beyond the scope of this paper to address such concerns. However, the fact of inequality is itself noteworthy and poorly appreciated.

In general, Asian American women usually are overrepresented in clerical or administrative support jobs. While there is a somewhat greater tendency for foreign-born college-educated Asian women to find clerical-related jobs, both native- and foreign-born women have learned that clerical work is the area where they are most easily employed. In fact, in 1970 a third of native-born Chinese women were doing clerical work. A decade later Filipino women were concentrated there. In addition Asian American women tend to be overrepresented as cashiers, file clerks, office machine operators, and typists. They are less likely to get jobs as secretaries or receptionists. The former occupations not only carry less prestige but generally [writes Bob H. Suzuki in *Amerasia Journal*] have "little or no decision-making authority, low mobility and low public contact."

In short, education may improve one's chances for success, but it cannot promise the American Dream. For Asian American women education seems to serve less as an opportunity for upward mobility than as protection against jobs as service or assembly workers, or as machine operatives—all areas where foreign-born Asian women are far more likely to find themselves.

In this essay I have attempted to direct our attention on the gap between achievement and reward, specifically the failure to reward monetarily those who have demonstrated competence. Asian American women, like Asian American men, have been touted as "model minorities," praised for their outstanding achievements. The concept of model minority, however, obscures the fact that one's accomplishments are not adequately recognized in terms of commensurate income or choice of occupation. By focusing on the achievements of one minority in relation to another, our attention is diverted from larger institutional and historical factors which influence a group's success. Each ethnic group has a different history, and a simplistic method of modeling which assumes the experience of all immigrants is the same ignores the sociostructural context in which a certain kind of achievement occurred. For example, World War II enabled many Asian Americans who were technically trained and highly educated to move into lucrative war-related industries. More recently, Korean immigrants during the 1960s were able to capitalize on the fast-growing demand for wigs in the United States. It was not simply cultural ingenuity or individual hard work which made them successful in this enterprise, but the fact that Korean immigrants were in the unique position of being able to import cheap hair products from their mother country.

Just as there are structural opportunities, so there are structural barriers. However, the persistent emphasis in American society on individual effort deflects attention away from such barriers and creates self-doubt among those who have not "made it." The myth that Asian Americans have succeeded as a group, when in actuality there are serious discrepancies between effort and achievement and between achievement and reward, adds still further to this self-doubt.

While others have also pointed out the myth of the model minority, I want to add that myths do have social functions. It would be a mistake to dismiss the model minority concept as merely a myth. Asian Americans are—however inappropriately—thrust into the role of being models for other minorities.

Competing Images

A closer look at the images associated with Asians as a model minority group suggests competing or contradictory themes. One image is that Asian Americans exemplify a competitive spirit enabling them to overcome structural barriers through perseverance and ingenuity. On the other hand, they are also seen as complacent, content with their social lot, and expecting little in the way of outside help. A third image is that Asian Americans are experts at assimilation, demonstrating that this society still functions as a melting pot. Their values are sometimes equated with white, middle-class, Protestant values of hard work, determination, and thrift. Opposing this image, however, is still another, namely that Asian Americans have succeeded because they possess cultural values unique to them as a group—their family-centeredness and long tradition of reverence for scholarly achievement, for example.

Perhaps, then, this is why so many readily accept the myth, whose tenacity is due to its being vague and broad enough to appeal to a variety of different groups. Yet to the extent that the myth is based on misconceptions, we are called upon to reexamine it more closely in an effort to narrow the gap between striving and achieving.

For Discussion

Chapter One

1. What arguments are made by John Bigler and Norman Asing about Chinese "coolies"? Why might Chinese immigrants take pains to argue that they are not indentured laborers?

2. What motivates the anti-Chinese movement, according to Otis Gibson? What evidence for his contentions do you find in his viewpoint and in the viewpoints by John Bigler, Norman Asing, and the California legislature?

3. Why was the Supreme Court decision in *Wong Kim Ark v. United States* important? How might the history of Asian Americans have been different if the dissenting opinion of Melville W. Fuller had instead become the law of the land?

Chapter Two

1. Do V.S. McClatchy, Kiichi Kanzaki, George Shima, and Elwood Mead have differing conceptions of the meaning of "assimilation" in their discussions of Japanese Americans? If so, what are their points of contention? Do you think assimilation should have been the primary goal of Asian Americans? Why or why not?

2. Compare the arguments attacking and defending the Japanese with the arguments on the Chinese in chapter one. What are the similarities? What are the differences?

3. Both Riley H. Allen and William C. Smith attempt to tell us what Asian Americans in Hawaii are thinking. Which author do you believe provides a more accurate picture? Explain your answer.

4. Compare and contrast the complaints and arguments of Filipino immigrants, as seen in the final two viewpoints, with those of the previous viewpoints concerning Japanese immigrants. Which issues are similar? Which vary? Are the differences the result of differences between Filipinos and Japanese or differences in the conditions they faced? Explain your answer.

Chapter Three

1. In your view, does Galen M. Fisher present convincing refutations of the arguments of the San Benito County Chamber of Commerce regarding the security risks of Japanese Americans? Why or why not? According to Ina Sugihara, what were the real motivations behind evacuation? Whose arguments seem most plausible? Explain.

2. On what conditions does Mike Masaoka accept the necessity of mass evacuation of Japanese Americans? Are his conditions adequately met by the arguments of the San Benito County Chamber of Commerce? Explain your answer.

3. Why, according to James M. Omura, were Japanese aliens better situated at the start of World War II than their American citizen children? What point is he trying to make? Do you believe such an argument, made before a congressional committee while the United States and Japan were at war, was tactically wise? Why or why not?

Chapter Four

1. Fox Butterfield and James W. Chin have opposing ideas on the relationship between discrimination and ethnic identity. Summarize these differences and explain how they might account for the authors' disparate conclusions on the persistence of discrimination.

2. Is the story of the Korean family profiled in Elizabeth Mehren's article an example of the economic exploitation of Asians posited by Joseph S. Chung? Why or why not?

3. Why does Deborah Woo believe the "model minority" label of Asian Americans to be a myth? On what specific issues does she disagree with David A. Bell on the state of Asian Americans? Which of the two authors do you believe provides a more accurate picture? Explain.

General Questions

1. Judging from the viewpoints presented in this volume, how important was race in the debates over Asian Americans? Has race been a defining part of the Asian American experience? Why or why not?

2. Are elements of the "model minority" description of Asian Americans, which is debated in chapter four, found in earlier descriptions of Asians presented in the first three chapters? What might this say about the evolving public image of Asian Americans?

Chronology

1790	Congress limits naturalized U.S. citizenship to "free white persons."
1849	In the *Passenger Cases* the Supreme Court rules that immigration is foreign commerce, which only Congress (and not the states) can regulate.
	The California gold rush signals the onset of the first significant Chinese immigration to the United States.
1852	The first group of 195 Chinese contract laborers land in Hawaii to work in its sugar plantations.
1854	The California Supreme Court rules that testimony by Chinese and other racial minorities against whites is invalid.
1862	Six Chinese district associations in San Francisco form a loose federation (referred to by some as the "Six Chinese Companies").
1865	The Central Pacific Railroad recruits Chinese workers.
1868	The U.S. Senate ratifies the Burlingame Treaty with China, which recognizes migration between the two countries.
	The first Japanese contract laborers arrive in Hawaii; the Japanese government bans subsequent emigration.
1869	Most of the more than ten thousand Chinese who labored on the construction of the transcontinental railroad lose their jobs upon its completion; many return to San Francisco and other urban centers.
	The first colony of Japanese settles in Gold Hill, California.
1871	Twenty-one Chinese are killed by mobs in Los Angeles, California.
1878	One Ah Yup is denied naturalization by the Circuit Court of San Francisco; the case sets a precedent for denying U.S. citizenship to Chinese immigrants.
1880	The United States and China sign a new treaty that gives the United States the unilateral right to "regulate, limit, or suspend" Chinese immigration.
	California revises its Civil Code to prohibit the issuance of marriage licenses to whites wishing to

	marry "Mongolians, Negroes, mulattos [or] persons of mixed blood."
1882	Chinese district association leaders in San Francisco form the Chinese Consolidated Benevolent Association (CCBA, also known as the Chinese Six Companies) to speak and act for the Chinese community. Similar associations are formed in other cities, including New York in 1883 and Honolulu and Vancouver, Canada, in 1884.
May 6, 1882	Congress passes the Chinese Exclusion Act, which suspends Chinese immigration for ten years and declares Chinese ineligible for citizenship.
1883	The kingdom of Hawaii limits Chinese immigration.
1884	A Chinese-language school is established in San Francisco by the Chinese Six Companies.
1885	Chinese are victims of violent attacks in Rock Springs, Wyoming, and Seattle, Washington.
	Japan's government lifts its ban on emigration; thirty thousand Japanese contract laborers immigrate to Hawaii between 1885 and 1894.
1890–1920	Three hundred thousand Japanese immigrate to the western United States.
1893	A U.S. law specifies that all Chinese seeking entry as merchants must have their status attested to by the testimony of two credible witnesses other than Chinese.
1898	The United States acquires the Philippines from Spain in the Spanish-American War. Filipino "wards" of the U.S. government gain the legal right to enter the United States.
	Hawaii is annexed by the United States. Congress passes a joint resolution banning Chinese laborers from immigrating to Hawaii.
	In *Wong Kim Ark v. United States*, the Supreme Court rules that people born in the United States of Chinese parents are U.S. citizens and cannot be excluded.
1900	The first significant anti-Japanese protests take place in the United States, with separate meetings in Seattle and San Francisco.
	Congress passes the Organic Act, making all U.S. laws applicable in Hawaii, thus ending contract labor on the islands; many freed Japanese workers move to the mainland seeking higher wages.
1903–1905	Seven thousand Koreans immigrate to Hawaii; the immigration flow stops when Japan establishes a

	protectorate over Korea and halts emigration.
1903	The Pensionado Act provides for Filipino students to be educated in the United States.
October 11, 1906	The San Francisco school board formally orders all Japanese students to attend the city's Chinese school; after the Japanese consul protests, President Theodore Roosevelt intervenes and persuades San Francisco authorities to reverse the decision in return for a promise to limit Japanese immigration.
1907	President Roosevelt signs an executive order prohibiting Japanese and Korean laborers in Hawaii from remigrating to the continental United States.
	210 Filipinos arrive in Hawaii to work in the sugar plantations; between 1907 and 1924, 46,000 men and 7,000 women will join them.
1907–1908	The so-called Gentlemen's Agreement is concluded between the United States and Japan, in which the Japanese government agrees not to issue laborers passports to the United States.
1909	The Japanese Association of America is founded by the Japanese consul general in San Francisco.
1910	A special facility for Asian immigrants is established on Angel Island in San Francisco Bay.
1913	The California legislature passes the Alien Land Act to prevent Japanese from owning land; the law is tightened in 1921 and 1923.
1917	Congress passes the Immigration Act establishing most of Asia as a "barred zone" and banning all Asian immigration, except from Japan and the Philippines.
1918	Asian Americans who enlisted and served in the U.S. Army in World War I receive the right to become naturalized U.S. citizens.
1920	To placate American critics, Japan stops issuing passports to "picture brides."
	In Hawaii, eighty-seven hundred Filipino and Japanese farm workers go on strike.
1922	The Supreme Court in *Ozawa v. United States* rules that Japanese aliens are ineligible for citizenship; a similar ruling is made concerning East Indians in *United States v. Thind* in 1924.
1924	Immigration Act bans immigration of all aliens ineligible for citizenship (which includes all Asians); the law effectively ends Japanese immigration and also prohibits entry of alien wives of U.S. citizens.
1930	Race riots break out in Watsonville, California, and other places, against Filipino farm laborers.

	The Japanese American Citizens League (JACL) is established.
1934	The Tydings-McDuffie Act promises independence to the Philippines in ten years and enacts limits on Filipino immigration.
December 7–8, 1941	Japan bombs Pearl Harbor; the United States declares war on Japan; two thousand Japanese community leaders are arrested in Hawaii and California and interned in Department of Justice camps.
February 19, 1942	President Franklin Roosevelt signs Executive Order 9066 authorizing the military to prescribe defense zones from which to exclude suspected enemy aliens; the order is used to authorize the evacuation and internment of Japanese Americans.
December 6, 1942	The Manzanar Riot, the most serious outbreak of violence in an internment camp, takes place.
December 1943	Congress repeals Chinese exclusion laws, grants Chinese Americans the right of naturalization, and establishes a small Chinese immigration quota.
1945	Congress passes the War Brides Act, which permits Asian women to enter the United States outside of any quota system; two hundred thousand Asian wives of American soldiers enter the United States in the years following World War II; Chinese American veterans are excluded from War Brides Act until passage of a 1947 amendment.
August 1945	Japan surrenders following the atomic bombing of Hiroshima and Nagasaki; at the time of surrender about forty-four thousand Japanese Americans are incarcerated in detention centers, which are closed in 1946.
1946	Congress extends the right of naturalization to immigrants from India and the Philippines.
	The United States grants independence to the Philippines.
	California voters reject a measure validating existing alien land laws.
1948	Congress passes the Evacuation Claims Act authorizing payments to Japanese Americans to compensate for economic losses during internment; payments cover only a fraction of actual losses.
	California repeals its interracial marriage law.
1949	The United States severs diplomatic relations with China after the communist takeover; five thousand Chinese in the United States, mostly university students, are granted refugee status.
1950–1953	The United States fights in the Korean War.

1952	Congress passes the McCarran-Walter Immigration Act, which ends all racial bars to naturalization.
	The California Supreme Court declares all previous alien land acts to be unconstitutional.
November 1956	Dalip Singh Saund of California, an immigrant born in India, becomes the first Asian American to be elected to Congress.
1959	Hawaii becomes America's fiftieth state; Hiram Fong, a Chinese American, is elected by the state to serve in the U.S. Senate.
1965	The Immigration and Naturalization Act scraps the national origins quota system of the 1924 act, placing Asian nations on an equal basis with other countries. Taking full effect by July 1, 1968, the reforms initiate a new wave of Asian immigration.
1968–1969	Student strikes at San Francisco State College and the University of California at Berkeley result in the creation of new courses in Asian American studies.
1974	In a case involving students in San Francisco's Chinatown, the Supreme Court, in *Lau v. Nichols*, rules that school districts must provide bilingual education for students who speak little or no English.
1975	Communists take over South Vietnam, Cambodia, and Laos; over the next decade more than 760,000 refugees from those Southeast Asian nations settle in the United States.
February 19, 1976	President Gerald Ford rescinds Executive Order 9066 and declares that the World War II internment of Japanese Americans was "wrong."
1980	The U.S. census reveals that Japanese Americans are now outnumbered by both Chinese and Filipino Americans; census figures also reveal that Asian Americans have a greater median family income ($22,075) than white Americans ($20,840).
August 1988	Congress passes legislation providing twenty thousand dollars be paid to each surviving World War II Japanese American internee.
1990	U.S. census counts 7.3 million Asian Americans, almost 3 percent of the U.S. population.

Annotated Bibliography

Asian Women United of California. *Making Waves*. Boston: Beacon Press, 1989. An anthology of writings, both personal and academic, by and about Asian American women.

Herbert R. Barringer, Robert W. Gardner, and Michael S. Lewin. *Asians and Pacific Islanders in the United States*. New York: Russell Sage Foundation, 1993. A detailed demographic study of the migration, education, employment, and income of Asian and Pacific Islanders in the United States during the 1980s.

Carlos Bulosan. *America Is in the Heart: A Personal History*. Seattle: University of Washington Press, 1981. A classic autobiographical account by a Filipino immigrant that describes his experiences as an itinerant laborer in the western United States.

Sucheng Chan. *Asian Americans: An Interpretive History*. Boston: Twayne, 1991. An excellent introduction to the history of Asians in the United States from the 1840s to the present.

Sucheng Chan, ed. *Entry Denied: Exclusion and the Chinese Community in America, 1882–1943*. Philadelphia: Temple University Press, 1991. A history of the exclusion movement and the Chinese American reaction to it.

Sucheng Chan, ed. *Hmong Means Free: Life in Laos and America*. Philadelphia: Temple University Press, 1994. A recent study of this group of refugees from Southeast Asia.

Philip P. Choy, Lorraine Dong, and Marlon K. Hom, eds. *The Coming Man: Nineteenth Century American Perceptions of the Chinese*. Seattle: University of Washington Press, 1994. An interesting study of magazine and newspaper illustrations that show how Chinese immigrants were perceived by many Americans in the nineteenth century.

Frank F. Chuman. *The Bamboo People: The Law and Japanese-Americans*. Del Mar, CA: Publisher's Inc., 1976. A general legal history of Japanese Americans, with emphasis on land and civil rights questions.

Fred Cordova. *Filipinos: Forgotten Asian Americans*. Dubuque, IA: Kendall/Hunt, 1983. A general study of Filipino immigrants, including information and photographs on their family life, music, and sports.

Roger Daniels. *Asian America*. Seattle: University of Washington Press, 1988. A comprehensive study of Chinese and Japanese Americans from 1850 to the present, with emphasis on their communities, their legal status, and the changing demographics of both groups.

Roger Daniels. *The Politics of Prejudice: The Anti-Japanese Movement in California and the Struggle for Japanese Exclusion.* Berkeley and Los Angeles: University of California Press, 1962. A detailed history of the efforts to exclude Japanese immigrants from the United States, which culminated in the passage of the Immigration Act of 1924, effectively halting Japanese immigration.

Roger Daniels. *Prisoners Without Trial: Japanese-Americans in World War II.* New York: Hill and Wang, 1993. A careful and critical study of Japanese American internment during World War II.

Roger Daniels, ed. *American Concentration Camps: A Documentary History of the Relocation and Incarceration of Japanese-Americans, 1942–1945.* New York: Garland Press, 1989. An important source of primary documents relating to the internment of Japanese Americans during World War II.

Nancy D. Donnelly. *Changing Lives of Refugee Hmong Women.* Seattle: University of Washington Press, 1994. A study of how Hmong refugees are adapting to American life.

James Fawcett and Benjamin Carino, eds. *Pacific Bridges: The New Immigration from Asia and the Pacific Islands.* Staten Island, NY: Center for Migration Studies, 1987. Essays on post-1965 Asian immigration.

Philip S. Foner and Daniel Rosenberg, eds. *Racism, Dissent, and Asian Americans from 1850 to the Present: A Documentary History.* Westport, CT: Greenwood Press, 1993. A study and primary source collection of those who defended Asian Americans and opposed immigrant exclusion.

Deborah Gesensway and Mindy Roseman. *Beyond Words: Images from America's Concentration Camps.* Ithaca, NY: Cornell University Press, 1987. A moving literary and visual history of the Japanese internment camps and the art work that many internees produced during their incarceration.

Jeff Gillenkirk and James Motlow, eds. *Bitter Melon: Stories from the Last Rural Chinese Town in America.* Seattle: University of Washington Press, 1987. Thirteen oral histories of Chinese Americans whose home, Locke, California, was founded in 1915 as a Chinese agricultural community.

Arthur A. Hansen and Betty E. Mitson, eds. *Voices Long Silent: An Oral Inquiry into the Japanese American Evacuation.* Fullerton, CA: Fullerton Oral History Project, 1974. An important contribution to the historical study of Japanese American relocation during World War II.

Bill Hosokawa. *JACL in Quest of Justice.* New York: Morrow, 1982. A sympathetic history of the Japanese American Citizens League and its efforts at accommodation to the larger American culture, especially during World War II.

Katsuyo K. Howard, comp. *Passages: An Anthology of the Southeast Asian Refugee Experience.* Fresno, CA: Southeast Asian Student Services, California State University, 1990. A moving collection of personal writings by students of English describing their experiences as refugees from Vietnam, Cambodia, and Laos.

Yuji Ichioka. *The Issei: The World of the First Generation Japanese Immigrants, 1885–1924.* New York: Free Press, 1988. A detailed history employing Japanese and American sources that examines the many obstacles Japanese Americans faced from American laws, American labor unions, and the Japanese government, among other sources.

Noel Kent. *Hawaii: Islands Under the Influence.* New York: Monthly Review Press, 1983. A critical study of the political economy of the Hawaiian sugar industry and the immigrants who labored within it.

Hyung-chan Kim. *Dictionary of Asian American History.* Westport, CT: Greenwood Press, 1986. A handy source of basic information on the Asian American experience in the United States, including eight hundred entries and fifteen historical and sociological essays on Asian and Pacific Islander immigrants.

Hyung-chan Kim. *A Legal History of Asian Americans, 1790–1990.* Westport, CT: Greenwood Press, 1994. A history of the laws and court decisions affecting the lives of Asian Americans.

Hyung-chan Kim, ed. *The Korean Diaspora.* Santa Barbara, CA: Clio Books, 1977. Historical and sociological essays concerning Korean immigration and assimilation in North America.

Harry H.L. Kitano. *Japanese Americans: The Evolution of a Subculture.* Englewood Cliffs, NJ: Prentice Hall, 1969. A brief overview of Japanese American immigration and a social and cultural analysis of the effects of assimilation.

Harry H.L. Kitano and Roger Daniels. *Asian Americans.* 2nd ed. Englewood Cliffs, NJ: Prentice Hall, 1995. A concise overview of Asian Americans, with chapters on Chinese, Japanese, Koreans, Pacific Islanders, East Indians, and Southeast Asians.

Tricia Knoll. *Becoming Americans: Asian Sojourners, Immigrants, and Refugees in the Western United States.* Portland, OR: Coast to Coast Books, 1982. A study that examines diverse Asian immigrant groups, including Chinese, Japanese, Korean, Filipino, Vietnamese, Laotian, and Cambodian.

Peter Kwong. *The New Chinatown.* New York: Hill and Wang, 1987. A journalistic look at New York City's Chinatown, with an emphasis on employment issues, economic ties to China, and gangs and gang violence, concluding that Chinese Americans should not be considered a model minority.

H. Mark Lai. *Island: Poetry and History of Chinese Immigrants on Angel Island, 1910–1940.* Seattle: University of Washington Press, 1991. A history of the debarkation point for thousands of Asian immigrants, many of whom left their writings on the walls of the facility.

Joann Faung Jean Lee. *Asian American Experiences in the United States.* Jefferson, NC: McFarland, 1992. A collection of transcribed oral histories from first- to fourth-generation Americans from China and other Asian countries as well as the Pacific Islands.

James Loewen. *The Mississippi Chinese: Between Black and White*. Cambridge, MA: Harvard University Press, 1971. A revealing historical study of a little-known facet of the Chinese American experience.

Iwata Masakazu. *Planted in a Good Soil*. New York: Peter Lang, 1992. A history of the various agricultural occupations of the Issei (first-generation Japanese Americans) in California and other states.

Charles J. McClain. *In Search of Equality: The Chinese Struggle Against Discrimination in Nineteenth Century America*. Berkeley and Los Angeles: University of California Press, 1994. A pathbreaking study of the legal struggles of Chinese Americans against discriminatory laws.

Robert McClellan. *The Heathen Chinee: A Study of American Attitudes Toward China, 1890–1905*. Columbus: Ohio State University Press, 1971. A critical analysis of American attitudes and policies toward China and Chinese Americans after the passage of the 1882 Chinese Exclusion Act.

Carey McWilliams. *Factories in the Field: The Story of Migratory Farm Labor in California*. Boston: Little, Brown, 1939. A pioneering effort in exposing the underside of what the author argues is the exploitation of immigrant labor.

H. Brett Melendy. *Asians in America: Filipinos, Koreans, and East Indians*. Boston: Twayne, 1977. An introductory survey of three Asian American groups, emphasizing their motivations for immigration and their encounters with racism once they arrived.

Stuart Creighton Miller. *The Unwelcome Immigrant: The American Image of the Chinese, 1752–1882*. Berkeley and Los Angeles: University of California Press, 1969. An intellectual and popular history of the American response to Chinese immigration leading up to the Chinese Exclusion Act of 1882.

John Modell. *The Economics and Politics of Racial Accommodation: The Japanese in Los Angeles, 1900–1942*. Urbana: University of Illinois Press, 1977. A careful and detailed examination of the efforts of Japanese Americans to assimilate into American society.

Royal F. Morales. *Makibaka: The Pilipino-American Struggle*. Los Angeles: Mountainview, 1974. An analysis of Filipino immigration and a discussion of the many issues these immigrants have faced.

Mei T. Nakano. *Japanese American Women: Three Generations, 1890–1990*. San Francisco: National Japanese American Historical Society, 1990. An examination of the lives of the first (Issei) and subsequent (Nisei, Sansei) generations of Japanese American women.

Victor G. Nee and Brett de Bary Nee. *Longtime Californ': A Documentary Study of an American Chinatown*. New York: Pantheon Books, 1973. An impressive documentary history of San Francisco's Chinese community.

Gary Y. Okihiro. *Margins and Mainstreams: Asians in American History and Culture*. Seattle: University of Washington Press, 1994. A collection of essays on Asian Americans in American history and on multiculturalism.

William Petersen. *Japanese Americans: Oppression and Success.* New York: Random House, 1971. A study of Japanese American immigration and settlement by the sociologist credited with creating the term "model minority."

David M. Reimers. *Still the Golden Door: The Third World Comes to America.* 2nd ed. New York: Columbia University Press, 1992. A thorough study of the background, passage, and consequences of the controversial Immigration Act of 1965 that opened the way for increased Asian immigration.

Alexander Saxton. *The Indispensable Enemy: Labor and the Anti-Chinese Movement in California.* Berkeley and Los Angeles: University of California Press, 1971. A historical case study of the origins, ideas, and methods of the anti-Chinese movement in California.

Craig Storti. *Incident at Bitter Creek: The Story of the Rock Springs Chinese Massacre.* Ames: Iowa State University Press, 1991. A dramatic account of one of the worst incidents of anti-Chinese violence in all of American history.

Ronald Takaki. *Strangers from a Different Shore.* Boston: Little, Brown, 1989. A voluminous historical overview written for the general reader that examines all of the major strains of Asian immigration to the United States from the mid–nineteenth century to the late twentieth century.

Henry T. Trueba, *Cultural Conflict and Adaptation: The Case of Hmong Children in American Society.* New York: Falmer Press, 1990. A study of how Hmong children are adapting to America and how their experiences are both similar to and different from previous generations of Asian immigrants.

William Wei. *The Asian American Movement: A Social History.* Philadelphia: Temple University Press, 1993. A history of the increasingly organized political response of Asian Americans to life in the United States.

Robert Wilson and Bill Hosokawa. *East to America: A History of the Japanese in the United States.* New York: Morrow, 1980. A detailed history of Japanese Americans, with special emphasis on their World War II experience.

Cheng-Tsu Wu, ed. *"Chink!" A Documentary History of Anti-Chinese Prejudice in America.* New York: World Publishing, 1972. A primary source collection of anti-Chinese writings from the 1850s to the 1970s.

Judy Yung. *Chinese Women of America: A Pictorial History.* Seattle: University of Washington Press, 1986. A pioneering study of the long-neglected subject of Chinese American women.

Index

238